A righte Merrie Christmasse!!!

Proof

L E — G — — — ♦ — ♦ — — ♦ — ♦

Love and Joye, come to You

THE
WASSAIL
SONG

A righte Merrie Christmasse!!!

The Story of Christ-tide

By John Ashton. Copper-
plate Etching of "The
Wassail Song," by Arthur
C. Behrend.

BENJAMIN BLOM New York/London 1968

First Published (n.d.)
Reissued 1968
by Benjamin Blom, Inc. Bronx, New York 10452
and 56 Doughty Street London, W.C. 1

Library of Congress Catalog Card Number 68-56543

Printed in the United States of America

A righte Merrie Christmasse!!!

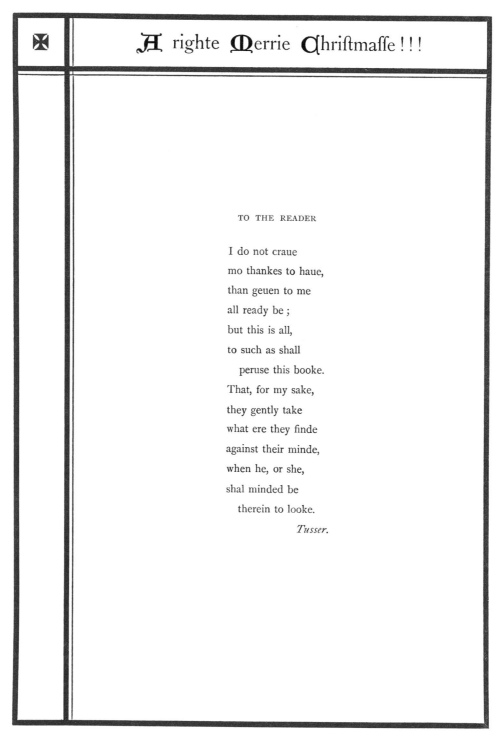

TO THE READER

I do not craue
mo thankes to haue,
than geuen to me
all ready be ;
but this is all,
to such as shall
    peruse this booke.
That, for my sake,
they gently take
what ere they finde
against their minde,
when he, or she,
shal minded be
    therein to looke.
                    Tusser.

A righte Merrie Christmasse!!!

PREFACE

IT is with a view of preserving the memory of Christmas that I have written this book.

In it the reader will find its History, Legends, Folklore, Customs, and Carols—in fact, an epitome of Old Christ-tide, forming a volume which, it is hoped, will be found full of interest.

JOHN ASHTON.

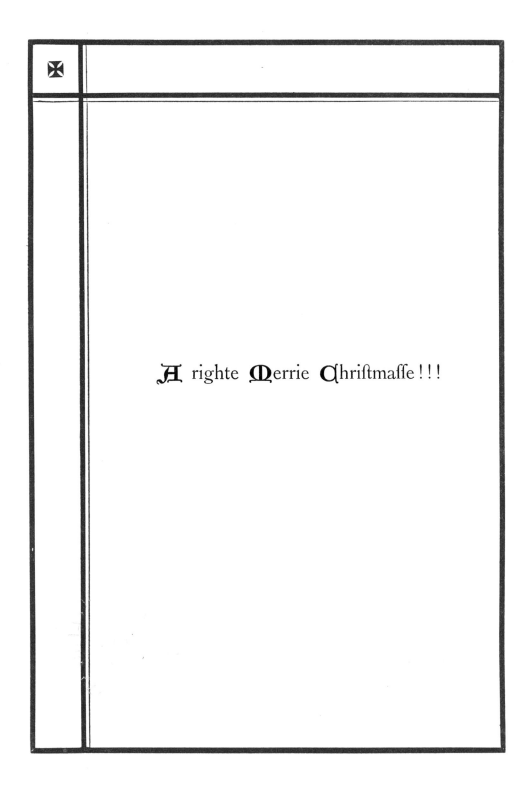

A righte Merrie Christmasse!!!

CONTENTS

CHAPTER I

CHAPTER II

CHAPTER III

CHAPTER IV

X

CHAPTER XXIII

CHAPTER XXIV

CHAPTER XXV

CHAPTER XXVI

CHAPTER XXVII

CHAPTER XXVIII

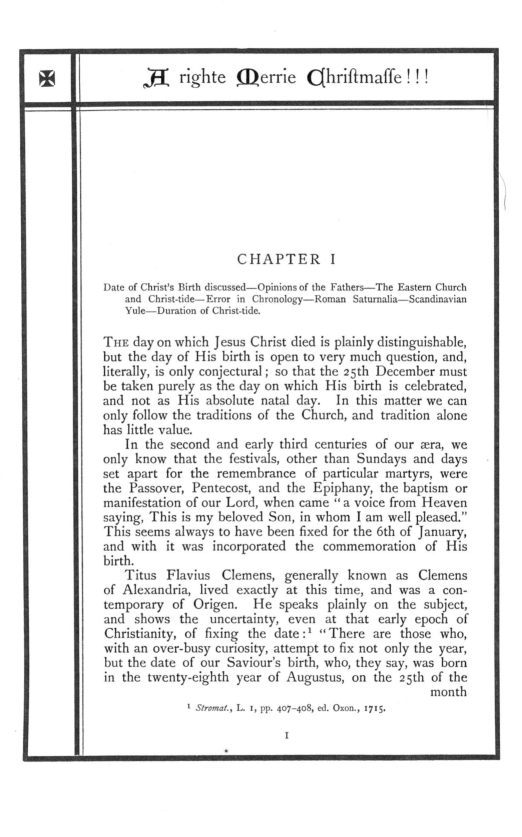

CHAPTER I

Date of Christ's Birth discussed—Opinions of the Fathers—The Eastern Church and Christ-tide—Error in Chronology—Roman Saturnalia—Scandinavian Yule—Duration of Christ-tide.

THE day on which Jesus Christ died is plainly distinguishable, but the day of His birth is open to very much question, and, literally, is only conjectural; so that the 25th December must be taken purely as the day on which His birth is celebrated, and not as His absolute natal day. In this matter we can only follow the traditions of the Church, and tradition alone has little value.

In the second and early third centuries of our æra, we only know that the festivals, other than Sundays and days set apart for the remembrance of particular martyrs, were the Passover, Pentecost, and the Epiphany, the baptism or manifestation of our Lord, when came "a voice from Heaven saying, This is my beloved Son, in whom I am well pleased." This seems always to have been fixed for the 6th of January, and with it was incorporated the commemoration of His birth.

Titus Flavius Clemens, generally known as Clemens of Alexandria, lived exactly at this time, and was a contemporary of Origen. He speaks plainly on the subject, and shows the uncertainty, even at that early epoch of Christianity, of fixing the date:[1] "There are those who, with an over-busy curiosity, attempt to fix not only the year, but the date of our Saviour's birth, who, they say, was born in the twenty-eighth year of Augustus, on the 25th of the
month

[1] *Stromat.*, L. 1, pp. 407–408, ed. Oxon., 1715.

I

month Pachon," *i.e.* the 20th of May.   And in another place he says: "Some say that He was born on the 24th or 25th of the month Pharmuthi," which would be the 19th or 20th of April.

But, perhaps, the best source of information is from the *Mémoires pour servir à l'histoire ecclésiastique des six premiers Siècles*, by Louis Sebastian le Nain de Tillemont, written at the very commencement of the eighteenth century,[1] and I have no hesitation in appending a portion of his fourth note, which treats " *Upon the day and year of the birth of Jesus Christ.*"

" It is thought that Jesus Christ was born in the night, because it was night when the angel declared His birth to the shepherds: in which S. Augustin says that He literally fulfilled David's words, *Ante luciferum genuite.*

" The tradition of the Church, says this father, is that it was upon the 25th of December.   Casaubon acknowledges that we should not immediately reject it upon the pretence that it is too cold a season for cattle to be at pasture, there being a great deal of difference between these countries and Judæa; and he assures us that, even in England, they leave the cows in the field all the year round.

" S. Chrysostom alleges several reasons to prove that Jesus Christ was really born upon the 25th of December; but they are weak enough, except that which he assures of, that it has always been the belief of the Western Churches. S. Epiphanius, who will have the day to have been the 6th of January, places it but at twelve days' distance.   S. Clement of Alexandria says that, in his time, some fixed the birth of Jesus Christ upon the 19th or 20th April; others, on the 20th of May.   He speaks of it as not seeing anything certain in it.

" It is cited from one John of Nice, that it was only under Pope Julius that the Festival of the Nativity was fixed at Rome upon the 25th of December.   Father Combesisius, who has published the epistle of this author, confesses that he is very modern: to which we may add that he is full of idle stories, and entirely ignorant of the history and discipline of antiquity.   So that it is better to rest upon the testimony

[1] Translated by T. Deacon in 1733-35, pp. 335-336.

2

testimony of S. Chrysostom, who asserts that, for a long time before, and by very ancient tradition, it was celebrated upon the 25th of December in the West, that is, in all the countries which reach from Thrace to Cadiz, and to the farthest parts of Spain. He names Rome particularly; and thinks that it might be found there that this was the true day of our Saviour's birth, by consulting the registers of the description of Judæa made at that time, supposing them still to be preserved there. We find this festival placed upon the 25th of December in the ancient Roman Calendar, which was probably made in the year 354. . . .

"We find by S. Basil's homily upon the birth of our Lord that a festival in commemoration of it was observed in Cappadocia, provided that this homily is all his; but I am not of opinion that it appears from thence either that this was done in January rather than December or any other month in the year, or that this festival was joined with that of the Baptism. On the contrary, the Churches of Cappadocia seem to have distinguished the Feast of the Nativity from that of the Epiphany, for S. Gregory Nazianzen says, that after he had been ordained priest, in the year 361, upon the festival of one mystery, he retired immediately after into Pontus, on that of another mystery, and returned from Pontus upon that of a third. Now we find that he returned at Easter, so that there is all imaginable reason to believe that he was ordained at Christmas, and retired upon the Epiphany. S. Basil died, in all probability, upon the 1st of January in the year 379, and S. Gregory Nyssen says that his festival followed close upon those of Christmas, S. Stephen, S. Peter, S. James, and S. John. We read in an oration ascribed to S. Amphilochius, that he died on the day of the Circumcision, between the Nativity of Jesus Christ and His Baptism. S. Gregory Nyssen says that the Feast of Lights, and of the Baptism of Jesus Christ, was celebrated some days after that of His Nativity. The other S. Gregory takes notice of several mysteries which were commemorated at Nazianzium with the Nativity, the Magi, etc., but he says nothing, in that place, of the Baptism. And yet, if the festival of Christmas was observed in Cappadocia upon the 25th of December, we must say that
S. Chrysostom

3

S. Chrysostom was ignorant of it, since he ascribes this practice only to Thrace and the more Western provinces. . . .

"In the year 377, or soon after, some persons who came from Rome, introduced into Syria the practice of celebrating our Lord's Nativity in the month of December, upon the same day as was done in the West; and this festival was so well received in that country that in less than ten years it was entirely established at Antioch, and was observed there by all the people with great solemnity, though some complained of it as an innovation. S. Chrysostom, who informs us of all this, speaks of it in such a manner as to make Father Thomassin say, not that the birth of Jesus Christ had till then been kept upon a wrong day, but that absolutely it had not been celebrated there at all.

"S. Chrysostom seems to say, that this festival was received at the same time by the neighbouring provinces to Antioch; but this must not be extended as far as to Egypt, as we learn from a passage in Cassian. This author seems to speak only of the time when he was in Scetæ (about 399), but also of that when he wrote his tenth conference (about the year 420 or 425). But it appears that, in the year 432, Egypt had likewise embraced the practice of Rome: for Paul of Emesa, in the discourse which he made then at Alexandria upon the 29th of Coiac, which is the 25th of December, says it was the day on which Jesus Christ was born. S. Isidore of Pelusium, in Egypt, mentions the Theophany and the Nativity of our Saviour, according to the flesh, as two different festivals. We were surprised to read in an oration of Basil of Seleucia, upon S. Stephen, that Juvenal of Jerusalem, who might be made bishop about the year 420, was the first who celebrated there our Saviour's Nativity."

The Armenian Church still keeps up the eastern 6th of January as Christmas day—and, as the old style of the calendar is retained, it follows that they celebrate the Nativity twenty-four days after we do: and modern writers make the matter more mixed—for Wiesseler thinks that the date of the Nativity was 10th January, whilst Mr. Greswell says it occurred on the 9th April B.C. 4.

It is not everybody that knows that our system of chronology is four years wrong—*i.e.* that Jesus Christ must have

4

have been born four years before *Anno Domini*, the year of our Lord. It happened in this way. Dionysius Exiguus, in 533, first introduced the system of writing the words *Anno Domini*, to point out the number of years which had elapsed since the Incarnation of our Lord; in other words he introduced our present chronology. He said the year 1 was the same as the year A.U.C. (from the building of Rome) 754; and this statement he based on the fact that our Saviour was born in the twenty-eighth year of the reign of Augustus; and he reckoned from A.U.C. 727, when the emperor first took the name of Augustus. The early Christians, however, dated from the battle of Actium, which was A.U.C. 723, thus making the Nativity 750. Now we believe that that event took place during Herod's reign, and we know that Herod died between the 13th March and 29th March, on which day Passover commenced, in A.U.C. 750, so that it stands to reason that our chronology is wrong.

Some think that the date of 25th December, which certainly began in the Roman Church, was fixed upon to avoid the multiplication of festivals about the vernal equinox, and to appropriate to a Christian use the existing festival of the winter solstice—the returning sun being made symbolical of the visit of Christ to our earth; and to withdraw Christian converts from those pagan observances with which the closing year was crowded, whilst the licence of the *Saturnalia* was turned into the merriment of Christmas.

This festival of the Saturnalia (of which the most complete account is given by Macrobius in his *Conviviorum Saturnaliorum*) dated from the remotest settlement of Latium, whose people reverenced Saturnus as the author of husbandry and the arts of life. At this festival the utmost freedom of social intercourse was permitted to all classes; even slaves were allowed to come to the tables of their masters clothed in their apparel, and were waited on by those whom they were accustomed to serve. Feasting, gaming, and revelry were the occupations of all classes, without discrimination of age, or sex, or rank. Processions crowded the streets, boisterous with mirth: these illuminated the night with lighted tapers of wax, which were also used as gifts between friends in the humbler walks of life. The season was one for the exchange of

5

of gifts of friendship, and especially of gifts to children. It began on the 17th December, and extended virtually, to the commencement of the New Year.

Prynne[1] speaks thus of Christmas: " If we compare our Bacchanalian Christmasses and New Year's Tides with these Saturnalia and Feasts of Janus, we shall finde such near affinytie betweene them both in regard of time (they being both in the end of December and on the first of January), and in their manner of solemnizing (both of them being spent in revelling, epicurisme, wantonesse, idlenesse, dancing, drinking, stage playes, and such other Christmas disorders now in use with Christians, were derived from these Roman Saturnalia and Bacchanalian Festivals; which should cause all pious Christians eternally to abominate them."

The Anglo-Saxons and early English knew not the words either of Christmas or Christ-tide. To them it was the season of Yule. Bede (*de temporum ratione*, c. 13), regards it as a term for the winter solstice. " Menses Giuli a conversione solis in auctum dici, quia unus eorum præcedit, alius subsequitur, nomina acceperunt": alluding to the Anglo-Saxon Calendar, which designated the months of December and January as *ærre-geola* and *æftera-geola*, the former and the latter Yule. Both Skeat and Wedgwood derive it from the old Norse *jôl*, which means feasting and revelry. Mr. J. F. Hodgetts, in an article entitled " Paganism in Modern Christianity" (*Antiquary*, December 1882, p. 257), says :—

"The ancient name (Yule) for Christmas is still used throughout all Scandinavia. The Swedes, Danes, and Norwegians wish each other a " glad Yule," as we say " A merry Christmas to you." This alone would serve to draw our attention to Scandinavia, even if no other reason existed for searching there for the origin of our great Christian Feast. The grand storehouses of Pagan lore, as far as the Northern nations of Teutonic race are concerned, are the two Eddas, and if we refer to the part, or chapter, of Snorri Sturlson's Edda, known as *Gylfa Ginning*, we shall find the twelfth name of Odin, the Father of the Gods, or Allfather, given as *Iàlg* or *Iàlkr* (pronounced *yolk* or *yulg*). The Christmas
tree

[1] *Histrio Mastix*, ed. 1633, p. 757.

6

tree, introduced into Russia by the Scandinavians, is called *ëlka* (pronounced *yolka*), and in the times just preceding, and just after, the conquest of Britain by the English, this high feast of Odin was held in mid-winter, under the name of *Iàlka tid*, or Yule-tide. It was celebrated at this season, because the Vikings, being then unable to go to sea, could assemble in their great halls and temples and drink to the gods they served so well. Another reason was, that it fell towards the end of the twelve mystic months that made up the mythical, as well as the cosmical, cycle of the year, and was therefore appropriately designated by the last of the names by which Odin is called in the Edda."

There are different opinions as to the duration of Christ-tide. The Roman Church holds that Christmas properly begins at Lauds on Christmas Eve, when the Divine Office begins to be solemnised as a Double, and refers directly to the Nativity of our Lord. It terminates on the 13th of January, the Octave day of the Epiphany. The evergreens and decorations remain in churches and houses until the 2nd of February, the Purification of the Blessed Virgin Mary.

But I think that if we in England are bound by ecclesiastical law as to the keeping of Christ-tide, it should, at least, be an English use—such as was observed before the domination of Rome in England. And, previous to the *Natale*, or Festival of the Nativity, the early Church ordained a preparatory period of *nine days*, called a *Novena*. These take the commencement of Christ-tide back to the 16th December, on which day the Sarum use ordained the Anthem, which commences, "O Sapientia, quæ ex ore Altissimi prodidisti," and at the present time this day is marked in the Calendar of the English Church Service Book as "O Sapientia." That this was commonly considered the commencement of Christ-tide is shown by the following anecdote of the learned Dr. Parr: —A lady asked him when Christmas commenced, so that she might know when to begin to eat mince pies. " Please to say Christmas pie, madam," replied the Doctor. " Mince pie is Presbyterian." " Well, Christmas pie—when may we begin to eat them?" " Look in your Prayer-book Calendar for December and there you will find ' O Sapientia.' Then Christmas pie—not before."

The

7

The Festival was considered of such high importance by the Anglo-Saxons that the ordinary Octave was not good enough; it must be kept up for *twelve* days. And Collier (*Eccl. Hist.*, 1840, vol. i. p. 285) says that a law passed in the days of King Alfred, "by virtue of which the *twelve days* after the Nativity of our Saviour are made festivals." This brings us to the feast of the Epiphany, 6th January, or "Twelfth Day," when Christmas ends—for the Epiphany has its own Octave to follow, and I think the general consensus of opinion is in favour of this ending.

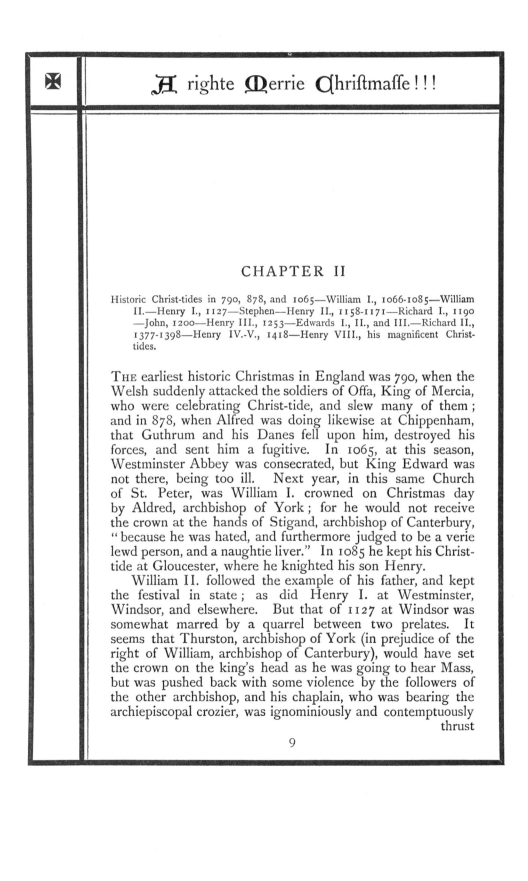
CHAPTER II

Historic Christ-tides in 790, 878, and 1065—William I., 1066-1085—William II.—Henry I., 1127—Stephen—Henry II., 1158-1171—Richard I., 1190—John, 1200—Henry III., 1253—Edwards I., II., and III.—Richard II., 1377-1398—Henry IV.-V., 1418—Henry VIII., his magnificent Christ-tides.

THE earliest historic Christmas in England was 790, when the Welsh suddenly attacked the soldiers of Offa, King of Mercia, who were celebrating Christ-tide, and slew many of them; and in 878, when Alfred was doing likewise at Chippenham, that Guthrum and his Danes fell upon him, destroyed his forces, and sent him a fugitive. In 1065, at this season, Westminster Abbey was consecrated, but King Edward was not there, being too ill. Next year, in this same Church of St. Peter, was William I. crowned on Christmas day by Aldred, archbishop of York; for he would not receive the crown at the hands of Stigand, archbishop of Canterbury, "because he was hated, and furthermore judged to be a verie lewd person, and a naughtie liver." In 1085 he kept his Christ-tide at Gloucester, where he knighted his son Henry.

William II. followed the example of his father, and kept the festival in state; as did Henry I. at Westminster, Windsor, and elsewhere. But that of 1127 at Windsor was somewhat marred by a quarrel between two prelates. It seems that Thurston, archbishop of York (in prejudice of the right of William, archbishop of Canterbury), would have set the crown on the king's head as he was going to hear Mass, but was pushed back with some violence by the followers of the other archbishop, and his chaplain, who was bearing the archiepiscopal crozier, was ignominiously and contemptuously thrust

9

thrust out of doors, cross and all. The strife did not end there, for both the prelates, together with the bishop of Lincoln, went to Rome to lay their case before the Pope for his decision.

Stephen, for a short time, kept Christ-tide royally; but the internal dissensions of his kingdom prevented him from continuing celebrating the festival in state. Henry II. kept his first Christ-tide at Bermondsey, where, to conciliate his subjects, he solemnly promised to expel all foreigners from England, whereupon some tarried not, but went incontinently. A curious event happened at Christmas 1158, when the king, then at Worcester, took the crown from his head and deposited it on the altar, never wearing it afterwards. In 1171 he spent the feast at Dublin, where, there being no place large enough, he built a temporary hall for the accommodation of his suite and guests, to which latter he taught the delights of civilisation in good cookery, masquings, and tournaments. The most famous Christ-tide that we hear of in the reign of Richard I. is that in 1190, when "the two Kings of England and France held their Christmasse this yeare at Messina, and still the King of England used great liberalitie in bestowing his treasure freelie amongst knights and other men of warre, so that it was thought he spent more in a moneth than anie of his predecessours ever spent in a whole yeare."

John kept Christ-tide in 1200 at Guildford, "and there gave to his servants manie faire liveries and suits of apparell. The archbishop of Canturburie did also the like at Canturburie, seeming in deed to strive with the king, which of them should passe the other in such sumptuous appareling of their men: whereat the king (and not without good cause) was greatlie mooved to indignation against him, although, for a time, he coloured the same." John took a speedy and very curious revenge. "From thence he returned and came to Canturburie, where he held his Easter, which fell that yeare on the day of the Annunciation of our Ladie, at which feast he sat crowned, together with his wife, queen Isabell, *the archbishop of Canturburie bearing the charges of them and their trains while they remained there.*" Next year he held the feast at Argenton in Normandy.

Henry III. celebrated the Nativity right royally in 1253 at

at York, "whither came Alexander the young King of Scots, and was there made knight by the King of England; and, on Saint Stephan's day, he married the ladie Margaret, daughter to the King of England, according to the assurance before time concluded. There was a great assemblie of noble personages at that feast. The Queene dowager of Scotland, mother to King Alexander, a Frenchwoman of the house of Coucie, had passed the sea, and was present there with a faire companie of lords and gentlemen. The number of knights that were come thither on the King of England's part were reckoned to be at the point of one thousand. The King of Scots had with him three score knights, and a great sort of other gentlemen comparable to knights. The King of Scots did homage to the King of England, at that time, for the realme of Scotland, and all things were done with great love and favour, although, at the beginning, some strife was kindled about taking up of lodgings. This assemblie of the princes cost the archbishop verie deerelie in feasting and banketting them and their traines. At one dinner it was reported he spent at the first course three score fat oxen."

Edward I. had, at two separate times, as Christmas guests Llewellyn of Wales and Baliol of Scotland. Edward II. kept one feast of the Nativity at York in 1311, revelling with Piers Gaveston and his companions; but that of 1326 was spent in prison at Kenilworth, whilst his wife and son enjoyed themselves at Wallingford. Strange and sad guests, too, must the captive King of France and David of Scotland have been at Edward III.'s Christ-tide feast in 1358 at Westminster.

Richard II. came to the throne 21st June 1377, a boy of eleven years, and I think Stow has made a mistake in a year in the following account, because at the date he gives he would have been king instead of prince.

"One other show, in the year 1377, made by the citizens for the disport of the young prince Richard, son to the Black Prince, in the feast of Christmas, in this manner:—On the Sunday before Candlemas, in the night, one hundred and thirty citizens, disguised and well horsed, in a mummery, with sound of trumpets, sackbuts, cornets, shalmes, and other minstrels, and innumerable torch lights of wax, rode from Newgate through Cheape,

Cheape, over the bridge, through Southwarke, and so to Kennington beside Lambheth, where the young prince remained with his mother and the Duke of Lancaster, his uncle, the Earls of Cambridge, Hertford, Warwicke, and Suffolke, with divers other lords. In the first rank did ride forty-eight in the likeness and habit of Esquires, two and two together, clothed in red coats and gowns of say or sandal, with comely visors on their faces; after them came forty-eight Knights, in the same livery of colour and stuff; then followed one richly arrayed like an Emperor; and, after him some distance, one stately attired like a Pope, whom followed twenty-four Cardinals; and, after them, eight or ten with black visors, not amiable, as if they had been legates from some foreign princes. These maskers, after they had entered Kennington, alighted from their horses, and entered the hall on foot; which done, the prince, his mother, and the lords, came out of the chamber into the hall, whom the said mummers did salute, showing by a pair of dice upon the table their desire to play with the prince, which they so handled, that the prince did always win when he cast them. Then the mummers set to the prince three jewels, one after the other, which were a bowl of gold, a cup of gold, and a ring of gold, which the prince won at three casts. Then they set to the prince's mother, the duke, the earls, and other lords, to every one a ring of gold, which they did also win. After which they were feasted, and the music sounded, the prince and lords danced on the one part with the mummers, which did also dance; which jollity being ended, they were again made to drink, and then departed in order as they came."

When he came to the throne as Richard II. he had very enlarged ideas on expenditure, and amongst others on Christmas feasts. He held one at Lichfield in 1398, where the Pope's Nuncio and several foreign noblemen were present, and he was obliged to enlarge the episcopal palace in order to accommodate his guests. Stow tells us: "This yeere King Richarde kept his Christmas at Liechfield, where he spent in the Christmas time 200 tunns of wine, and 2000 oxen with their appurtenances." But then he is said to have had 2000 cooks, and cookery was then elevated into a science: so much so, that the earliest cookery book that has

come

come down to us is *The Forme of Cury*, which "was compiled of the chef Mairt Cok of Kyng Richard the Secunde,
Kyng of .nglond aftir the Conquest." Twenty-eight oxen,
three hundred sheep, an incredible number of fowls, and all
kinds of game were slaughtered every morning for the use of
his household. It seems incredible, but see what old John
Hardyng, the metrical chronicler, says :—

> Truly I herd Robert Ireleffe saye,
>> Clerke of the grene cloth, y^t to the household,
> Came euery daye for moost partie alwaye,
>> Ten thousand folke by his messis tould,
> That folowed the hous aye as thei would,
>> And in the kechin three hundred seruitours,
>> And in eche office many occupiours ;

> And ladies faire with their gentilwomen,
>> Chamberers also and launderers,
> Three hundred of them were occupied then.

Of the Christ-tides of Henry IV. there are no events
recorded, except that Stow states that "in the 2nd of his
reign, he then keeping his Christmas at Eltham, twelve
aldermen and their sons rode in a mumming, and had great
thanks," but Henry V. had at least one sweet Christmas day.
It was in the year 1418, when he was besieging Rouen, and
Holinshed thus describes the sufferings of the garrison.
"If I should rehearse (according to the report of diverse
writers) how deerelie dogs, rats, mise, and cats were sold
within the towne, and how greedilie they were by the poore
people eaten and devoured, and how the people dailie died
for fault of food, and young infants laie sucking in the streets
on their mother's breasts, lieng dead, starved for hunger ;
the reader might lament their extreme miseries. A great
number of poore sillie creatures were put out at the gates,
which were by the Englishmen that kept the trenches, beaten
and driven backe againe to the same gates, which they found
closed and shut against them. And so they laie betweene
the wals of the citie and the trenches of the enimies, still
crieing for helpe and releefe, for lacke whereof great numbers
of them dailie died.
"Howbeit, King Henrie, moved with pitie, upon Christmasse

masse daie, in the honor of Christes Nativitie, refreshed all
the poore people with vittels, to their great comfort and his
high praise."

There are no notable Christ-tides until we come to the
reign of Henry VIII. In the second year of his reign he
kept Christmas quietly at Richmond, the queen being near
her confinement, which event taking place on the first of
January, she was sufficiently recovered to look at the festivities on Twelfth day. "Against the twelfe daie, or the daie
of the Epiphanie, at night, before the banket in the hall at
Richmond, was a pageant devised like a mounteine, and set
with stones; on the top of which mounteine was a tree of
gold, the branches and boughes frised with gold, spreading on
everie side over the mounteine, with roses and pomegranates,
the which mounteine was, with vices, brought up towards the
king, and out of the same came a ladie apparelled in cloth of
gold, and the children of honour called the henchmen, which
were freshlie disguised, and danced a morice before the
king; and, that done, re-entered the mounteine, which was
then drawen backe, and then was the wassail or banket
brought in, and so brake up Christmasse."

However the queen was better next year, and " In this
yeare the king kept his Christmasse at Greenewich, where
was such abundance of viands served to all comers of anie
honest behaviour, as hath beene few times seene. And
against New Yeeres night was made in the hall a castell,
gates, towers, and dungeon, garnished with artillerie and
weapon, after the most warlike fashion : and on the front of
the castell was written *Le forteresse dangereux*, and, within
the castell were six ladies cloathed in russet sattin, laid all
over with leaves of gold, and everie one knit with laces of
blew silke and gold. On their heads, coifs and caps all of
gold. After this castell had beene caried about the hall, and
the queene had beheld it, in came the king with five other,
apparelled in coats, the one half of russet sattin, the other
halfe of rich cloth of gold; on their heads caps of russet
sattin embrodered with works of fine gold bullion.

" These six assaulted the castell. The ladies seeing them
so lustie and couragious, were content to solace with them,
and upon further communication to yeeld the castell, and so
they

14

they came downe and dansed a long space. And after, the
ladies led the knights into the castell, and then the castell
suddenlie vanished out of their sights. On the daie of the
Epiphanie at night, the king, with eleven other, were disguised, after the manner of Italie; called a maske, a thing
not seene before, in England; they were apparelled in garments long and broad, wrought all with gold, with visors and
caps of gold. And, after the banket done, these maskers
came in, with six gentlemen disguised in silke, bearing staffe
torches, and desired the ladies to danse : some were content,
and some refused. And, after they had dansed, and com-
muned togither, as the fashion of the maske is, they tooke
their leave and departed, and so did the queene and all the
ladies."

In 1513, "The king kept a solemne Christmasse at
Greenwich, with danses and mummeries in most princelie
manner. And on the Twelfe daie at night came into the hall
a mount, called *the* rich mount. The mount was set full of
rich flowers of silke, and especiallie full of broome slips full of
cods, the branches were greene sattin, and the flowers flat
gold of damaske, which signified Plantagenet. On the top
stood a goodlie beacon giving light ; round about the beacon
sat the king and five others, all in cotes and caps of right
crimsin velvet, embrodered with flat gold of damaske, their
cotes set full of spangles of gold. And foure woodhouses
(? *wooden horses*) drew the mount till it came before the
queene, and then the king and his companie descended and
dansed. Then, suddenlie, the mount opened, and out came
six ladies in crimsin sattin and plunket, embrodered with
gold and pearle, with French hoods on their heads, and they
dansed alone. Then the lords of the mount tooke the ladies
and dansed together ; and the ladies re-entered, and the
mount closed, and so was conveied out of the hall. Then
the king shifted him, and came to the queene, and sat at
the banket, which was verie sumptuous."

1514, "This Christmasse, on New Yeares night, the
king, the Duke of Suffolke, and two other were in mantels of
cloath of silver, lined with blew velvet ; the silver was
pounced in letters, that the velvet might be seene through ;
the mantels had great capes like to the Portingall slops, and
all

all their hosen, dublets, and coats were of the same fashion cut, and of the same stuffe. With them were foure ladies in gowns, after the fashion of Savoie, of blew velvet, lined with cloath of gold, the velvet all cut, and mantels like tipets knit togither all of silver, and on their heads bonets of burned gold: the foure torch-bearers were in sattin white and blew. This strange apparell pleased much everie person, and in especiall the queene. And thus these foure lords and foure ladies came into the queenes chamber with great light of torches, and dansed a great season, and then put off their visors, and were all well knowne, and then the queene hartily thanked the king's grace for her goodlie pastime and desport.

"Likewise on the Twelve night, the king and the queene came into the hall at Greenewich, and suddenlie entered a tent of cloath of gold; and before the tent stood foure men of armes, armed at all points, with swords in their hands; and, suddenlie, with noise of trumpets entered foure other persons all armed, and ran to the other foure, and there was a great and fierce fight. And, suddenlie, out of a place like a wood, eight wild men, all apparelled in greene mosse, made with sleved silke, with ouglie weapons, and terrible visages, and there fought with the knights eight to eight: and, after long fighting, the armed knights drove the wild men out of their places, and followed the chase out of the hall, and when they were departed, the tent opened, and there came out six lords and six ladies richlie apparelled, and dansed a great time. When they had dansed their pleasure, they entered the tent againe, which was conveied out of the hall: then the king and queene were served with a right sumptuous banket."

In 1515, "The king kept a solemne Christmasse at his manor of Eltham; and on the Twelfe night, in the hall was made a goodlie castell, wounderously set out: and in it certeine ladies and knights; and when the king and queene were set, in came other knights and assailed the castell, where manie a good stripe was given; and at the last the assailants were beaten awaie. And then issued out knights and ladies out of the castell, which ladies were rich and strangelie disguised; for all their apparell was in braids of gold, fret with moving spangles of silver and gilt, set on crimsin sattin, loose and not

fastned;

16

fastned; the men's apparell of the same sute made like Julis of Hungarie, and the ladies heads and bodies were after the fashion of Amsterdam. And when the dansing was done, the banket was served in of five hundred dishes, with great plentie to everie bodie."

In 1517, "the king kept his Christmasse at his manor of Greenwich, and on the Twelfe night, according to the old custome, he and the queene came into the hall; and when they were set, and the queene of Scots also, there entered into the hall a garden artificiall, called the garden of *Esperance*. This garden was towred at everie corner, and railed with railes gilt; all the banks were set with flowers artificiall of silke and gold, the leaves cut of green sattin, so that they seemed verie flowers. In the midst of this garden was a piller of antique worke, all gold set with pearles and stones, and on the top of the piller, which was six square, was a lover, or an arch embowed, crowned with gold; within which stood a bush of roses red and white, all of silk and gold, and a bush of pomegranats of the like stuffe. In this garden walked six knights, and six ladies richlie apparelled, and then they descended and dansed manie goodlie danses, and so ascended out of the hall, and then the king was served with a great banket."

In 1518 was the fearful plague of the "sweating sickness," and the chronicler says "this maladie was so cruell that it killed some within three houres, some merrie at dinner, and dead at dinner." It even invaded the sanctity of the Court, and the king reduced his *entourage*, and kept no Christmas that year.

In 1520, "the king kept his Christmas at Greenwich with much noblenesse and open Court. On Twelfe daie his grace and the earle of Devonshire, with foure aids, answered at the tournie all commers, which were sixteene persons. Noble and rich was their apparell, but in feats of armes the king excelled the rest."

The next one recorded is that of 1524, when "before the feast of Christmasse, the lord Leonard Graie, and the lord John Graie, brethren to the Marquesse Dorset, Sir George Cobham, sonne to the lord Cobham, William Carie, Sir John Dudleie, Thomas Wiat, Francis Pointz, Francis Sidneie, Sir Anthonie Browne, Sir Edward Seimor, Oliver Manners, Percivall

17

Percivall Hart, Sebastian Nudigate, and Thomas Calen, esquiers of the king's houshold, enterprised a challenge of feats of armes against the feast of Christmas, which was proclaimed by Windsore the herald, and performed at the time appointed after the best manners, both at tilt, tourneie, barriers, and assault of a castell erected for that purpose in the tilt-yard at Greenewich, where the king held a roiall Christmasse that yeare, with great mirth and princelie pastime."

Of the next Christ-tide we are told, "In this winter there was great death in London, so that the terme was adjourned : and the king kept his Christmasse at Eltham, with a small number, and therefore it was called the Still Christmasse."

In 1526, "the king kept a solemne Christmasse at Greenewich with revelles, maskes, disguisings and bankets ; and the thirtith daie of December, was an enterprise of iusts made at the tilt by six gentlemen, against all commers, which valiantlie furnished the same, both with speare and sword ; and like iustes were kept the third daie of Januarie, where were three hundred speares broken. That same night, the king and manie yoong gentlemen with him, came to Bridewell, and there put him and fifteene other, all in masking apparell, and then tooke his barge and rowed to the cardinal's place, where were at supper a great companie of lords and ladies, and then the maskers dansed, and made goodlie pastime ; and when they had well dansed, the ladies plucked awaie their visors, and so they were all knowen, and to the king was made a great banket."

This is the last recorded Christ-tide of this reign, and, doubtless, as the king grew older and more sedate, he did not encourage the sports which delighted him in his hot youth.

CHAPTER III

Historic Christ-tides—Edward VI., 1551—Mary—Elizabeth—James I.—The
Puritans—The Pilgrim Fathers—Christmas's Lamentation—Christ-tide
in the Navy, 1625.

ONLY one is noted in the reign of Edward VI., that of 1551,
of which Holinshed writes, "Wherefore, as well to remove
fond talke out of men's mouths, as also to recreat and
refresh the troubled spirits of the young king; who seemed
to take the trouble of his uncle[1] somewhat heavilie; it was
devised, that the feast of Christ's nativitie, commonlie called
Christmasse, then at hand, should be solemnlie kept at Greenwich, with open houshold and frank resorte to Court (which
is called keeping of the hall), what time of old ordinarie
course there is alwaies one appointed to make sport in the
Court, called commonlie lord of misrule : whose office is not
unknowne to such as have beene brought up in noble men's
houses, and among great house-keepers, which use liberall
feasting in that season.   There was, therefore, by orders of
the Councell, a wise gentleman, and learned, named George
Ferrers, appointed to that office for this yeare; who, being of
better credit and estimation than commonlie his predecessors
had beene before, received all his commissions and warrants
by the name of the maister of the king's pastimes.   Which
gentleman so well supplied his office, both in shew of sundrie
sights and devises of rare inventions, and in act of diverse
interludes, and matters of pastime plaied by persons, as not
onely satisfied the common sort, but, also, were very well liked
and

[1] The Duke of Somerset had just been condemned to death, and was beheaded the 22nd
January following.

and allowed by the councell, and others of skill in the like
pastimes ; but, best of all, by the yoong king himselfe, as
appeered by his princelie liberalitie in rewarding that service.

"On mondaie, the fourth of Januarie, the said lord of
merie disports came by water to London, and landed at the
Tower wharffe, where he was received by Vanse, lord of
misrule to John Mainard, one of the shiriffes of London, and
so conducted through the citie with a great companie of
yoong lords and gentlemen to the house of Sir George Barne,
lord maior, where he, with the cheefe of his companie dined,
and, after, had a great banket : and at his departure the lord
maior gave him a standing cup with a cover of silver and
guilt, of the value of ten pounds, for a reward, and also set a
hogshed of wine, and a barrell of beere at his gate, for his
traine that followed him. The residue of his gentlemen and
servants dined at other aldermen's houses, and with the
shiriffes, and then departed to the tower wharffe againe, and
so to the court by water, to the great commendation of the
maior and aldermen, and highlie accepted of the king and
councell."

Mary does not seem to have kept up state Christ-tide
except on one occasion, the year after her marriage with
Philip, when a masque was performed before her.

Elizabeth continued the old tradition, but they are only
mentioned and known by the Expenses books. It is said
that at Christmas 1559 she was displeased with something in
the play performed before her, and commanded the players to
leave off. There was also a masque for her amusement on
Twelfth Night.

Of James I.'s first Christ-tide in England we have the
following in a letter from the Lady Arabella Stuart to the
Earl of Shrewsbury, 3rd December 1603 :—

"The Queen intendeth to make a mask this Christmass,
to which my lady of Suffolk and my lady Walsingham have
warrants to take of the late Queen's apparell out of the
Tower at their discretion. Certain gentlemen, whom I may
not yet name, have made me of theyr counsell, intend
another. Certain gentlemen of good sort another. It is said
there shall be 30 playes. The king will feast all the Embas-
sadours this Christmass."

The

The death of the infant Princess Mary in September 1607 did not interfere with James I. keeping Christmas right royally in that year. There were masques and theatricals—nay, the king wanted a play acted on Christmas night—and card-playing went on for high sums, the queen losing £300 on the eve of Twelfth night.

It was, probably, the exceeding license of Christ-tide that made the sour Puritans look upon its being kept in remembrance, as vain and superstitious; at all events, whenever in their power, they did their best to crush it. Take, for instance, the first Christmas day after the landing of the so-called "Pilgrim Fathers" at Plymouth Rock in 1620, and read the deliberate chilliness and studied slight of the whole affair, which was evidently more than the ship's master could bear.

"Munday, the 25 Day, we went on shore, some to fell tymber, some to saw, some to riue, and some to carry, so that no man rested all that day, but towards night, some, as they were at worke, heard a noyse of some Indians, which caused vs all to goe to our Muskets, but we heard no further, so we came aboord againe, and left some twentie to keepe the court of gard; that night we had a sore storme of winde and raine. Munday the 25 being Christmas day, we began to drinke water aboord, but at night, the Master caused vs to have some Beere, and so on board we had diverse times now and then some Beere, but on shore none at all."

That this working on Christmas day was meant as an intentional slight—for these pious gentlemen would not work on the Sunday—is, I think, made patent by the notice by William Bradford, of how they kept the following Christmas.

"One ye day called Christmas-day, ye Gov'r caled them out to worke (as was used), but ye most of this new company excused themselves, and said it went against their consciences to worke on ye day. So ye Gov'r tould them that if they made it a mater of conscience, he would spare them till they were better informed. So he led away yᵉ rest, and left them: but when they came home at noone from their worke, he found them in ye streete at play, openly; some pitching ye barr, and some at stoole ball, and such like sports. So he went to them and tooke away their implements, and told them

them it was against his conscience that they should play, and others worke. If they made ye keeping of it matter of devotion, let them kepe their houses, but there should be no gameing or revelling in ye streets. Since which time nothing hath been attempted that way, at least, openly."

But we shall hear more of the Puritans and Christ-tide, only my scheme is to treat the season chronologically, and, consequently, there must be a slight digression; and the following ballad, which must have been published in the time of James I., because of the allusion to yellow starch (Mrs. Turner having been executed for the poisoning of Sir Thomas Overbury in 1615), gives us

CHRISTMAS'S LAMENTATION

Christmas is my name, far have I gone,
　　Without regard; without regard.
Whereas great men by flocks there be flown,
　　To London-ward—to London Ward.
There they in pomp and pleasure do waste
That which Old Christmas was wonted to feast,
　　　Well a day!
Houses where music was wont for to ring,
Nothing but bats and owlets do sing.
　　Well a day, Well a day.
　　　Well a day, where should I stay?

Christmas beef and bread is turn'd into stones,
　　Into stones and silken rags;
And Lady Money sleeps and makes moans,
　　And makes moans in misers' bags;
Houses where pleasures once did abound,
Nought but a dog and a shepherd is found,
　　　Well a day!
Places where Christmas revels did keep,
Now are become habitations for sheep.
　　Well a day, Well a day,
　　　Well a day, where should I stay?

Pan, the shepherds' god, doth deface,
　　Doth deface Lady Ceres' crown,
And the tillage doth go to decay,
　　To decay in every town;

Landlords

Landlords their rents so highly enhance,
That Pierce, the ploughman, barefoot may dance;
    Well a day!
Farmers that Christmas would still entertain,
Scarce have wherewith themselves to maintain,
    Well a day, etc.

Come to the countryman, he will protest,
   Will protest, and of bull-beef boast;
And, for the citizen, he is so hot,
   Is so hot, he will burn the roast.
The courtier, sure good deeds will not scorn,
Nor will he see poor Christmas forlorn?
    Well a day!
Since none of these good deeds will do,
Christmas had best turn courtier too,
    Well a day, etc.

Pride and luxury they do devour,
   Do devour house keeping quite;
And soon beggary they do beget,
   Do beget in many a knight.
Madam, forsooth, in her coach must wheel
Although she wear her hose out at heel,
    Well a day!
And on her back wear that for a weed,
Which me and all my fellows would feed.
    Well a day, etc.

Since pride came up with the yellow starch,
   Yellow starch—poor folks do want,
And nothing the rich men will to them give,
   To them give, but do them taunt;
For Charity from the country is fled,
And in her place hath nought left but need;
    Well a day!
And corn is grown to so high a price,
It makes poor men cry with weeping eyes.
    Well a day, etc.

Briefly for to end, here do I find,
   I do find so great a vocation,
That most great houses seem to attain,
   To attain a strong purgation;
Where purging pills such effects they have shew'd,
That forth of doors they their owners have spued;
    Well a day!

And

23

And where'er Christmas comes by, and calls,
Nought now but solitary and naked walls.
     Well a day, etc.

Philemon's cottage was turn'd into gold,
     Into gold, for harbouring Jove :
Rich men their houses up for to keep,
     For to keep, might their greatness move ;
But, in the city, they say, they do live,
Where gold by handfulls away they do give ;—
     I'll away,
And thither, therefore, I purpose to pass,
Hoping at London to find the Golden Ass.
     I'll away, I'll away,
     I'll away, for here's no stay.

A little light upon this ballad may possibly be found in a letter from John Chamberlain to Sir Dudley Carleton (21st December 1627) :—"Divers lords and personages of quality have made means to be dispensed withall for going into the Country this Christmas according to the proclamation ; but it will not be granted, so that they pack away on all sides for fear of the worst."

As we are now getting near the attempted suppression of Christmas under the Puritan *régime*, it may be as well to notice the extreme licence to which the season's holiday and festivities had reached — and perhaps a more flagrant case than the following can scarcely be given. On 13th January 1626 the Commissioners of the Navy write to the Duke of Buckingham that they have received information from persons who have been on board the *Happy Entrance* in the Downs, and the *Nonsuch* and *Garland* at Gore-end, that for these Christmas holidays, the captains, masters, boatswains, gunners, and carpenters, were not aboard their ships, nor gave any attendance to the service, leaving the ships a prey to any who might have assaulted them. The Commissioners sent down clothes for the sailors, and there were no officers to take charge of them, and the pressed men ran away as fast as the Commissioners sent them down. If they had beaten up and down, they might have prevented the loss of two English ships taken by the Dunkirkers off Yarmouth."

This

This, naturally, was a state of things which could not be allowed, and on January 15 the Duke of Buckingham wrote to Sir Henry Palmer as to the officers and men quitting their ships at Christmas time, and called upon him "presently to repair on board his own ship, and to charge the officers of all the ships composing his fleet, not to depart from their ships without order."

CHAPTER IV

Attempts of Puritans to put down Christ-tide—Attitude of the people—Preaching before Parliament—"The Arraignment, etc., of Christmas."

As soon as the Puritans became at all powerful, their iconoclastic zeal naturally attacked Christmas, and the Scotchmen, such as Baillie, Rutherford, Gillespie, and Henderson, in the Westminster Assembly of Divines, tried in 1643 to get the English observance of Christmas abolished —but they only succeeded so far as coming to a resolution that whilst preaching on that day, "withal to cry down the superstition of that day." Next year they were happier in their efforts, as is shortly told in *Parliamentary History*, December 19, 1644. "The lords and commons having long since appointed a day for a Fast and Humiliation, which was to be on the last Wednesday in every Month, it happening to fall on Christmas day this month, the Assembly of Divines sent to acquaint the lords with it: and, to avoid any inconveniences that might be by some people keeping it as a Feast, and others as a Fast, they desired that the Parliament would publish a Declaration the next Lord's day in the Churches of London and Westminster; that that day might be kept as it ought to be, that the whole kingdom might have comfort thereby. The houses agreed to this proposal, and directed the following Ordinance to be published; which bore this title—

"AN ORDINANCE FOR THE BETTER OBSERVATION OF THE FEAST OF THE NATIVITY OF CHRIST.

"Whereas some doubts have been raised whether the
next

26

next Fast shall be celebrated, because it falleth on the day which, heretofore, was usually called the Feast of the Nativity of our Saviour; the lords and commons do order and ordain that public notice be given, that the Fast appointed to be kept on the last Wednesday in every month, ought to be observed until it be otherwise ordered by both houses; and that this day particularly is to be kept with the more solemn humiliation, because it may call to remembrance our sins and the sins of our forefathers, who have turned this Feast, pretending the memory of Christ, into an extreme forgetfulness of him, by giving liberty to carnal and sensual delights; being contrary to the life which Christ himself led here upon earth, and to the spiritual life of Christ in our souls; for the sanctifying and saving whereof Christ was pleased both to take a human life, and to lay it down again.

"The lords ordered That the Lord Mayor of London take care that this Ordinance should be dispersed to all churches and chapels, within the line of communication and the bills of mortality. Afterwards it was made general through the kingdom; in consequence of which Christmas day was no longer observed as a Festival, by law, till the Restoration."

But the popular love of Christmas could not be done away with by restrictive legislation, as the movers therein very well knew, *teste* Lightfoot, who, in his Journal, says "Some of our members were sent to the houses to desire them to give an order that the next Fast day might be solemnly kept, because the people will be ready to neglect it, being Christmas day."

Nor was anything neglected to repress this Christ-tide, because its keeping was inbred in the people, and they hated this sour puritanical feeling, and the doing away with their accustomed festivities. Richard Kentish told the House of Commons so in very plain language. Said he: "The people of England do hate to be reformed; so now, a prelatical priest, with a superstitious service book, is more desired, and would be better welcome to the generality of England, than the most learned, laborious, conscientious preacher, whether Presbyterian or Independent. These

These poor simple creatures are mad after superstitious festivals, after unholy holidays."

The houses of Parliament baked their pie for themselves, and deservedly had to eat it; for two red hot gospellers, Calamy and Sedgewick, preached on the iniquity of keeping Christ-tide to the Lords in Westminster Abbey; whilst in the contiguous Church of S. Margaret, Thorowgood and Langley expatiated on the same theme to the Commons, and, as if they could not have enough of so good a thing, *all four sermons were printed by order of the Houses.*

Calamy in his sermon said, "This day is the day which is commonly called the Feast of Christ's Nativity, or Christmas Day, a day that hath hitherto been much abused in superstition and profaneness. I have known some that have preferred Christmas Day before the Lord's Day, and have cried down the Lord's Day and cried up Christmas Day. I have known those that would be sure to receive the Sacrament on Christmas Day though they did not receive it all the year after. This was the superstition of this day, and the profaneness was as great. There were some that did not play cards all the year long, yet they must play at Christmas. This year, God, by a providence hath buried this Feast in a Fast, and I hope it will never rise again. You have set out, Right Honourable, a strict Order for the keeping of it, and you are here to-day to observe your own Order, and I hope you will do it strictly." And he finished with a prayer, in which he begged they might have grace "to be humbled, especially for the old superstition and profaneness of this Feast."

But although the English people were crushed for a time under the iron heel of the Puritan boot, they had no sympathy with their masters, nor their ways—*vide* the rebound, immediately after Oliver Cromwell's death, and the return to the old state of things, which has never altered since, except as a matter of fashion. Yet, even then, there were protests against this effacement of Christ-tide, and many have been handed down to us, differing naturally very much in style. One really amusing one has the merit of being short: and when the reader of this book has perused it, I believe he will thank me for having reproduced it. It is—
"The

"THE

ARRAIGNMENT

Conviction and Imprisonment

of

CHRISTMAS

On *S. Thomas Day* last,

And

How he broke out of Prison in the Holidayes and got away, onely left his hoary hair, and gray beard, sticking between two Iron Bars of a Window.

With

An Hue and Cry after CHRISTMAS, and a Letter from *Mr. Woodcock*, a Fellow in Oxford, to a Malignant Lady in LONDON.

And divers passages between the Lady and the Cryer, about Old Christmas: And what shift he was fain to make to save his life, and great stir to fetch him back again.

With divers other Witty Passages.

"Printed by *Simon Minc'd Pye*, for *Cissely Plum-Porridge;* And are to be sold by *Ralph Fidler*, Chandler, at the signe of the *Pack of Cards* in *Mustard - Alley*, in *Brawn Street*. 1645."

This

This little Tract commenced with the supposed Letter,

"Lady,

"*I Beseech you, for the love of Oxford, hire a Cryer (I will see him paid for his paines), to cry old father Christmas, and keep him with you (if you can meet with him, and stay him), till we come to London, for we expect to be there shortly, and then we will have all things as they were wont, I warrant you; hold up your spirits, and let not your old friends be lost out of your favour, for his sake, who is*

"Your ever servant,

"Jo. WOODCOCK.

"*Lady*—Honest Crier, I know thou knewest old Father Christmas; I am sent to thee from an honest schollar of Oxford (that hath given me many a hug and kisse in Christmasse time when we have been merry) to cry Christmas, for they hear that he is gone from hence, and that we have lost the poor old man; you know what marks he hath, and how to cry him.

"*Cryer*—Who shall pay me for my paines?

"*Lady*—Your old friend, *Mr. Woodcock*, of Oxford. Wilt thou take his word?

"*Cryer*—I will cry him, I warrant you, through the Citie and Countrie, and it shall go hard but I will finde him out; I can partly ghesse who can tell some newes of him, if any people in England can, for I am acquainted with all his familiar friends. Trust me in this businesse, I will bring you word within fewe dayes.

Ho-o-o-o-o-o-o yes, ho-o-o-o-o-o yes, ho-o-o-o-o-o yes;

Any man or woman, whether Popish or Prelaticall, Superstitious or Judaicall, or what person so ever, of any Tribe or Trullibub,[1] that can give any knowledge, or tell any tidings of an old, old, old, very old, grey-bearded Gentleman, called Christmas,

---

[1] This word has an indefinite meaning. Sometimes it is synonymous with entrails— as "tripes and trullibubs"; sometimes it is meant for something very trifling, and then is occasionally spelt "trillibubs." Why introduced here, no one can tell.

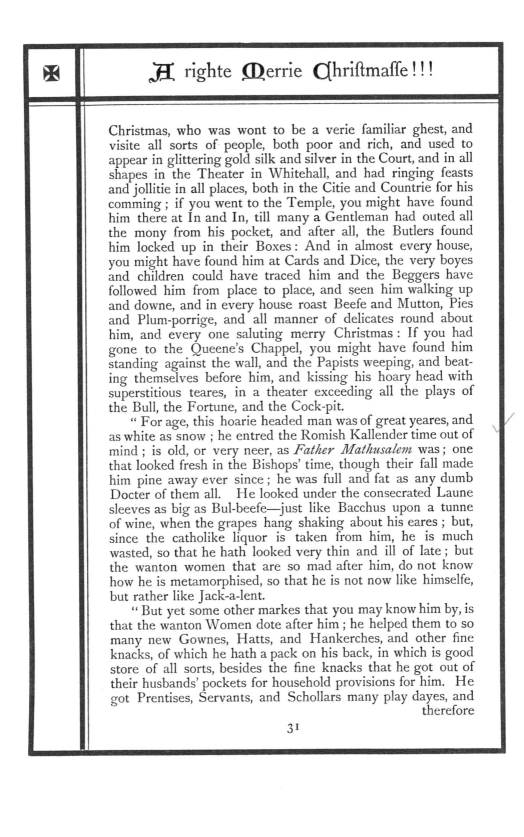

Christmas, who was wont to be a verie familiar ghest, and visite all sorts of people, both poor and rich, and used to appear in glittering gold silk and silver in the Court, and in all shapes in the Theater in Whitehall, and had ringing feasts and jollitie in all places, both in the Citie and Countrie for his comming; if you went to the Temple, you might have found him there at In and In, till many a Gentleman had outed all the mony from his pocket, and after all, the Butlers found him locked up in their Boxes: And in almost every house, you might have found him at Cards and Dice, the very boyes and children could have traced him and the Beggers have followed him from place to place, and seen him walking up and downe, and in every house roast Beefe and Mutton, Pies and Plum-porrige, and all manner of delicates round about him, and every one saluting merry Christmas: If you had gone to the Queene's Chappel, you might have found him standing against the wall, and the Papists weeping, and beating themselves before him, and kissing his hoary head with superstitious teares, in a theater exceeding all the plays of the Bull, the Fortune, and the Cock-pit.

"For age, this hoarie headed man was of great yeares, and as white as snow; he entred the Romish Kallender time out of mind; is old, or very neer, as *Father Mathusalem* was; one that looked fresh in the Bishops' time, though their fall made him pine away ever since; he was full and fat as any dumb Docter of them all. He looked under the consecrated Laune sleeves as big as Bul-beefe—just like Bacchus upon a tunne of wine, when the grapes hang shaking about his eares; but, since the catholike liquor is taken from him, he is much wasted, so that he hath looked very thin and ill of late; but the wanton women that are so mad after him, do not know how he is metamorphised, so that he is not now like himselfe, but rather like Jack-a-lent.

"But yet some other markes that you may know him by, is that the wanton Women dote after him; he helped them to so many new Gownes, Hatts, and Hankerches, and other fine knacks, of which he hath a pack on his back, in which is good store of all sorts, besides the fine knacks that he got out of their husbands' pockets for household provisions for him. He got Prentises, Servants, and Schollars many play dayes, and therefore

31

therefore was well beloved by them also, and made all merry with Bagpipes, Fiddles, and other musicks, Giggs, Dances, and Mummings, yea, the young people had more merry dayes and houres before him whilst he stayd, which was in some houses 12 dayes, in some 20, in some more, in some lesse, than in all the yeare againe."

   ·   ·   ·   ·   ·   ·   ·

"All you, therefore, that by your diligent inquirie, can tell me anie tidings of this ould man called Christmas, and tell me where he may be met withall ; whether in any of your streets, or elsewhere, though in never so straitned a place ; in an Applewoman's staul or Grocer's Curren Tub, in a Cooke's Oven or the Maide's Porrige pot, or crept into some corner of a Translater's shop, where the Cobler was wont so merrily to chant his Carolls ; whosoever can tel what is become of him, or where he may be found, let them bring him back againe into England, to the Crier, and they shall have a Benediction from the Pope, an hundred oaths from the Cavaliers, 40 kisses from the Wanton Wenches, and be made Pursevant to the next Arch Bishop. Malignants will send him a piece of Braune, and everie Prentice boy will give him his point (? *pint of wine*) next holie Thursday, the good Wives will keepe him in some corners of their mince pies, and the new Nuncio Ireland will returne him to be canonized the next Reformation of the Calender.

*   "And so Pope save Christmas.*

"*Cryer*—Lady, I am come to tell you what returne I can make you of the crying of old Father Christmas, which I have done, and am now here to give you an answer.

"*Lady*—Well said, honest Cryer, Mr. Woodcock will remember you for it.

"*Cryer*—The poor old man upon St. Thomas his day was arraigned, condemned, and after conviction cast into prison amongst the King's Souldiers ; fearing to be hanged, or some other execution to be done upon him, and got out at so narrow a passage, between two Iron Bars of a Window, that nothing but onely his old gray beard and hoarie haire of his head stuck there, but nothing else to be seen of him ; and, if you will have that, compound for it, lest it be sold among the sequestred

sequestred goods, or burnt with the next Popish pictures, by the hand of the hangman.

"*Lady*—But is old, old, good old Christmas gone? Nothing but the hair of his good, grave old head and beard left! Well I will have that, seeing I cannot have more of him, one lock whereof will serve *Mr. Woodcock* for a token. But what is the event of his departure?

"*Cryer*—The poor are sory for it, for they go to every door a-begging as they were wont to do (*Good Mrs., somewhat against this good Time*); but Time was transformed (*Away, begone, here is not for you*); and so they, instead of going to the Ale-house to be drunk, were fain to work all the Holidayes. The Schollers came into the Hall, where their hungry stomacks had thought to have found good Brawn and Christmas pies, Roast Beef and Plum-porridge; but no such matter. Away, ye prophane, these are superstitious meats; your stomacks must be fed with wholesome doctrine. Alas, poor tallow-faced Chandlers, I met them mourning through the streets, and complaining that they could get no vent for their Mustard, for want of Brawn.

"*Lady*—Well, if ever the Catholiques or Bishops rule again in England, they will set the Church dores open on Christmas day, and we shall have Masse at the High Altar, as was used when the day was first instituted, and not have the holy Eucharist barred out of School, as School boyes do their Masters against the festival![1] What! shall we have our mouths shut to welcome old Christmas? No, no, bid him come by night over the Thames, and we will have a back door open to let him in. I will, myself, give him his diet for one year, to try his fortune this time twelve month, it may prove better."

[1] This Saturnalia of barring out the Schoolmaster at Christmas—just before breaking up—was in use certainly as late as 1888. Vide *Notes and Queries*, 7th series, vol. vi. p. 484.

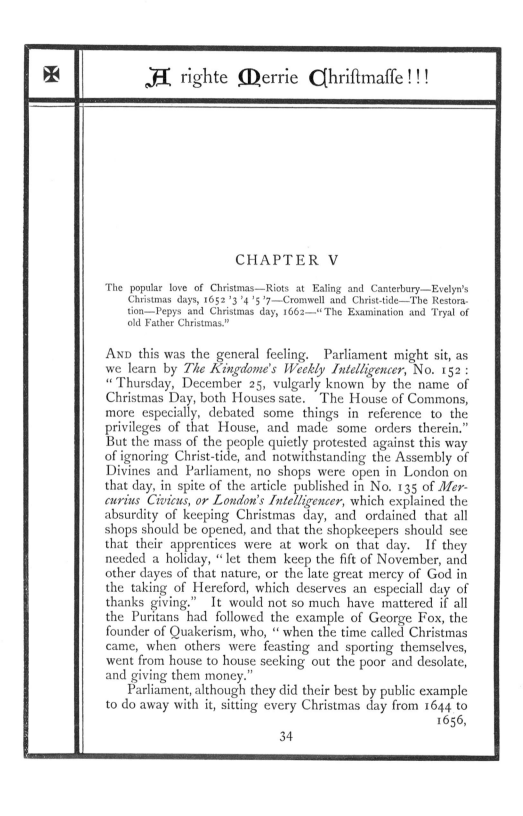

CHAPTER V

The popular love of Christmas—Riots at Ealing and Canterbury—Evelyn's
Christmas days, 1652 '3 '4 '5 '7—Cromwell and Christ-tide—The Restoration—Pepys and Christmas day, 1662—"The Examination and Tryal of
old Father Christmas."

AND this was the general feeling. Parliament might sit, as
we learn by *The Kingdome's Weekly Intelligencer*, No. 152:
"Thursday, December 25, vulgarly known by the name of
Christmas Day, both Houses sate. The House of Commons,
more especially, debated some things in reference to the
privileges of that House, and made some orders therein."
But the mass of the people quietly protested against this way
of ignoring Christ-tide, and notwithstanding the Assembly of
Divines and Parliament, no shops were open in London on
that day, in spite of the article published in No. 135 of *Mer-
curius Civicus, or London's Intelligencer*, which explained the
absurdity of keeping Christmas day, and ordained that all
shops should be opened, and that the shopkeepers should see
that their apprentices were at work on that day. If they
needed a holiday, "let them keep the fift of November, and
other dayes of that nature, or the late great mercy of God in
the taking of Hereford, which deserves an especiall day of
thanks giving." It would not so much have mattered if all
the Puritans had followed the example of George Fox, the
founder of Quakerism, who, "when the time called Christmas
came, when others were feasting and sporting themselves,
went from house to house seeking out the poor and desolate,
and giving them money."

Parliament, although they did their best by public example
to do away with it, sitting every Christmas day from 1644 to
1656,

1656, could not extinguish the deep-rooted feeling in favour of its being kept up in the old-fashioned way, and, in London, at Christmas 1646, those who opened their shops were very roughly used, so much so that in 1647 they asked the Parliament to protect them in future. Certainly, in that year, the shops were all closed, but the irrepressible love of Christmas could not be controlled, and the porters of Cornhill bedecked the conduit with "Ivy, Rosmary, and Bays," and similar decorations were exhibited in other parts of the City—a proceeding which sorely exercised the Lord Mayor and the City Marshal, who rode about, with their followings, setting fire to the harmless green stuff—the doing of which occasioned great mirth among the Royalist party.

There were riots about the keeping of Christmas in several parts of the country—notably one at Ealing, in Middlesex ; but there was a famous one at Canterbury,[1] the particulars of which are given in a short tract, which I here reprint, as it shows the feeling in the country :

"Upon Wednesday, *Decem.* 22, the Cryer of *Canterbury* by the appointment of Master *Major*,[2] openly proclaimed that Christmas day, and all other Superstitious Festivals should be put downe, and that a Market should be kept upon *Christmas day*.

"Which not being observed (but very ill taken by the Country) the towne was thereby unserved with provision, and trading very much hindered; which occasioned great discontent among the people, caused them to rise in a Rebellious way.

"The *Major* being slighted, and his Commands observed only of a few who opened their Shops, to the number of 12 at the most : They were commanded by the multitude to shut up again, but refusing to obey, their ware was thrown up and down, and they, at last, forced to shut in.

"The *Major* and his assistants used their best endeavours to qualifie this tumult, but the fire being once kindled, was not easily quenched.

"The *Sheriffe* laying hold of a fellow, was stoutly resisted ; which the *Major* perceiving, took a Cudgell, and strook the
man :

---

[1] "Canterbury Christmas ; or, A True Relation of the Insurrection in Canterbury on Christmas Day last, with the great hurt that befell divers persons thereby."
[2] Mayor.

man : who, being now puny, pulled up his courage, and knockt down the *Major*, whereby his Cloak was much torne and durty, besides the hurt he received.

"The *Major* hereupon made strict Proclamation for keeping the Peace, and that every man depart to his own house.

"The multitude hollowing thereat, in disorderly manner; the *Aldermen* and *Constables* caught two or three of the rout, and sent them to the Jaile, but they soon broke loose, and Jeered Master *Alderman*.

"Soone after, issued forth the Commanders of this Rabble, with an addition of Souldiers, into the high street, and brought with them two Foot-balls, whereby their company increased. Which the *Major* and *Aldermen* perceiving, took what prisoners they had got, and would have carried them to the Jayle. But the multitude following after to the *King's Bench*, were opposed by Captain *Bridg*, who was straight knoct down, and had his head broke in two places, not being able to withstand the multitude, who, getting betwixt him and the Jayle, rescued their fellowes, and beat the *Major* and *Aldermen* into their houses, and then cried *Conquest*.

"Where, leaving them to breath a while, they went to one *White's*, a Barber (a man noted to be a busie fellow), whose windowes they pulled downe to the ground : The like they did to divers others, till night overtook them, and they were forced to depart, continuing peaceable the next day, it being the Saboth.

"On *Munday* morning, the Multitude comming, the Major set a strong watch with Muskets and Holbards in the City, both at the Gates and at *S. Andrews* Church, the Captaine of the Guard was *White* the Barber.

"Till noon, they were quiet, then came one *Joyce*, a Hackney man, whom *White* bid stand, the fellow asked what the matter was, and withall called him *Roundhead;* whereat *White* being moved, cocked his Pistoll and would have shot him, but the Major wisht him to hold : Neverthelesse he shot, and the fellow fell down, but was not dead. Whence arose a sudden clamour that a man was murdered, whereupon the people came forth with clubs, and the *Major* and *Aldermen* made haste away ; the Towne rose againe, and the Country came in, took possession of the Gates, and made enquiry for *White;* they

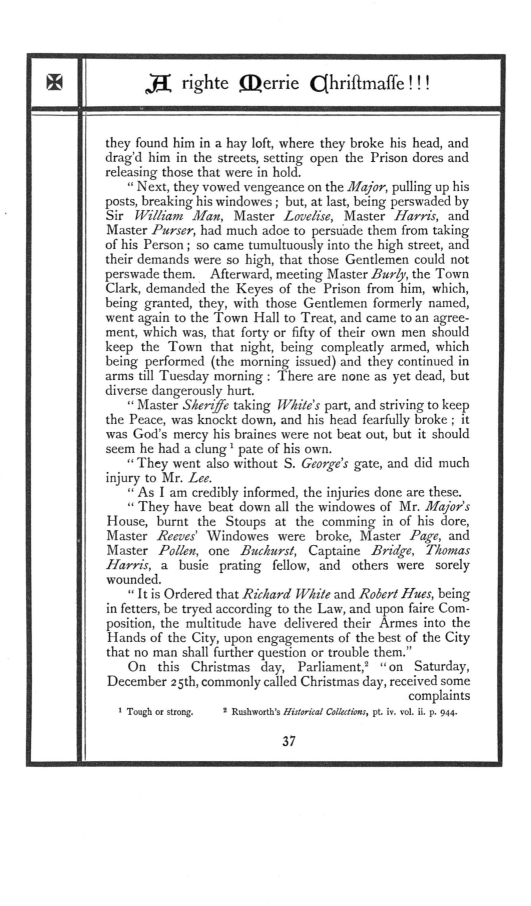
they found him in a hay loft, where they broke his head, and drag'd him in the streets, setting open the Prison dores and releasing those that were in hold.

"Next, they vowed vengeance on the *Major*, pulling up his posts, breaking his windowes; but, at last, being perswaded by Sir *William Man*, Master *Lovelise*, Master *Harris*, and Master *Purser*, had much adoe to persuade them from taking of his Person; so came tumultuously into the high street, and their demands were so high, that those Gentlemen could not perswade them. Afterward, meeting Master *Burly*, the Town Clark, demanded the Keyes of the Prison from him, which, being granted, they, with those Gentlemen formerly named, went again to the Town Hall to Treat, and came to an agreement, which was, that forty or fifty of their own men should keep the Town that night, being compleatly armed, which being performed (the morning issued) and they continued in arms till Tuesday morning : There are none as yet dead, but diverse dangerously hurt.

"Master *Sheriffe* taking *White's* part, and striving to keep the Peace, was knockt down, and his head fearfully broke; it was God's mercy his braines were not beat out, but it should seem he had a clung [1] pate of his own.

"They went also without S. *George's* gate, and did much injury to Mr. *Lee*.

"As I am credibly informed, the injuries done are these.

"They have beat down all the windowes of Mr. *Major's* House, burnt the Stoups at the comming in of his dore, Master *Reeves'* Windowes were broke, Master *Page*, and Master *Pollen*, one *Buchurst*, Captaine *Bridge*, *Thomas Harris*, a busie prating fellow, and others were sorely wounded.

"It is Ordered that *Richard White* and *Robert Hues*, being in fetters, be tryed according to the Law, and upon faire Composition, the multitude have delivered their Armes into the Hands of the City, upon engagements of the best of the City that no man shall further question or trouble them."

On this Christmas day, Parliament,[2] "on Saturday, December 25th, commonly called Christmas day, received some complaints

---

[1] Tough or strong.   [2] Rushworth's *Historical Collections*, pt. iv. vol. ii. p. 944.

complaints of the countenancing of malignant ministers in some parts of London, where they preach and use the Common Prayer Book, contrary to the order of Parliament, and some delinquent Ministers have power given them to examine and punish churchwardens, sequestrators, and others that do countenance delinquent ministers to preach, and commit them, if they see cause ; upon which some were taken into Custody."   One instance of this is given in Whitelocke's *Memorials* (p. 286).   " Mr. Harris, a Churchwarden of St. Martius, ordered to be committed for bringing delinquents to preach there, and to be displaced from his office of Church-warden."

And so it went on, the Parliament and Nonconformists doing their best to suppress Christ-tide, and the populace stubbornly refusing to submit, as is shown in a letter from Sir Thomas Gower to Mr. John Langley, on December 28, 1652.[1] " There is little worth writing, most of the time being spent in endeavouring to take away the esteem held of Christmas Day, to which end, order was made that whoever would open shops should be protected by the State ; yet I heard of no more than two who did so, and one of them had better have given £50, his wares were so dirtyed ; and secondly, that no sermons should be preached, which was observed (for aught I hear) save at Lincoln's Inn."

Evelyn, who was a staunch Episcopalian, writes in deep despondency as to the keeping of Christ-tide.   " 1652, Dec. 25, Christmas day, no Sermon any where, no church being permitted to be open, so observed it at home.   The next day, we went to Lewisham, where an honest divine preached."   " 1653, Dec. 25, Christmas-day.   No churches, or public assembly.   I was fain to pass the devotions of that Blessed day with my family at home."   " 1654, Dec. 25, Christmas-day.   No public offices in Churches, but penalties on observers, so as I was constrained to celebrate it at home."

On November 27, 1655, Cromwell promulgated an edict, prohibiting all ministers of the Church of England from preaching or teaching in any schools, and Evelyn sadly notes the fact.   " Dec. 25.   There was no more notice taken of

Christmas

[1] Hist. MSS. Commission Reports, v. p. 192.

Christmas day in Churches.   I went to London, where Dr.
Wild preached the funeral sermon of Preaching,[1] this being
the last day; after which, Cromwell's proclamation was to
take place, that none of the Church of England should dare
either to preach, or administer Sacraments, teach school, etc.,
on pain of imprisonment or exile.   So this was the mourn-
fullest day that in my life I had seen, or the Church of
England herself, since the Reformation ; to the great rejoicing
of both Papist and Presbyter.   So pathetic was his discourse,
that it drew many tears from the auditory.   Myself, wife, and
some of our family received the Communion : God make me
thankful, who hath hitherto provided for us the food of our
souls as well as bodies !   The Lord Jesus pity our distressed
Church, and bring back the captivity of Zion !'"

His next recorded Christ-tide was an eventful one for
him, and he thus describes it : "1657, Dec. 25. I went to
London with my wife to celebrate Christmas day, Mr.
Gunning preaching in Exeter Chapel, on Michah vii. 2.
Sermon ended, as he was giving us the Holy Sacrament, the
Chapel was surrounded with soldiers, and all the Communicants
and assembly surprised and kept prisoners by them, some in
the house, others carried away.   It fell to my share to be
confined to a room in the house, where yet I was permitted
to dine with the master of it, the Countess of Dorset, Lady
Hatton, and some others of quality who invited me.   In the
afternoon, came Colonel Whalley, Goffe, and others, from
Whitehall, to examine us one by one ; some they committed
to the Marshal, some to prison.   When I came before them,
they took my name and abode, examined me why, contrary to
the ordinance made, that none should any longer observe the
superstitious time of the Nativity (so esteemed by them), I
durst offend, and particularly be at Common Prayers, which
they told me was but the Mass in English, and particularly
pray for Charles Stuart, for which we had no Scripture.   I
told them we did not pray for Charles Stuart, but for all
Christian Kings, Princes, and Governors.   They replied, in
doing so we prayed for the King of Spain, too, who was their
enemy, and a Papist, with other frivolous and ensnaring
questions

---

[1] His text was 2 Cor. xiii. 9.

39

questions and much threatening ; and, finding no colour to
detain me, they dismissed me with much pity of my ignorance.
These were men of high flight and above ordinances, and
spake spiteful things of our Lord's Nativity. As we went up
to receive the Sacrament, the miscreants held their muskets
against us, as if they would have shot us at the Altar, but yet
suffering us to finish the Office of the Communion, as, perhaps,
not having instructions what to do, in case they found us in
that action. So I got home late the next day : blessed be
God !"

Cromwell himself seems to have been somewhat ashamed
of these persecutions and severities, for [1] (25th December
1657) "Some Congregations being met to observe this day,
according to former solemnity, and the *Protector* being moved
that Souldiers might be sent to repress them, he advised
against it, as that which was contrary to the *Liberty of Conscience* so much owned and pleaded for by the *Protector* and
his friends ; but, it being contrary to Ordinances of Parliament (which were also opposed in the passing of them) that
these days should be so solemnized, the *Protector* gave way to
it, and those meetings were suppressed by the Souldiers."

But his life was drawing to a close, and with the Restoration of the king came also that of Christ-tide, and there was no
longer any need of concealment, as Pepys tells us how he spent
his Christmas day in 1662. "Had a pleasant walk to White
Hall, where I intended to have received the Communion with
the family, but I came a little too late. So I walked up into
the house, and spent my time looking over pictures, particularly the ships in King Henry the VIII.ths voyage to Bul-
laen ; marking the great difference between those built then
and now. By and by down to the Chapel again, where
Bishop Morley[2] preached upon the Song of the Angels,
'Glory to God on high, on earth peace, and good will towards
men.' Methought he made but a poor Sermon, but long, and,
reprehending the common jollity of the Court for the true joy
that shall and ought to be on these days ; he particularized
concerning their excess in playes and gaming, saying that he
whose office it is to keep the gamesters in order and within
bounds,

---

[1] Whitelock's *Memorials*, ed. 1682, p. 666.   [2] Bishop of Winchester, died 1684.

bounds, serves but for a second rather in a duell, meaning the groome-porter. Upon which it was worth observing how far they are come from taking the reprehensions of a bishop seriously, that they all laugh in the Chapel when he reflected on their ill actions and courses. He did much press us to joy in these public days of joy, and to hospitality; but one that stood by whispered in my eare that the Bishop do not spend one groate to the poor himself. The Sermon done, a good anthem followed with vialls, and the King come down to receive the Sacrament. But I staid not, but, calling my boy from my Lord's lodgings, and giving Sarah some good advice, by my Lord's order, to be sober, and look after the house, I walked home again with great pleasure, and there dined by my wife's bed side with great content, having a mess of brave plum-porridge and a roasted pullet for dinner, and I sent for a mince pie abroad, my wife not being well, to make any herself yet."

The popular love of Christmas is well exemplified in a little 16mo book, printed in 1678, entitled "The Examination and Tryal of old Father CHRISTMAS ; Together with his Clearing by the Jury, at the Assizes held at the Town of *Difference*, in the County of *Discontent*." The Jury was evidently a packed one. "Then saith the *Clerk* to the *Cryer*, count them— *Starve-mouse*, one, *All-pride*, two, *Keep-all*, three, *Love-none*, four, *Eat-alone*, five, *Give-little*, six, *Hoard-corn*, seven, *Grutch-meat*, eight, *Knit-gut*, nine, *Serve-time*, ten, *Hate-good*, eleven, *Cold-kitchen*, twelve.

"Then saith the *Cryer*, all you bountiful Gentlemen of the Jury, answer to your names, and stand together, and hear your Charge.

"With that there was such a lamentable groan heard, enough to turn Ice into Ashes, which caused the *Judge*, and the rest of the Bench, to demand what the matter was ; it was replied that the grave old Gentleman, *Christmas*, did sound (*swoon*) at the naming of the Jury ; then it was commanded that they should give him air, and comfort him up, so that he might plead for himself : and here, I cannot pass by in silence, the love that was expressed by the Country people, some shreeking and crying for the old man ; others striving to hold him up, others hugging him, till they had almost broke the back

41

back of him, others running for Cordials and strong waters, insomuch that, at last they had called back his wandring spirits, which were ready to take their last farewel."

Christmas challenged this jury, and another was empannelled consisting of Messrs *Love-friend, Hate-strife, Free-man, Cloath-back, Warm-gut, Good-work, Neighbour-hood, Open-house, Scorn-use, Soft-heart, Merry-man, and True-love.* His Indictment was as follows :

"*Christmas*, thou art here indicted by the name of *Christmas*, of the Town of *Superstition*, in the County of *Idolatry*, and that thou hast, from time to time, abused the people of this Common-wealth, drawing and inticing them to Drunkenness, Gluttony, and unlawful Gaming, Wantonness, Uncleanness, Lasciviousness, Cursing, Swearing, abuse of the Creatures, some to one Vice, and some to another; all to Idleness : what sayest thou to thy Inditement, guilty or not guilty? He answered, Not guilty, and so put himself to the Trial."

After the witnesses against him were heard, Christmas was asked what he could say in his defence.

"*Judge.*—Old *Christmas*, hold up thy head, and speak for thy self. Thou hast heard thy inditement, and also what all these Witnesses have evidenced against thee; what sayest thou now for thy self, that sentence of condemnation should not be pronounced against thee?

"*Christmas.*—Good my Lord, be favourable to an old man, I am above One thousand six hundred years old, and was never questioned at Sizes or Sessions before : my Lord, look on these white hairs, are they not a Crown of Glory? . . .

"And first, my Lord, I am wronged in being indited by a wrong name, I am corruptly called *Christmas*, my name is *Christ-tide* or time.

"And though I generally come at a set time, yet I am with him every day that knows how to use me.

"My Lord, let the Records be searcht, and you shall find that the Angels rejoyced at my coming, and sung *Gloria in excelsis;* the Patriarchs and Prophets longed to see me.

"The Fathers have sweetly imbraced me, our modern Divines all comfortably cherisht me; O let me not be despised now I'm old. Is there not an injunction in *Magna Charta,*

Charta, that commands men to inquire for the old way, which is the good way; many good deeds do I do, O, why do the people hate me? We are commanded to be given to Hospitality, and this hath been my practice from my youth upward: I come to put men in mind of their redemption, to have them love one another, to impart with something here below, that they may receive more and better things above; the wise man saith *There is a time for all things*, and why not for thankfulness? I have been the cause that at my coming, Ministers have instructed the people every day in publick, telling the people how they should use me, and other delights, not to effeminate, or corrupt the mind, and bid them abhor those pleasures from which they should not rise bettered, and that they should by no means turn pass-time into Trade: And if that at any time they have stept an Inch into excess, to punish themselves for it, and be ever after the more careful to keep within compass.

"And did also advise them to manage their sports without Passion; they would also tell the people that their feasts should not be much more than nature requires, and grace moderates; not pinching, nor pampering; And whereas they say that I am the cause they sit down to meat, and rise up again graceless, they abundantly wrong me: I have told them that before any one should put his hand in the dish, he should look up to the owner, and hate to put one morsel in his mouth unblessed: I tell them they ought to give thanks for that which is paid for already, knowing that neither the meat, nor the mouth, nor the man, are of his own making: I bid them fill their bellies, not their eyes, and rise from the board, not glutted, but only satisfied, and charge them to have a care that their guts be no hindrances to their brains or hands, and that they should not lose themselves in their feasts, but bid them be soberly merry, and wisely free. I also advise them to get friendly Thrift to be there Caterer, and Temperance to carve at the board, and be very watchful that obscenity, detraction and scurrility be banisht the table; but let their discourse be as savoury as the meat, and so feed as though they did live to eat, and, at last, rise as full of thankfulness, as of food; this hath, this is, and this shall be my continual practice.

"Now,

"Now, concerning the particulars that these folks charge me with, I cannot answer them, because I do not remember them; my memory is but weak, as old men's use to be; but, methinks, they seem to be the seed of the Dragon; they send forth of their mouths whole floods of impious inventions against me, and lay to my charge things which I am not guilty of, which hath caused some of my friends to forsake me, and look upon me as a stranger: my brother *Good-works* broke his heart when he heard on it, my sister *Charity* was taken with the Numb-palsie, so that she cannot stretch out her hand . . . ."

Counsel was heard for him as well as witnesses examined on his behalf, and the Jury "brought him in, *Not Guilty*, with their own judgement upon it. That he who would not fully celebrate *Christmas* should forfeit his estate. The Judge being a man of old integrity, was very well pleased, and *Christmas* was released with a great deal of triumph and exaltation."

44

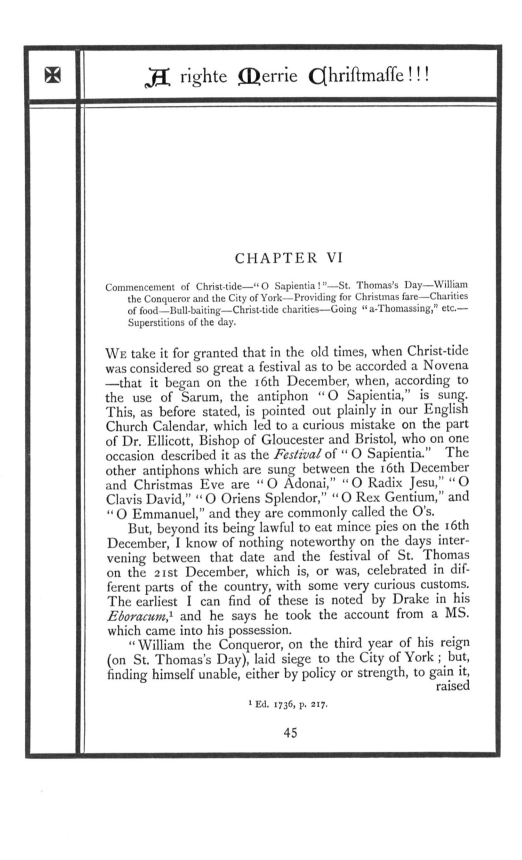

CHAPTER VI

Commencement of Christ-tide—"O Sapientia!"—St. Thomas's Day—William
the Conqueror and the City of York—Providing for Christmas fare—Charities
of food—Bull-baiting—Christ-tide charities—Going "a-Thomassing," etc.—
Superstitions of the day.

WE take it for granted that in the old times, when Christ-tide
was considered so great a festival as to be accorded a Novena
—that it began on the 16th December, when, according to
the use of Sarum, the antiphon "O Sapientia," is sung.
This, as before stated, is pointed out plainly in our English
Church Calendar, which led to a curious mistake on the part
of Dr. Ellicott, Bishop of Gloucester and Bristol, who on one
occasion described it as the *Festival* of "O Sapientia." The
other antiphons which are sung between the 16th December
and Christmas Eve are "O Adonai," "O Radix Jesu," "O
Clavis David," "O Oriens Splendor," "O Rex Gentium," and
"O Emmanuel," and they are commonly called the O's.

But, beyond its being lawful to eat mince pies on the 16th
December, I know of nothing noteworthy on the days inter-
vening between that date and the festival of St. Thomas
on the 21st December, which is, or was, celebrated in different parts of the country, with some very curious customs.
The earliest I can find of these is noted by Drake in his
Eboracum,[1] and he says he took the account from a MS.
which came into his possession.

"William the Conqueror, on the third year of his reign
(on St. Thomas's Day), laid siege to the City of York ; but,
finding himself unable, either by policy or strength, to gain it,
raised

---

[1] Ed. 1736, p. 217.

45

raised the siege, which he had no sooner done but by accident he met with two fryers at a place called Skelton, not far from York, and had been to seek reliefe for their fellows and themselves against Christmas: the one having a wallet full of victualls and a shoulder of mutton in his hand, with two great cakes hanging about his neck; the other having bottles of ale, with provisions, likewise of beife and mutton in his wallett.

"The King, knowing their poverty and condition, thought they might be serviceable to him towards the attaining York, wherefore (being accompanied with Sir John Fothergill, general of the field, a Norman born), he gave them money, and withall a promise that, if they would lett him and his soldiers into their priory at a time appointed, he would not only rebuild their priory, but indowe it likewise with large revenues and ample privileges. The fryers easily consented, and the Conqueror as soon sent back his army, which, that night, according to agreement, were let into the priory by the two fryers, by which they immediately made themselves masters of all York; after which Sir Robert Clifford, who was governor thereof, was so far from being blamed by the Conqueror for his stout defence made the preceding days, that he was highly esteemed and rewarded for his valour, being created Lord Clifford, and there knighted, with the four magistrates then in office—viz., Horongate, Talbot (who after came to be Lord Talbott), Lassells, and Erringham.

"The Arms of the City of York at that time was, *argent*, a cross, *gules*, viz. St. George's Cross. The Conqueror charged the cross with five lyons, passant gardant, *or*, in memory of the five worthy captains, magistrates, who governed the city so well, that he afterwards made Sir Robert Clifford governour thereof, and the other four to aid him in counsell; and, the better to keep the City in obedience, he built two castles, and double-moated them about; and, to shew the confidence and trust he put in these old but new-made officers by him, he offered them freely to ask whatsoever they would of him before he went, and he would grant their request; wherefore they (abominating the treachery of the two fryers to their eternal infamy), desired that, on St. Thomas's Day, for ever, they might have a fryer of the priory
of

of St. Peter's to ride through the city on horseback, with his face to the horse's tayle : and that, in his hand, instead of a bridle, he should have a rope, and in the other a shoulder of mutton, with one cake hanging on his back and another on his breast, with his face painted like a Jew ; and the youth of the City to ride with him, and to cry and shout 'Youl, Youl !' with the officers of the City riding before and making proclamation, that on this day the City was betrayed ; and their request was granted them ; which custom continued till the dissolution of the said fryory ; and afterwards, in imitation of the same, the young men and artizans of the City, on the aforesaid St. Thomas's day, used to dress up one of their own companions like a fryer, and call him Youl, which custom continued till within these threescore years, there being many now living which can testify the same. But upon what occasion since discontinued, I cannot learn ; this being done in memory of betraying the City by the said fryers to William the Conqueror."

St. Thomas's day used to be utilised in laying in store of food at Christ-tide for the purpose of properly keeping the feast of the Nativity. In the Isle of Man it was the custom for the people to go on that day to the mountains in order to capture deer and sheep for the feast ; and at night bonfires blazed on the summit of every "fingan," or cliff, to provide for which, at the time of casting peats, every person put aside a large one, saying, "Faaid mooar moaney son oie'l fingan "—that is, *A large turf for Fingan's Eve.*

Beef was sometimes left to the parish by deceased benefactors, as in the case of Boteler's Bull Charity at Biddenham, Bedfordshire, of which Edwards says :[1] "This is an ancient annual payment of £5 out of an estate at Biddenham, formerly belonging to the family of Boteler, and now the property of Lord Viscount Hampden, which is due and regularly paid on St. Thomas's Day to the overseers of the poor, and is applicable by the terms of the original gift (of which no written memorial is to be found), or by long-established usage, to the purchase of a bull, which is killed and

[1] *A Collection of Old English Customs and Curious Bequests and Charities,* London, 1842, p. 64.

47

and the flesh thereof given among the poor persons of the parish.

"For many years past, the annual fund being insufficient to purchase a bull, the deficiency has been made good out of other charities belonging to the parish. It was proposed some years ago by the vicar that the £5 a year should be laid out in buying meat, but the poor insisted on the customary purchase of a bull being continued, and the usage is, accordingly, kept up. The price of the bull has varied of late years from £9 to £14. The Churchwardens, Overseers, and principal inhabitants assist at the distribution of the meat."

He gives another instance[1] of a gift of beef and barley at Nevern, Pembrokeshire : "William Rogers, by will, June 1806, gave to the Minister and Churchwardens of Nevern and their successors £800 three per cent. Consols, to be transferred by his executors within six months after his decease ; and it was his will that the dividends should be laid out annually, one moiety thereof in good beef, the other moiety in good barley, the same to be distributed on every St. Thomas's Day in every year by the Minister and Churchwardens, to and among the poor of the said parish of Nevern.

"After the payment of £1 to a solicitor in London, and a small amount for a stamp and postage, the dividends (£24) are expended in the purchase of beef and barley, which is distributed by the Churchwarden on 21st December to all the poor of the parish, in shares of between two and three gallons of barley, and between two and three pounds of beef."

Yet another example of Christmas beef for the poor—this time rather an unpleasant one :[2] "The cruel practice of bull-baiting was continued annually on St. Thomas's Day in the quaint old town of Wokingham, Berks, so lately as 1821. In 1822, upon the passing of the Act against cruelty to Animals, the Corporation resolved on abolishing the custom. The alderman (as the chief Magistrate is called there) went with his officers in procession and solemnly pulled up the bull-ring, which had, from immemorial time been fixed in the market-place. The bull-baiting was regarded with no ordinary attachment

---

[1] *A Collection of Old English Customs and Curious Bequests and Charities*, London, 1842, p. 24. [2] *Notes and Queries*, second series, v. 35.

attachment by 'the masses'; for, besides the love of 'sport,' however barbarous, it was here connected with something more solid—the Christmas dinner.

"In 1661, George Staverton gave by will, out of his Staines house, four pounds to buy a bull for the use of the poor of Wokingham parish, to be increased to six pounds after the death of his wife and her daughter; the bull to be baited, and then cut up, 'one poor's piece not exceeding another's in bigness.' Staverton must have been an amateur of the bull-bait; for he exhorts his wife, if she can spare her four pounds a-year, to let the poor have the bull at Christmas next after his decease, and so forward.

"Great was the wrath of the populace in 1822 at the loss, not of the beef—for the corporation duly distributed the meat —but of the baiting. They vented their rage for successive years in occasional breaches of the peace. They found out— often informed by the sympathising farmer or butcher—where the devoted animal was domiciled; proceeded at night to liberate him from stall or meadow, and to chase him across the country with all the noisy accompaniments imaginable. So long was this feeling kept alive, that thirteen years after- wards—viz. in 1835—the mob broke into the place where one of the two animals to be divided was abiding, and baited him, in defiance of the authorities, in the market-place; one enthusiastic amateur, tradition relates, actually lying on the ground and seizing the miserable brute by the nostril, *more canino*, with his own human teeth! This was not to be endured, and a sentence of imprisonment in Reading Gaol gave the *coup de grace* to the sport. The bequest of Staver- ton now yields an income of £20, and has for several years past been appropriated to the purchase of two bulls. The flesh is divided, and distributed annually on St. Thomas's Day, by the alderman, churchwardens, and overseers to nearly every poor family (between 200 and 300), without regard to their receiving parochial relief. The produce of the offal and hides is laid out in the purchase of shoes and stockings for the poor women and children. The bulls' tongues are recognised by courtesy as the perquisites of the alderman and town-clerk."

But there were other kindly gifts to the poor, *vide* one at
Farnsfield,

49

Farnsfield, Nottinghamshire, where Samuel Higgs,[1] by his will dated May 11, 1820 (as appears from the church tablet), gave £50 to the vicar and churchwardens of this parish, and directed that the interest should be given every year on 21st December, in equal proportions, to ten poor men and women who could repeat the Lord's Prayer, the Creed, and the Ten Commandments before the vicar or such other person as he should appoint to hear them. The interest is applied according to the donor's orders, and the poor persons appointed to partake of the charity continue to receive it during their lives.

Take another case, at Tainton, Oxfordshire,[2] where a quarter of barley meal is provided annually at the expense of Lord Dynevor, the lord of the manor, and made into loaves called cobbs. These used to be given away in Tainton Church to such of the poor children of Burford as attended. A sermon is preached on St. Thomas's Day, according to directions supposed to be contained in the will of Edmund Harman, 6s. 8d. being also paid out of Lord Dynevor's estate to the preacher. The children used to make so much riot and disturbance in the church, that about 1809 it was thought better to distribute the cobbs in a stable belonging to one of the churchwardens, and this course has been pursued ever since.

At Slindon, Sussex,[3] a sum of £15 was placed in the Arundel Savings Bank, in the year 1824, the interest of which is distributed on St. Thomas's Day. It is said that this money was found many years since on the person of a beggar, who died by the roadside, and the interest of it has always been appropriated by the parish officers for the use of the poor.

Where these gifts were not distributed, as a rule, the poor country folk went round begging for something wherewith to keep the festival of Christ-tide; and for this they can scarcely be blamed, for agricultural wages were very low, and mostly paid in kind, so that the labourer could never lay by for a rainy day, much less have spare cash to spend in festivity. Feudality was not wholly extinct, and they naturally

[1] *Edwards*, p. 209.   [2] *Ibid.*, p. 25.   [3] *Ibid.*, p. 129.

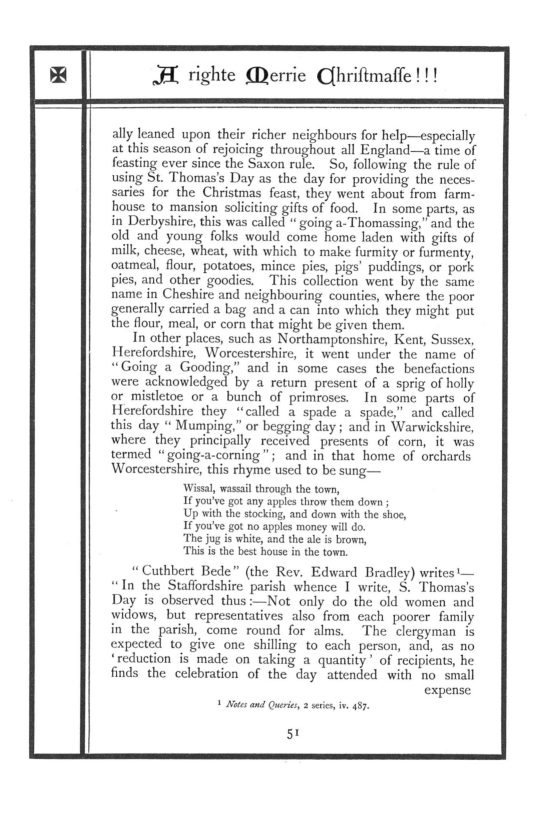

ally leaned upon their richer neighbours for help—especially at this season of rejoicing throughout all England—a time of feasting ever since the Saxon rule. So, following the rule of using St. Thomas's Day as the day for providing the necessaries for the Christmas feast, they went about from farm-house to mansion soliciting gifts of food. In some parts, as in Derbyshire, this was called "going a-Thomassing," and the old and young folks would come home laden with gifts of milk, cheese, wheat, with which to make furmity or furmenty, oatmeal, flour, potatoes, mince pies, pigs' puddings, or pork pies, and other goodies. This collection went by the same name in Cheshire and neighbouring counties, where the poor generally carried a bag and a can into which they might put the flour, meal, or corn that might be given them.

In other places, such as Northamptonshire, Kent, Sussex, Herefordshire, Worcestershire, it went under the name of "Going a Gooding," and in some cases the benefactions were acknowledged by a return present of a sprig of holly or mistletoe or a bunch of primroses. In some parts of Herefordshire they "called a spade a spade," and called this day "Mumping," or begging day; and in Warwickshire, where they principally received presents of corn, it was termed "going-a-corning"; and in that home of orchards Worcestershire, this rhyme used to be sung—

> Wissal, wassail through the town,
> If you've got any apples throw them down;
> Up with the stocking, and down with the shoe,
> If you've got no apples money will do.
> The jug is white, and the ale is brown,
> This is the best house in the town.

"Cuthbert Bede" (the Rev. Edward Bradley) writes[1]— "In the Staffordshire parish whence I write, S. Thomas's Day is observed thus:—Not only do the old women and widows, but representatives also from each poorer family in the parish, come round for alms. The clergyman is expected to give one shilling to each person, and, as no 'reduction is made on taking a quantity' of recipients, he finds the celebration of the day attended with no small expense

[1] *Notes and Queries*, 2 series, iv. 487.

expense. Some of the parishioners give alms in money, others in kind. Thus, some of the farmers give corn, which the miller grinds *gratis*. The day's custom is termed 'Gooding.' In neighbouring parishes no corn is given, the farmers giving money instead; and in some places the money collected is placed in the hands of the clergyman and churchwardens, who, on the Sunday nearest to S. Thomas's Day, distribute it at the vestry. The fund is called S. Thomas's Dole, and the day itself is termed Doleing Day."

There is very little folk-lore about this day. Halliwell says that girls used to have a method of divination with a "S. Thomas's Onion," for the purpose of finding their future husbands. The onion was peeled, wrapped in a clean handkerchief, and then being placed under their heads, the following lines were said :

> Good S. Thomas, do me right,
> And see my true love come to-night,
> That I may see him in the face,
> And him in my kind arms embrace.

A writer in *Notes and Queries*[1] says. "A Nottinghamshire maid-servant tells me :—'One of my mistresses was brought up at Ranskill, or not far from there. She used to say that when she and her sister were children they always hid under the nurse's cloak if they went out to a party on S. Thomas's Day. They were told that S. Thomas came down at that time and sat on the steeple of the church.'"

[1] 7 series, x. p. 487.

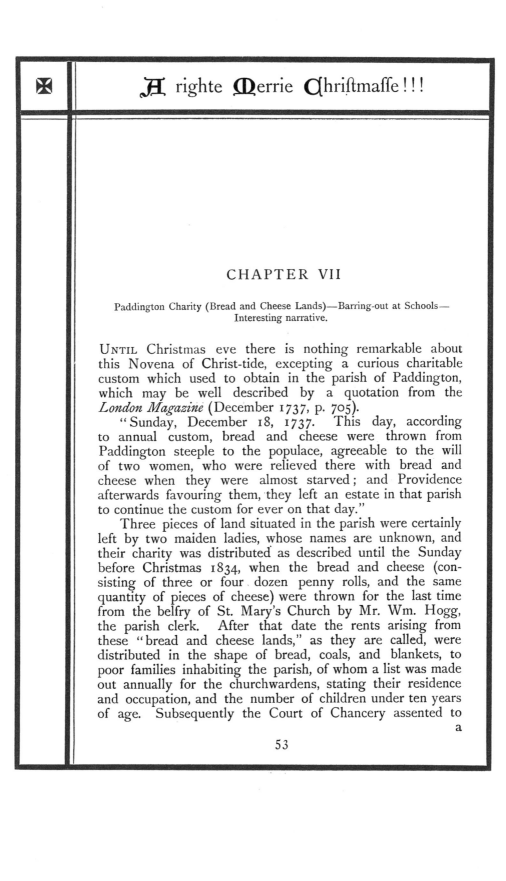

CHAPTER VII

Paddington Charity (Bread and Cheese Lands)—Barring-out at Schools—
Interesting narrative.

UNTIL Christmas eve there is nothing remarkable about
this Novena of Christ-tide, excepting a curious charitable
custom which used to obtain in the parish of Paddington,
which may be well described by a quotation from the
London Magazine (December 1737, p. 705).

"Sunday, December 18, 1737. This day, according
to annual custom, bread and cheese were thrown from
Paddington steeple to the populace, agreeable to the will
of two women, who were relieved there with bread and
cheese when they were almost starved; and Providence
afterwards favouring them, they left an estate in that parish
to continue the custom for ever on that day."

Three pieces of land situated in the parish were certainly
left by two maiden ladies, whose names are unknown, and
their charity was distributed as described until the Sunday
before Christmas 1834, when the bread and cheese (consisting of three or four dozen penny rolls, and the same
quantity of pieces of cheese) were thrown for the last time
from the belfry of St. Mary's Church by Mr. Wm. Hogg,
the parish clerk. After that date the rents arising from
these "bread and cheese lands," as they are called, were
distributed in the shape of bread, coals, and blankets, to
poor families inhabiting the parish, of whom a list was made
out annually for the churchwardens, stating their residence
and occupation, and the number of children under ten years
of age. Subsequently the Court of Chancery assented to

a

a scheme whereby the rents are portioned amongst the national schools, etc.

A curious custom used to obtain in some schools just before the Christmas holidays, of *barring-out* the master, and keeping him out of the schoolroom until the boys' grievances had been listened to and promise of redress given; and the best account of this custom that I have ever met with is in the *Gentleman's Magazine* for 1828, vol. ii. p. 404, etc.

"It was a few days before the usual period of the Christmas Holidays arrived, when the leading scholars of the head form determined on reviving the ancient but obsolete custom of *barring-out* the master of the school. Many years had elapsed since the attempt had succeeded; and many times since that period had it been made in vain. The scholars had heard of the glorious feats of their forefathers in their boyish years, when they set the lash of the master at defiance for days together. Now, alas! all was changed; the master, in the opinion of the boys, reigned a despot absolute and uncontrolled; the merciless cruelty of his rod, and the heaviness of his tasks, were insupportable. The accustomed holidays had been rescinded; the usual Christmas feast reduced to a non-entity, and the chartered rights of the scholars were continually violated. These grievances were discussed *seriatim;* and we were all unanimously of opinion that our wrongs should, if possible, be redressed. But how the object should be effected was a momentous and weighty affair. The master was a clergyman of the old school, who for the last forty years had exercised an authority hitherto uncontrolled, and who had no idea of enforcing scholastic discipline without the exercise of the whip. The consequences of a failure were terrible to think upon; but then the anticipation of success, and the glory attendant upon the enterprise, if successful, were sufficient to dispel every fear.

"At the head of the Greek class was one whose very soul seemed formed for the most daring attempts. He communicated his intentions to a chosen few, of which the writer was one, and offered to be the leader of the undertaking if we would promise him our support. We hesitated; but he he represented the certainty of success with such feeling eloquence that he entirely subdued our opposition. He stated that Addison had acquired immortal fame by a similar enterprise. He told us that almost every effort in the sacred cause of freedom had succeeded. He appealed to our classical recollections :—Epaminondas and Leonidas were worthy of our example ; Tarquin and Cæsar, as tyrants, had fallen before the united efforts of freedom ; we had only to be unanimous, and the rod of this scholastic despot would be for ever broken. We then entered enthusiastically into his views. He observed that delays were dangerous ; 'the barring-out,' he said, 'should take place the very next morning to prevent the possibility of being betrayed.' On a previous occasion (he said), some officious little urchin had told the master the whole plot, several days having been allowed to intervene between the planning of the project and its execution, and, to the astonishment of the boys, it appeared they found the master at his desk two hours before his usual time, and had the mortification of being congratulated on their early attendance, with an order to be there every morning at the same hour !

"To prevent the occurrence of such a defeat we determined on organising our plans that very night. The boys were accordingly told to assemble after school hours at a well-known tombstone in the neighbouring Churchyard, as something of importance was under consideration. The place of meeting was an elevated parallelogram tombstone, which had always served as a kind of council table to settle our little disputes as well as parties of pleasure. Here we all assembled at the appointed time. Our leader took his stand at one end of the stone, with the head boys who were in the secret on each side of him. 'My boys (he laconically observed), to-morrow morning we are to *bar-out* the flogging parson, and to make him promise that he will not flog us hereafter without a cause, nor set us long tasks or deprive us of our holidays. The boys of the Greek form will be your Captains, and I am to be your Captain-General. Those that are cowards had better retire and be satisfied with future floggings ; but you, who have courage, and know what it is to have been flogged for nothing,

55

nothing, come here and sign your names.' He immediately pulled out a pen and a sheet of paper; and having tied some bits of thread round the finger-ends of two or three boys, with a pin he drew blood to answer for ink, and to give more solemnity to the act. He signed the first, the Captains next, and the rest in succession. Many of the lesser boys slunk away during the ceremony; but on counting the names we found we mustered upwards of forty—sufficient, it was imagined, even to carry the school by storm. The Captain-General then addressed us: 'I have the key of the school, and shall be there at seven o'clock. The old Parson will arrive at nine, and every one of you must be there before eight to allow us one hour for barricading the doors and windows. Bring with you as much provision as you can; and tell your parents that you have to take your dinners in school. Let every one of you have some weapon of defence; you who cannot obtain a sword, pistol, or poker, must bring a stick or cudgel. Now, all go home directly, and be sure to arrive early in the morning.'

"Perhaps a more restless and anxious night was never passed by young recruits on the eve of a general battle. Many of us rose some hours before the time; and at seven o'clock, when the school door was opened, there was a tolerably numerous muster. Our Captain immediately ordered candles to be lighted, and a rousing fire to be made (for it was a dark December's morning). He then began to examine the store of provisions, and the arms which each had brought. In the meantime, the arrival of every boy with additional material was announced by tremendous cheers.

"At length the Church Clock struck eight. 'Proceed to barricade the doors and windows,' exclaimed the Captain, 'or the old lion will be upon us before we are prepared to meet him.' In an instant the old oaken door rang on its heavy hinges. Some, with hammers, gimlets, and nails, were eagerly securing the windows, while others were dragging along the ponderous desks, forms, and everything portable, to blockade, with certain security, every place which might admit of ingress. This operation being completed, the Captain mounted the master's rostrum, and called over the list of names, when he found

found only two or three missing. He then proceeded to classify them into divisions, or companies of six, and assigned to each its respective Captain. He prescribed the duties of each company. Two were to guard the large casement window, where, it was expected, the first attack would be made; this was considered the post of honour, and, consequently, the strongest boys, with the most formidable weapons, were selected, whom we called Grenadiers. Another company, whom we considered as the Light Infantry, or Sharp Shooters, were ordered to mount a large desk in the centre of the School; and, armed with squibs, crackers, and various missiles, they were to attack the enemy over the heads of the Combatants. The other divisions were to guard the back windows and door, and to act according to the emergency of the moment. Our leader then moved some resolutions (which, in imitation of Brutus, he had cogitated during the previous night), to the effect that each individual should implicitly obey his own Captain; that each Captain should follow the orders of the Captain-general, and that a *corps de réserve* should be stationed in the rear, to enforce this obedience, and prevent the combatants from taking to flight. The resolutions were passed amid loud vociferations.

"We next commenced an examination of the various weapons, and found them to consist of one old blunderbuss, one pistol, two old swords, a few rusty pokers, and sticks, stones, squibs, and gunpowder in abundance. The firearms were immediately loaded with blank powder; the swords were sharpened, and the pokers heated in the fire. These weapons were assigned to the most daring company, who had to protect the principal window. The missiles were for the light infantry, and all the rest were armed with sticks.

"We now began to manœuvre our companies, by marching them into line and column, so that every one might know his own situation. In the midst of this preparation, the sentinel whom we had placed at the window, loudly vociferated, 'The parson! The parson's coming!'

"In an instant all was confusion. Every one ran he knew not where; as if eager to fly, or screen himself from observation. Our captain immediately mounted a form, and called to the captains of the two leading companies to take their stations.

57

stations. They immediately obeyed ; and the other companies followed their example ; though they found it much more difficult to manœuvre when danger approached than they had a few minutes before ! The well-known footstep, which had often struck on our ears with terror, was now heard to advance along the portico. The muttering of his stern voice sounded in our ears like the lion's growl. A death-like silence prevailed : we scarcely dared to breathe : the palpitations of our little hearts could, perhaps, alone be heard. The object of our dread then went round to the front window, for the purpose of ascertaining whether any one was in the school. Every footstep struck us with awe : not a word, not a whisper was heard. He approached close to the window ; and with an astonished countenance stood gazing upon us, while we were ranged in battle array, motionless statues, and silent as the tomb. 'What is the meaning of this?' he impatiently ex-claimed. But no answer could he obtain, for who would then have dared to render himself conspicuous by a reply ? Pallid countenances and livid lips betrayed our fears. The courage, which one hour before was ready to brave every danger, appeared to be fled. Every one seemed anxious to conceal himself from view : and there would, certainly, have been a general flight through the back windows had it not been for the prudent regulation of a *corps de réserve*, armed with cudgels, to prevent it.

"'You young scoundrels, open the door instantly,' he again exclaimed ; and, what added to our indescribable horror, in a fit of rage he dashed his hand through the window, which consisted of diamond-shaped panes, and appeared as if deter-mined to force his way in.

"Fear and trepidation, attended by an increasing commo-tion, now possessed us all. At this critical moment every eye turned to our captain, as if to reproach him for having brought us into this terrible dilemma. He alone stood unmoved ; but he saw that none would have courage to obey his commands. Some exciting stimulus was necessary. Suddenly waving his hand, he exclaimed aloud, 'Three cheers for the barring-out, and success to our cause !' The cheers were tremendous ; our courage revived ; the blood flushed in our cheeks ; the parson was breaking in ; the moment was critical. Our Captain,

58

Captain, undaunted, sprang to the fire-place—seized a heated poker in one hand, and a blazing torch in the other. The latter he gave to the captain of the sharp shooters, and told him to prepare a volley; when, with red-hot poker, he fearlessly advanced to the window seat; and, daring his master to enter, he ordered an attack—and an attack, indeed, was made, sufficiently tremendous to have repelled a more powerful assailant. The missiles flew at the ill-fated window from every quarter. The blunderbuss and the pistol were fired; squibs and crackers, inkstands and rulers, stones, and even burning coals, came in showers about the casement, and broke some of the panes into a thousand pieces; while blazing torches, heated pokers, and sticks, stood bristling under the window. The whole was scarcely the work of a minute: the astonished master reeled back in dumb amazement. He had, evidently, been struck with a missile or with the broken glass; and probably fancied that he had been wounded by the fire-arms. The schools now rang with the shouts of 'Victory,' and continued cheering. 'The enemy again approaches,' cried the captain; 'fire another volley;—stay, he seeks a parley — hear him.' 'What is the meaning, I say, of this horrid tumult?' 'The barring-out, the barring-out!' a dozen voices instantly exclaimed. 'For shame,' says he, in a tone evidently subdued; what disgrace are you bringing upon yourselves and the schools. What will the Trustees—what will your parents say? William,' continued he, addressing the captain, 'open the door without further delay.' 'I will, Sir,' he replied, 'on your promising to pardon us, and give us our lawful holidays, of which we have lately been deprived; and not set us tasks during the holidays.' 'Yes, yes,' said several squealing voices, 'that is what we want; and not to be flogged for nothing.' 'You insolent scoundrels! you consummate young villains!' he exclaimed, choking with rage, and at the same time making a furious effort to break through the already shattered window, 'open the door instantly, or I'll break every bone in your hides.' 'Not on those conditions,' replied our Captain, with provoking coolness;— 'Come on, my boys, another volley.' No sooner said than done, and even with more fury than before. Like men driven to despair, who expect no quarter on surrendering, the little urchins

59

urchins daringly mounted the window seat, which was a broad, old-fashioned one, and pointed the fire arms and heated poker at him ; whilst others advanced with the squibs and missiles. 'Come on, my lads,' said the captain, 'let this be our Thermopylæ, and I will be your Leonidas.' And, indeed, so daring were they, that each seemed ready to emulate the Spartans of old. The master, perceiving their determined obstinacy, turned round, without further remonstrance, and indignantly walked away.

"Relieved from our terrors, we now became intoxicated with joy. The walls rang with repeated hurrahs! In the madness of enthusiasm, some of the boys began to tear up the forms, throw the books about, break the slates, locks, and cupboards, and act so outrageously that the captain called them to order ; not, however, before the master's desk and drawers had been broken open, and every play thing which had been taken from the scholars restored to its owner.

"We now began to think of provisions. They were all placed on one table and dealt out in rations by the Captains of each company. In the meantime, we held a council of war, as we called it, to determine on what was to be done.

"In a recess at the east end of the school there stood a large oak chest, black with age, whose heavy hinges had become corroded with years of rust. It was known to contain the records and endowments of the school ; and, as we presumed, the regulations for the treatment of the scholars. The oldest boy had never seen its inside. Attempts, dictated by insatiable curiosity, had often been made to open it ; but it was deemed impregnable. It was guarded by three immense locks, and each key was in the possession of different persons. The wood appeared to be nearly half a foot thick, and every corner was plaited with iron. All eyes were instinctively directed to this mysterious chest. Could any means be devised for effecting an entrance? was the natural question. We all proceeded to reconnoitre ; we attempted to move it, but in vain : we made some feeble efforts to force the lid ; it was firm as a block of marble. At length, one daring urchin brought, from the fire-place, a red-hot poker, and began to bore through its sides. A universal shout was given. Other pokers were brought, and to work they went. The smoke and

and tremendous smell which the old wood sent forth rather alarmed us. We were apprehensive that we might burn the records instead of obtaining a copy of them. This arrested our progress for a few minutes.

"At this critical moment a shout was set up that the parson and a constable was coming! Down went the pokers; and, as if conscience-stricken, we were all seized with consternation. The casement window was so shattered that it could easily be entered by any resolute fellow. In the desperation of the moment we seized the desks, forms, and stools to block it up; but, in some degree, our courage had evaporated, and we felt reluctant to act on the offensive. The old gentleman and his attendant deliberately inspected the windows and fastenings : but, without making any attempt to enter, they retreated for the purpose, we presumed, of obtaining additional assistance. What was now to be done? The master appeared obdurate, and we had gone too far to recede. Some proposed to drill a hole in the window seat, fill it with gunpowder, and explode it if any one attempted to enter. Others thought we had better prepare to set fire to the school sooner than surrender unconditionally. But the majority advised what was, perhaps, the most prudent resolution, to wait for another attack ; and, if we saw no hopes of sustaining a longer defence, to make the best retreat we could.

"The affair of the Barring Out had now become known, and persons began to assemble round the windows, calling out that the master was coming with assistance, and saying everything to intimidate us. Many of us were completely jaded with the over-excitement we had experienced since the previous evening. The school was hot, close, and full of smoke. Some were longing for liberty and fresh air ; and most of us were now of opinion that we had engaged in an affair which it was impossible to accomplish. In this state of mind we received another visit from our dreaded master. With his stick he commenced a more furious attack than before; and, observing us less turbulent, he appeared determined to force his way in spite of the barricadoes. The younger boys thought of nothing but flight and self-preservation, and the rush to the back windows became general. In the midst of **this**

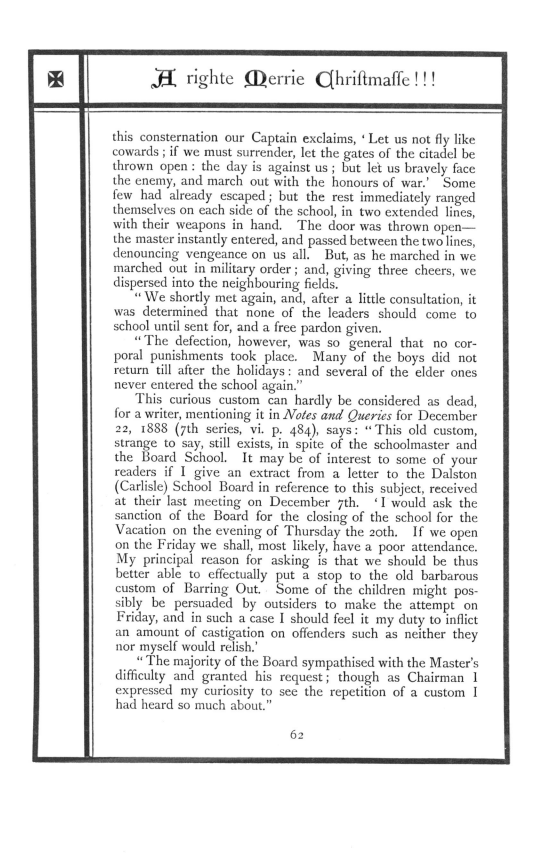
this consternation our Captain exclaims, ‘Let us not fly like cowards ; if we must surrender, let the gates of the citadel be thrown open : the day is against us ; but let us bravely face the enemy, and march out with the honours of war.’ Some few had already escaped ; but the rest immediately ranged themselves on each side of the school, in two extended lines, with their weapons in hand. The door was thrown open— the master instantly entered, and passed between the two lines, denouncing vengeance on us all. But, as he marched in we marched out in military order ; and, giving three cheers, we dispersed into the neighbouring fields.

“We shortly met again, and, after a little consultation, it was determined that none of the leaders should come to school until sent for, and a free pardon given.

“The defection, however, was so general that no corporal punishments took place. Many of the boys did not return till after the holidays : and several of the elder ones never entered the school again.”

This curious custom can hardly be considered as dead, for a writer, mentioning it in *Notes and Queries* for December 22, 1888 (7th series, vi. p. 484), says : “This old custom, strange to say, still exists, in spite of the schoolmaster and the Board School. It may be of interest to some of your readers if I give an extract from a letter to the Dalston (Carlisle) School Board in reference to this subject, received at their last meeting on December 7th. ‘I would ask the sanction of the Board for the closing of the school for the Vacation on the evening of Thursday the 20th. If we open on the Friday we shall, most likely, have a poor attendance. My principal reason for asking is that we should be thus better able to effectually put a stop to the old barbarous custom of Barring Out. Some of the children might possibly be persuaded by outsiders to make the attempt on Friday, and in such a case I should feel it my duty to inflict an amount of castigation on offenders such as neither they nor myself would relish.’

“The majority of the Board sympathised with the Master’s difficulty and granted his request ; though as Chairman I expressed my curiosity to see the repetition of a custom I had heard so much about.”

CHAPTER VIII

The Bellman—Descriptions of him—His verses. The Waits—Their origin—
Ned Ward on them—Corporation Waits—York Waits (17th Century)—
Essay on Waits—Westminster Waits—Modern Waits.

BEFORE the advent of Christmas the Bellman, or Watchman, left at each house a copy of verses ostensibly breathing good-will and a happy Christmas to the occupants, but in reality as a reminder to them of his existence, and that he would call in due time for his Christmas box. The date of the institution of the Bellman is not well defined. In Tegg's *Dictionary of Chronology*, 1530 is given, but no authority for the statement is adduced; Machyn, in his diary, is more definite "[the xij. day of January 1556-7, in Alderman Draper's ward called] chordwenerstrett ward, a belle man [went about] with a belle at evere lane, and at the ward [end to] gyff warnyng of ffyre and candyll lyght, [and to help the] poure, and pray for the ded." Their cry being, "Take care of your fire and candle, be charitable to the poor, and pray for the dead."

Shakespeare knew him, for in *Macbeth* (Act II. sc. 2) he says:

> It was the owl that shriek'd, the fatal bell man,
> Which gives the stern'st good night.

And Milton mentions him in *Il Penseroso:*

> Or the bellman's drowsy charm,
> To bless the doors from nightly harm.

Herrick also celebrates *The Bellman:*

> From noise of Scare-fires rest ye free,
> From Murders *Benedicite.*

From

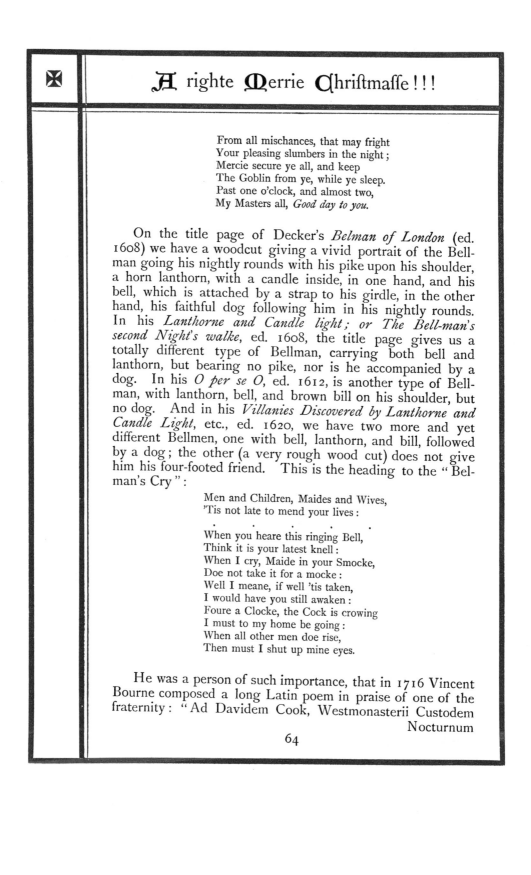
From all mischances, that may fright
Your pleasing slumbers in the night;
Mercie secure ye all, and keep
The Goblin from ye, while ye sleep.
Past one o'clock, and almost two,
My Masters all, *Good day to you.*

On the title page of Decker's *Belman of London* (ed. 1608) we have a woodcut giving a vivid portrait of the Bellman going his nightly rounds with his pike upon his shoulder, a horn lanthorn, with a candle inside, in one hand, and his bell, which is attached by a strap to his girdle, in the other hand, his faithful dog following him in his nightly rounds. In his *Lanthorne and Candle light; or The Bell-man's second Night's walke,* ed. 1608, the title page gives us a totally different type of Bellman, carrying both bell and lanthorn, but bearing no pike, nor is he accompanied by a dog. In his *O per se O,* ed. 1612, is another type of Bellman, with lanthorn, bell, and brown bill on his shoulder, but no dog. And in his *Villanies Discovered by Lanthorne and Candle Light,* etc., ed. 1620, we have two more and yet different Bellmen, one with bell, lanthorn, and bill, followed by a dog; the other (a very rough wood cut) does not give him his four-footed friend. This is the heading to the "Belman's Cry":

Men and Children, Maides and Wives,
'Tis not late to mend your lives:

.   .   .   .   .

When you heare this ringing Bell,
Think it is your latest knell:
When I cry, Maide in your Smocke,
Doe not take it for a mocke:
Well I meane, if well 'tis taken,
I would have you still awaken:
Foure a Clocke, the Cock is crowing
I must to my home be going:
When all other men doe rise,
Then must I shut up mine eyes.

He was a person of such importance, that in 1716 Vincent Bourne composed a long Latin poem in praise of one of the fraternity: "Ad Davidem Cook, Westmonasterii Custodem
Nocturnum

64

Nocturnum et Vigilantissimum," a translation of which runs thus, in the last few lines:

> Should you and your dog ever call at my door,
> You'll be welcome, I promise you, nobody more.
> May you call at a thousand each year that you live,
> A shilling, at least, may each householder give;
> May the "Merry Old Christmas" you wish us, befal,
> And your self, and your dog, be the merriest of all!

At Christ-tide it was their custom to leave a copy of verses, mostly of Scriptural character, and generally very sorry stuff, at every house on their beat, with a view to receiving a Christmas box; and this was an old custom, for Gay notices it in his *Trivia* (book ii.) written in 1715:

> Behold that narrow street which steep descends,
> Whose building to the slimy shore extends;
> Here Arundel's fam'd structure rear'd its frame,
> The street, alone, retains the empty name;
> Where Titian's glowing paint the canvass warm'd,
> And Raphael's fair design, with judgment, charm'd,
> Now hangs the *bellman's song*, and pasted here
> The coloured prints of Overton appear.

Another ante-Christmas custom now falling into desuetude is the waits, who originally were musical watchmen, who had to give practical evidence of their vigilance by playing on the hautboy, or flageolet, at stated times during the night. In the household of Edward IV. there is mentioned in the *Liber niger Domus Regis*, "A Wayte, that nightely from Mychelmas to Shreve Thorsdaye *pipe the watch* within this courte fowere tymes; in the Somere nightes three tymes, and maketh *bon gayte* at every chambre doare and offyce, as well for feare of pyckeres and pillers."[1]

These waits afterwards became bands of musicians, who were ready to play at any festivities, such as weddings, etc., and almost every city and town had its band of waits; the City of London had its Corporation Waits, which played before the Lord Mayor in his inaugural procession, and at banquets

[1] Pickers and stealers.

banquets and other festivities. They wore blue gowns, red sleeves and caps, and every one had a silver collar about his neck. Ned Ward thus describes them in his *London Spy* (1703).

"At last bolted out from the corner of a street, with an *ignis fatuus* dancing before them, a parcel of strange hobgoblins, covered with long frieze rugs and blankets, hooped round with leather girdles from their cruppers to their shoulders, and their noddles buttoned up into caps of martial figure, like a Knight Errant at tilt and tournament, with his wooden head locked in an iron helmet; one, armed, as I thought with a lusty faggot-bat, and the rest with strange wooden weapons in their hands, in the shape of clyster pipes, but as long almost as speaking trumpets. Of a sudden they clapped them to their mouths, and made such a frightful yelling that I thought *he* would have been dissolving, and the terrible sound of the last trumpet to be within an inch of my ears . . . 'Why, what,' says he, 'don't you love musick? These are the topping tooters of the town, and have gowns, silver chains and salaries for playing *Lilli-borlero* to my Lord Mayor's horse through the City.'"

That these Corporation Waits were no mean musicians we have the authority of Morley, who, in dedicating his *Consort Lessons* to the Lord Mayor and Aldermen in 1599, says:

"As the ancient custom of this most honourable and renowned city hath been ever to retain and maintain excellent and expert musicians to adorn your Honours' favours, feasts and solemn meetings—to these, your Lordships' Wayts, I recommend the same—to your servants' careful and skilful handling."

These concert lessons were arranged for six instruments —viz. two viols (treble and bass), a flute, a cittern (a kind of guitar, strung with wire), a treble lute, and a pandora, which was a large instrument, similar to a lute, but strung with wire in lieu of catgut.

The following is a description of the York Waits, end of seventeenth century:

> In a Winter's morning,   'Ere the cock did crow,
> Long before the dawning,   Or stars their light withdraw,
>   Wak'd

Wak'd by a hornpipe pretty,
Play'd along York City,
By th' help of o'er night's bottle
Damon made this ditty. . . .
In a winter's night,
By moon or lanthorn light,
Through hail, rain, frost, or snow
Their rounds the music go ;
Clad each in frieze or blanket
(For either, heav'n be thanked),
Lin'd with wine a quart,
Or ale a double tankard.
Burglars send away,
And, bar guests dare not stay ;
Of claret, snoring sots
Dream o'er their pipes and pots,

.   .   .   .   .   .

Candles, four in the pound,
Lead up the jolly Round,

While Cornet shrill i' th' middle
Marches, and merry fiddle,
Curtal with deep hum, hum,
Cries we come, come,
And theorbo loudly answers,
Thrum, thrum, thrum, thrum,
    thrum.
But, their fingers frost-nipt,
So many notes are o'erslipt,
That you'd take sometimes
The Waits for the Minster chimes :
Then, Sirs, to hear their musick
Would make both me and you sick,
And much more to hear a roopy
    fiddler call
(With voice, as Moll would cry,
" Come, shrimps, or cockles buy ").
" Past three, fair frosty morn,
Good morrow, my masters all."

With regard to their modern practice of playing during the night-tide, we find the following explanation in an *Essay on the Musical Waits at Christmas*, by John Cleland, 1766. Speaking of the Druids, he says : " But, whatever were their reasons for this preference, it is out of doubt that they generally chose the dead of night for the celebration of their greatest solemnities and festivals. Such assemblies, then, whether of religion, of ceremony, or of mere merriment, were promiscuously called *Wakes*, from their being nocturnal. The master of the *Revels* (*Reveils*) would, in good old English, be termed the Master of the *Wakes*. In short, such nocturnal meetings are the *Wakes* of the Britons ; the *Reveillons* of the French ; the *Medianoche* of the Spaniards ; and the *Pervigilia* of the Romans. The Custom of *Wakes* at burials (*les vigiles des morts*) is at this moment, in many parts, not discontinued.

" But, at the antient *Yule* (or Christmas time, especially), the dreariness of the weather, the length of the night, would naturally require something extraordinary, to wake and rouse men from their natural inclination to rest, and to a warm bed, at that hour. The summons, then, to the *Wakes* of that season were given by music, going the rounds of invitation to the mirth or festivals which were awaiting them. In this there was some propriety, some object ; but where is there
any

67

any in such a solemn piece of banter as that of music going the rounds and disturbing people in vain? For, surely, any meditation to be thereby excited on the holiness of the ensuing day could hardly be of great avail, in a bed, between sleeping and waking. But such is the power of custom to perpetuate absurdities.

"However, the music was called *The Wakeths*, and, by the usual tendency of language to euphony, softened into *Waits*, as *workth* into *wort*, or *checkths* into *chess*, etc."

Another authority, Jones, in his *Welsh Bards*, 1794, says: "Waits are musicians of the lower order, who commonly perform on Wind instruments, and they play in most towns under the windows of the chief inhabitants, at midnight, a short time before Christmas; for which they collect a Christmas box, from house to house. They are said to derive their name of *Waits*, for being always in waiting to celebrate weddings and other joyous events happening within their district. There is a building at Newcastle called *Waits' Tower*, which was, formerly, the meeting-house of the town band of musicians."

The town waits certainly existed in Westminster as late as 1822, and they were elected by the Court of Burgesses of that city—*vide* a magazine cutting of that date: "*Christmas Waits.*—Charles Clapp, Benjamin Jackson, Denis Jelks, and Robert Prinset, were brought to Bow Street Office by O. Bond, the constable, charged with performing on several musical instruments in St. Martin's Lane, at half-past twelve o'clock this morning, by Mr. Munroe, the authorized principal Wait, appointed by the Court of Burgesses for the City and Liberty of Westminster, who alone considers himself entitled, by his appointment, to apply for Christmas boxes. He also urged that the prisoners, acting as Minstrels, came under the meaning of the Vagrant Act, alluded to in the 17th Geo. II.; however, on reference to the last Vagrant Act of the present king, the word 'minstrels' is omitted; consequently, they are no longer cognizable under that Act of Parliament; and, in addition to that, Mr. Charles Clapp, one of the prisoners, produced his indenture of having served seven years as an apprentice to the profession of a musician to Mr. Clay, who held the same appointment as Mr. Munroe does under the

Court

Court of Burgesses. The prisoners were discharged, after receiving an admonition from Mr. Halls, the sitting magistrate, not to collect Christmas boxes."

In an article, "Concerning Christmas," in *Belgravia* (vol. 6, new series, p. 326), we read: "It may not, perhaps, be generally known that, in the year of grace 1871, 'Waits' are regularly sworn before the Court of Burgesses at Westminster, and act under the authority of a warrant, signed by the clerk, and sealed with the arms of the city and liberty; in addition to which they are bound to provide themselves with a silver badge, also bearing the arms of Westminster."

The modern waits have entirely departed from any pretence of allusion to Christ-tide, and play indifferently the last things out in dance music, operatic airs, or music-hall songs; and they act upon people according to their various temperaments, some liking to "hear the waits," whilst others roundly anathematise them for disturbing their slumbers.

CHAPTER IX

Christ-tide Carols—The days of Yule—A Carol for Christ-tide—"Lullaby"—
The Cherry-tree Carol—Dives and Lazarus.

THE singing of carols is now confined to Christmas day; but
it was not always so, appropriate carols being sung during the
Christ-tide preceding the day of the Nativity—such, for
instance, as the following examples. The first is taken from
Sloane MS. 2593, in the British Museum, and in this one I
have preserved the old spelling, which is ascribed to the time
of Henry VI. It will be seen that Christ-tide is prolonged
till Candlemas day, the Feast of the Purification of the Blessed
Virgin Mary, which is kept on the 2nd of February, on which
day all Christ-tide decorations are taken down.

Make we myrth
For Crystes byrth,
    And syng we ȝole[1] tyl Candelmes.

The fyrst day of ȝole have we in mynd,
How God was man born of oure kynd:
For he the bondes wold onbynd
    Of all oure synnes and wykednes.

The secund day we syng of Stevene,
That stoned and steyyd up even
To God that he saw stond in hevyn,
    And crounned was for hys prouesse.

The iij day longeth to sent Johan,
That was Cristys darlyng, derer non,
Whom he betok, whan he shuld gon,
    Hys moder der for hyr clennesse,

The

---

[1] Yule.

The iiij day of the chyldren ʒong,
That Herowd to deth had do with wrong,
And Crist thei coud non tell with tong,
But with ther blod bar hym wytnesse.

The v day longeth to sent Thomas,[1]
That as a strong pyller of bras,
Held up the chyrch, and sclayn he was,
For he sted with ryʒtwesnesse.

The viij day tok Jhesu hys name,
That saved mankynd fro syn and shame,
And circumsysed was for no blame,
But for ensample of meknesse.

The xij day offerd to hym kynges iij,
Gold, myr, and cence, thes gyftes free,
For God, and man, and kyng was he,
Thus worschyppyd thei his worthynes.

On the xl day cam Mary myld,
Unto the temple with hyr chyld,
To shew hyr clen that never was fylyd,
And therwith endyth Chrystmes.

The following is taken from a MS. of the latter half of the fifteenth century, which Mr. Thomas Wright edited for the Percy Society in 1847. The spelling is even more archaic than the above, so that it is modernised, and a gloss given for all those words which may not be easily understood wherever possible :—

This endris[2] night
I saw a sight,
    A star as bright as day ;
And ever among
A maiden sung,
    Lullay, by by, lullay.

The lovely lady sat and sang, and to her Child said—
My son, my brother, my father dear, why lyest Thou thus in hayd.
    My sweet bird,
    Thus it is betide   Though

---

[1] St. Thomas à Becket, of Canterbury, was commemorated on 29th December.   [2] Last.

Though Thou be King veray ;[1]
But, nevertheless,
I will not cease
To sing, by by, lullay.

The Child then spake in His talking, and to His mother said—
I bekyd[2] am King, in Crib[3] there I be laid;
For Angels bright
Down to Me light,
Thou knowest it is no nay ;
And of that sight
Thou mays't be light
To sing, by by, lullay.

Now, sweet Son, since Thou art King, why art Thou laid in stall?
Why not Thou ordained Thy bedding in some great King his hall?
Me thinketh it is right
That King or Knight
Should lie in good array ;
And then among
It were no wrong
To sing, by by, lullay.

Mary, mother, I am thy child, though I be laid in stall,
Lords and dukes shall worship Me, and so shall Kings all ;
Ye shall well see
That Kings three
Shall come the twelfth day ;
For this behest
Give me thy breast
And sing, by by, lullay.

Now tell me, sweet Son, I pray Thee, Thou art my love and dear,
How should I keep Thee to Thy pay,[4] and make Thee glad of cheer ;
For all Thy will
I would fulfil
Thou witest[5] full well, in fay,[6]
And for all this
I will Thee kiss
And sing, by by, lullay.

My

---

[1] True. [2] I am renowned as. [3] Manger. [4] Satisfaction.
[5] Knowest. [6] In faith.

My dear mother, when time it be, thou take Me up aloft,
And set Me upon thy knee, and handle Me full soft ;
　　　And in thy arm,
　　　Thou wilt Me warm,
　　　　　And keep night and day ;
　　　If I weep,
　　　And may not sleep,
　　　　　Thou sing, by by, lullay.

Now, sweet Son, since it is so, that all thing is at Thy will,
I pray Thee grant me a boon, if it be both right and skill.[1]
　　　That child or man,
　　　That will or can
　　　　　Be merry upon my day ;
　　　To bliss them bring,
　　　And I shall sing
　　　　　Lullay, by by, lullay.

A very popular carol, too, was that of the Legend of the Cherry Tree, which is very ancient, and is one of the scenes in the fifteenth of the Coventry Mysteries, which were played in the fifteenth century, on *Corpus Christi Day.*

Joseph was an old man,
　And an old man was he,
And he married Mary
　The Queen of Galilee.

When Joseph was married,
　And Mary home had brought,
Mary proved with child,
　And Joseph knew it not.

Joseph and Mary walked
　Through a garden gay,
Where the cherries they grew
　Upon every tree.

O, then bespoke Mary,
　With words both meek and mild,
"O, gather me cherries, Joseph,
　They run so in my mind."

And then replied Joseph,
　With his words so unkind,
"Let him gather thee cherries,
　That got thee with child."

O, then bespoke our Saviour,
　All in His mother's womb,
"Bow down, good cherry tree,
　To My mother's hand."

The uppermost sprig
　Bowed down to Mary's knee,
"Thus you may see, Joseph,
　These cherries are for me."

"O, eat your cherries, Mary,
　O, eat your cherries now,
O, eat your cherries, Mary,
　That grow upon the bough."

The parable of Dives and Lazarus was a great favourite at Christ-tide, as, presumably, it served to stir up men to deeds of charity towards their poorer brethren ; but the follow-
　　　　　　　　　　　　　　　　　　　　　　ing

[1] Reasonable.

ing carol, parts of which are very curious, has nothing like the antiquity of the foregoing examples :—

As it fell out upon a day,
  Rich Dives made a feast,
And he invited all his guests,
  And gentry of the best.

Then Lazarus laid him down, and
  down,
  And down at Dives' door,
" Some meat, some drink, brother
  Dives,
  Bestow upon the poor."

" Thou art none of my brother,
  Lazarus,
  That lies begging at my door,
No meat, nor drink will I give thee,
  Nor bestow upon the poor."

Then Lazarus laid him down, and
  down,
  And down at Dives' wall,
" Some meat, some drink, brother
  Dives,
  Or with hunger starve I shall."

" Thou art none of my brother,
  Lazarus,
  That lies begging at my wall,
No meat, nor drink will I give thee,
  But with hunger starve you shall."

Then Lazarus laid him down, and
  down,
  And down at Dives' gate,
" Some meat, some drink, brother
  Dives,
  For Jesus Christ, His sake."

" Thou art none of my brother,
  Lazarus,
  That lies begging at my gate,
No meat, nor drink I'll give to thee,
  For Jesus Christ, His sake."

Then Dives sent out his merry men,
  To whip poor Lazarus away,
But they had no power to strike a
  stroke,
  And flung their whips away.

Then Dives sent out his hungry dogs,
  To bite him as he lay.
But they had no power to bite at all,
  So licked his sores away.

As it fell out upon a day,
  Poor Lazarus sickened and died,
There came an Angel out of heaven,
  His soul there for to guide.

" Rise up, rise up, brother Lazarus,
  And come along with me,
For there's a place in heaven provided
  To sit on an Angel's knee."

As it fell out upon a day,
  Rich Dives sickened and died,
There came a serpent out of hell,
  His soul there for to guide.

" Rise up, rise up, brother Dives,
  And come along with me,
For there's a place in hell provided,
  To sit on a serpent's knee."

Then Dives lifting his eyes to heaven,
  And seeing poor Lazarus blest,
" Give me a drop of water, brother
  Lazarus,
  To quench my flaming thirst.

" Oh ! had I as many years to abide,
  As there are blades of grass,
Then there would be an ending day ;
  But in hell I must ever last.

" Oh ! was I now but alive again,
  For the space of one half hour,
I would make my will, and then secure
  That the devil should have no
  power."

CHAPTER X

Christmas Eve—Herrick thereon—The Yule Log—Folk-lore thereon—The Ashen Faggot—Christmas Candles—Christmas Eve in the Isle of Man—Hunting the Wren—Divination by Onions and Sage—A Custom at Aston—"The Mock"—Decorations and Kissing Bunch—"Black Ball"—Guisers and Waits—Ale Posset.

ALL the festivals of the Church are preceded by a vigil, or eve, and, considering the magnitude of the festival of Christmas, it is no wonder that the ceremonial attaching to the eve of the Nativity outvies all others. What sings old Herrick of it?

> Come, bring with a noise,
> My merrie, merrie boyes,
> The Christmas Log to the firing;
> While my good Dame, she
> Bids ye all be free;
> And drink to your hearts' desiring.
>
> With the last yeere's brand,
> Light the new block, And
> For good success in his spending,
> On your Psalterie play,
> That sweet luck may
> Come while the Log is teending.[1]
>
> Drink now the strong Beere,
> Cut the white loafe heere,
> The while the meat is a shredding;
> For the rare Mince pie,
> And the Plums stand by
> To fill the Paste that's a-kneading.

Bringing

---

[1] Lighting, burning.

75

Bringing in the Yule log, clog, or block—for it is indifferently called by any of these names, was a great function on Christmas eve—and much superstitious reverence was paid to it, in order to insure good luck for the coming year. It had to be lit "with the last yeere's brand," and Herrick gives the following instructions in *The Ceremonies for Candlemasse day*.

> Kindle the Christmas Brand, and then
> Till Sunne-set, let it burne ;
> Which quencht, then lay it up agen,
> Till Christmas next returne.

> Part must be kept, wherewith to teend
> The Christmas Log next yeare ;
> And, where 'tis safely kept, the Fiend
> Can do no mischief there.

But, even if lit with the remains of last year's log, it seems to be insufficient, unless the advice to the maids who light it be followed.

> Wash your hands, or else the fire
> Will not teend to your desire ;
> Unwasht hands, ye Maidens, know,
> Dead the Fire, though ye blow.

In some parts of Devonshire a curious custom in connection with the Yule log is still kept up, that of burning the Ashton or ashen faggot. It is well described by a writer in *Notes and Queries*.[1]

"Of the olden customs, so many of which are dying out, that of burning an 'ashen faggot' on Christmas Eve, still holds its own, and is kept up at many farm houses.

"Among the various gleanings of the Devon Association Folk-Lore Committee is recorded a notice of this custom. We are there informed that, on Christmas eve, 1878, the customary faggot was burned at *thirty-two* farms and cottages in the Ashburton postal district alone.

"The details of the observance vary in different families ; but some, being common to all, may be considered as held necessary to the due performance of the rite. For example, the

[1] Sixth series, vol. ii. p. 508.

the faggot must contain as large a log of ash as possible, usually the trunk of a tree, remnants of which are supposed to continue smouldering on the hearth the whole of the twelve days of Christmas.   This is the Yule dog of our forefathers, from which a fire can be raised by the aid of a pair of bellows, at any moment day or night, in token of the ancient custom of open hospitality at such a season.   Then the faggot must be bound together with as many binders of twisted hazel as possible.   Remembering that the Ash and Hazel were sacred trees with the Scandinavians, their combined presence in forming the faggot may once have contained some mystic signification.   Also, as each binder is burned through, a quart of cider is claimed by the Company.   By this, some hidden connexion between the pleasures of the party and the loosening bands of the faggot is typified.   While the fire lasts, all sorts of amusements are indulged in—all distinction between master and servant, neighbour and visitor, is for the time set aside.

> The heir, with roses in his shoes,
> That night might village partner choose ;
> The lord, underogating, share
> The vulgar game of ' post and pair.'
> All hailed, with uncontrolled delight,
> And general voice, the happy night,
> That to the cottage, as the crown,
> Brought tidings of Salvation down.

" In some houses, when the faggot begins to burn up, a young child is placed on it, and his future pluck foretold by his nerve or timidity.   May not this be a remnant of the dedication of children to the Deity by passing them through the sacred fire ?

" Different reasons are given for burning Ash.   By some, it is said that when our Saviour was born, Joseph cut a bundle of Ash, which, every one knows, burns very well when green ; that, by this, was lighted a fire, by which He was first dressed in swaddling clothes.

" The gipsies have a legend that our Saviour was born out in a field like themselves, and brought up by an Ash fire. The holly, ivy, and pine, they say, hid him, and so, now, are always green, whilst the ash and the oak showed where He
was

77

was hiding, and they remain dead all the winter. Therefore the gipsies burn Ash at Christmas.

"We can well understand how the pleasures of the ashen faggot are looked forward to with delight by the hard-working agricultural labourer, for whom few social enjoyments are provided. The harvest home, in these days of machinery, seems lost in the usual routine of work, and the shearing feast, when held, is confined to the farmer's family, or shepherd staff, and is not a general gathering. Moreover, these take place in the long busy days of summer, when extra hands and strangers are about the farm doing job work. But, with Christmas, things are different. Work is scarce ; only the regular hands are on the farm, and there is nothing to prevent following out the good old custom of our ancestors, of feasting, for once, those among whom one's lot is cast.

> England was Merry England, when
> Old Christmas brought his sports again.
> 'Twas Christmas broached the mightiest ale ;
> 'Twas Christmas told the merriest tale :
> A Christmas gambol oft could cheer
> The poor man's heart through half the year."

To add to the festivity and light, large candles are burnt, the bigger the better ; but, as the custom of keeping Christmas descended from "Children of a larger growth" to those of lesser, so did the size of the candles decrease in proportion, until they reached the minimum at which we now know them. In the Isle of Man they had a custom which has, probably, dropped into desuetude, of all going to church on Christmas eve, each bearing the largest candle procurable. The churches were well decorated with holly, and the service, in commemoration of the Nativity, was called *Oiel Verry*. Waldron, in his *Description of the Isle of Man*, says, " On the 24th of December, towards evening, all the servants in general have a holiday ; they go not to bed all night, but ramble about till the bells ring in all the churches, which is at twelve o'clock : prayers being over, they go to hunt the wren ; and, after having found one of these poor birds, they kill her and lay her on a bier, with the utmost solemnity, bringing her to the parish church, and burying her with a whimsical kind of solemnity,

78

solemnity, singing dirges over her in the Manks language, which they call her knell; after which Christmas begins."

There are many peculiar customs appertaining to Christmas eve. Burton, in his *Anatomy of Melancholy*, says, "'Tis their only desire, if it may be done by art, to see their husband's picture in a glass; they'll give anything to know when they shall be married; how many husbands they shall have, by *Cromnyomantia*, a kind of divination, with onions laid on the altar at Christmas eve." This seems to be something like that which we have seen practised on St. Thomas's day—or that described in Googe's *Popish Kingdome*.

> In these same days, young wanton gyrles that meet for marriage be,
> Doe search to know the names of them that shall their husbands be;
> Four onyons, five, or eight, they take, and make in every one
> Such names as they doe fancie most, and best to think upon.
> Then near the chimney them they set, and that same onyon then
> That firste doth sproute doth surely beare the name of their good man.

In Northamptonshire another kind of divination, with the same object, used to be practised: the girl who was anxious to ascertain her lot in the married state, went into the garden and plucked twelve sage leaves, under the firm conviction that she would be favoured with a glimpse of the shadowy form of her future husband as he approached her from the opposite end of the ground; but she had to take great care not to damage or break the sage stock, otherwise the consequences would be fearful. But then, in this county, the ghosts of people who had been buried at cross roads had liberty to walk about and show themselves on Christmas eve, so that the country folk did not care to stir out more than necessary on the vigil. At Walton-le-Dale, in Lancashire, the inmates of most of the houses sat up on Christmas eve, with their doors open, whilst one of the party read the narrative of St. Luke, the saint himself being supposed to pass through the house.

A contributor to the *Gentleman's Magazine*, 7th February 1795, gives the following account of a custom which took place annually on the 24th of December, at the house of a gentleman residing at Aston, near Birmingham. "As soon as supper is over, a table is set in the hall. On it is placed

a

79

a brown loaf, with twenty silver threepences stuck on the top of it, a tankard of ale, with pipes and tobacco; and the two oldest servants have chairs behind it, to sit as judges, if they please. The steward brings the servants, both men and women, by one at a time, covered with a winnow sheet, and lays their right hand on the loaf, exposing no other part of the body. The oldest of the two judges guesses at the person, by naming a name, then the younger judge, and, lastly, the oldest again. If they hit upon the right person, the steward leads the person back again; but, if they do not, he takes off the winnow sheet, and the person receives a threepence, makes a low obeisance to the judges, but speaks not a word. When the second servant was brought, the younger judge guessed first and third; and this they did alternately, till all the money was given away. Whatever servant had not slept in the house the preceding night forfeited his right to the money. No account is given of the origin of this strange custom, but it has been practised ever since the family lived there. When the money is gone, the servants have full liberty to drink, dance, sing, and go to bed when they please."

In Cornwall, in many villages, Christmas merriment begins on the vigil, when the "mock" or Yule log is lighted by a portion saved from last year's fire. The family gather round the blaze, and amuse themselves with various games; and even the younger children are allowed, as a special favour, to sit up till a late hour to see the fun, and afterwards "to drink to the mock." In the course of the evening the merriment is increased by the entry of the "goosey dancers" (guised dancers), the boys and girls of the village, who have rifled their parents' wardrobes of old coats and gowns and, thus disguised, dance and sing, and beg money to make merry with. They are allowed, and are not slow to take, a large amount of license in consideration of the season. It is considered to be out of character with the time, and a mark of an ill-natured churlish disposition, to take offence at anything they do or say. This mumming is kept up during the week.

A very graphic description of Christmas eve in a Derbyshire cottage is given in *Notes and Queries*.[1] "For several weeks

[1] Fifth series, viii. p. 481.

weeks before Christmas the cottager's household is much busier than usual in making preparations for the great holiday. The fatted pig has been killed, as a matter of course, and Christmas pies, mince pies, and many other good things made from it in readiness for the feast. The house has been thoroughly cleaned, and all made 'spick and span.' The lads of the house, with those of their neighbours, have been learning their parts, and getting ready their dresses for the 'Christmas guising,' and the household daily talk is full flavoured of Christmas.

"The lasses have made their own special preparations, and for two or three days before Christmas Eve have been getting ready the accustomed house decorations—short garlands of holly and other evergreens for the tops of cupboards, pictures, and other furniture—and making up the most important decoration of all, 'the kissing-bunch.'

"This 'kissing-bunch' is always an elaborate affair. The size depends upon the couple of hoops—one thrust through the other—which form its skeleton. Each of the ribs is garlanded with holly, ivy, and sprigs of other greens, with bits of coloured ribbons and paper roses, rosy cheeked apples, specially reserved for this occasion, and oranges. Three small dolls are also prepared, often with much taste, and these represent our Saviour, the mother of Jesus, and Joseph. These dolls generally hang within the kissing-bunch by strings from the top, and are surrounded by apples, oranges tied to strings, and various brightly coloured ornaments. Occasionally, however, the dolls are arranged in the kissing-bunch to represent a manger scene.

"When the preparations are completed, the house is decorated during the day of Christmas eve. Every leaded window-pane holds its sprig of holly, ivy, or box; the ornaments on and over the mantel-shelf receive like attention, and every ledge and corner is loaded with green stuff. Mistletoe is not very plentiful in Derbyshire; but, generally, a bit is obtainable, and this is carefully tied to the bottom of the kissing-bunch, which is then hung in the middle of the house-place, the centre of attraction during Christmas-tide.

"While all this is going on, the housewife is very busy.
'Black-ball'

'Black-ball' has to be made; the 'elderberry wine' to be got out; 'sugar, spice, and all that's nice' and needful placed handy. The shop has to be visited, and the usual yearly gift of one, two, or three Christmas candles received. With these last, as every one knows, the house is lit up at dusk on Christmas Eve.

"Without the 'black-ball' just mentioned, the Christmas rejoicings in a cottage would not be complete. 'Black-ball' is a delicacy compounded of black treacle and sugar boiled together in a pan, to which, when boiling, is added a little flour, grated ginger, and spices. When it is boiled enough, it is poured into a large shallow dish, and, when partially cooled, is cut into squares and lengths, then rolled or moulded into various shapes. When quite cool, it is very hard, and very toothsome to young Derbyshire.

"After an early tea-meal, the fire is made up with a huge Yule-log; all the candles, oil and fat lamps lit, and everything is bright and merry-looking. The head of the family sits in the chimney corner with pipe and glass of ale, or mulled elder wine. The best table is set out, and fairly loaded with Christmas and mince pies, oranges, apples, nuts, 'black-baw,' wine, cakes, and green cheese, and the whole family, with the guests, if any, set about enjoying themselves. Romping games are the order of the eve, broken only when the 'guisers'—of whom there are always several sets—or waits arrive. The 'guisers' are admitted indoors, and go through the several acts of their play. At the conclusion 'Betsy Belzebub' collects coppers from the company, and glasses of ale and wine are given to the players. The Waits, or 'Christmas Singers' as they are mostly called, sing their carols and hymns outside the house, and during the performance cakes and ale, wine, and other cheer are carried out to them. So the Eve passes on.

"At nine or ten o'clock is brewed a large bowl of 'poor man's punch'—ale posset! This is the event of the night. Ale posset, or milk and ale posset as some call it, is made in this wise. Set a quart of milk on the fire. While it boils, crumble a twopenny loaf into a deep bowl, upon which pour the boiling milk. Next, set two quarts of good ale to boil, into which grate ginger and nutmeg, adding a quantity of sugar.

sugar. When the ale nearly boils, add it to the milk and bread in the bowl, stirring it while it is being poured in.

"The bowl of ale posset is then placed in the centre of the table. All the single folks gather round, each provided with a spoon. Then follows an interesting ceremony. A wedding ring, a bone button, and a fourpenny piece are thrown into the bowl, and all begin to eat, each dipping to the bottom of the bowl. He or she who brings up the ring will be the first married; whoever brings up the button will be an old maid or an old bachelor; and he or she who brings out the coin will become the richest. As may be imagined, this creates great fun. When seven shilling gold pieces were in circulation, this was the coin always thrown into the posset.

"The games are resumed when the posset is eaten, or possibly all gather round the fire, and sing or tell stories, whiling away the hours till the stroke of twelve, when all go outside the house to listen, whilst the singers, who have gathered at some point in the village, sing 'Christians, awake!' or 'Hark! the Herald Angels Sing'; and so comes to an end the cottager's one hearth-stone holiday of the whole year."

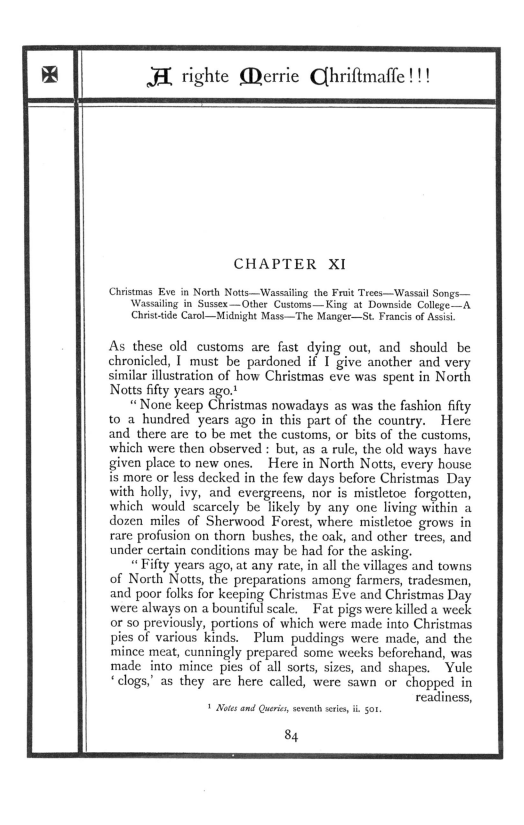
CHAPTER XI

Christmas Eve in North Notts—Wassailing the Fruit Trees—Wassail Songs—Wassailing in Sussex—Other Customs—King at Downside College—A Christ-tide Carol—Midnight Mass—The Manger—St. Francis of Assisi.

As these old customs are fast dying out, and should be chronicled, I must be pardoned if I give another and very similar illustration of how Christmas eve was spent in North Notts fifty years ago.[1]

"None keep Christmas nowadays as was the fashion fifty to a hundred years ago in this part of the country. Here and there are to be met the customs, or bits of the customs, which were then observed : but, as a rule, the old ways have given place to new ones. Here in North Notts, every house is more or less decked in the few days before Christmas Day with holly, ivy, and evergreens, nor is mistletoe forgotten, which would scarcely be likely by any one living within a dozen miles of Sherwood Forest, where mistletoe grows in rare profusion on thorn bushes, the oak, and other trees, and under certain conditions may be had for the asking.

"Fifty years ago, at any rate, in all the villages and towns of North Notts, the preparations among farmers, tradesmen, and poor folks for keeping Christmas Eve and Christmas Day were always on a bountiful scale. Fat pigs were killed a week or so previously, portions of which were made into Christmas pies of various kinds. Plum puddings were made, and the mince meat, cunningly prepared some weeks beforehand, was made into mince pies of all sorts, sizes, and shapes. Yule 'clogs,' as they are here called, were sawn or chopped in readiness,

[1] *Notes and Queries*, seventh series, ii. 501.

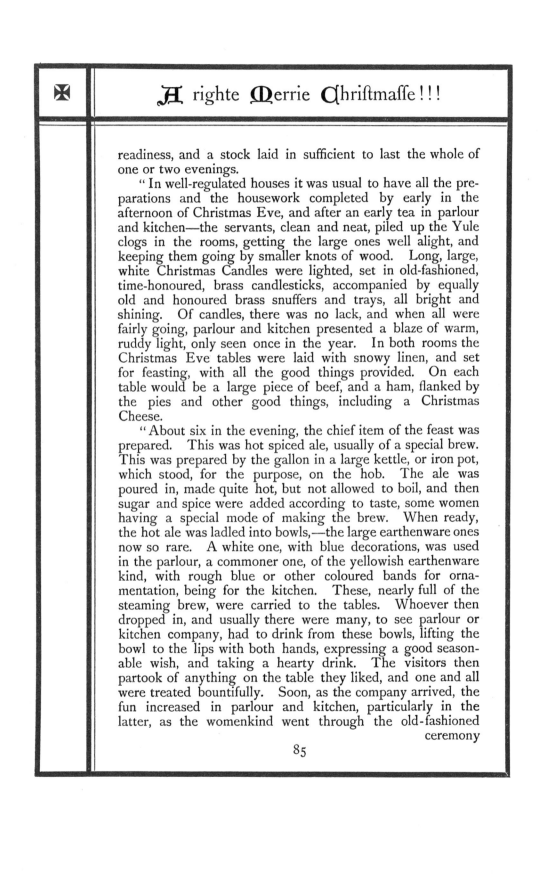
readiness, and a stock laid in sufficient to last the whole of one or two evenings.

"In well-regulated houses it was usual to have all the preparations and the housework completed by early in the afternoon of Christmas Eve, and after an early tea in parlour and kitchen—the servants, clean and neat, piled up the Yule clogs in the rooms, getting the large ones well alight, and keeping them going by smaller knots of wood. Long, large, white Christmas Candles were lighted, set in old-fashioned, time-honoured, brass candlesticks, accompanied by equally old and honoured brass snuffers and trays, all bright and shining. Of candles, there was no lack, and when all were fairly going, parlour and kitchen presented a blaze of warm, ruddy light, only seen once in the year. In both rooms the Christmas Eve tables were laid with snowy linen, and set for feasting, with all the good things provided. On each table would be a large piece of beef, and a ham, flanked by the pies and other good things, including a Christmas Cheese.

"About six in the evening, the chief item of the feast was prepared. This was hot spiced ale, usually of a special brew. This was prepared by the gallon in a large kettle, or iron pot, which stood, for the purpose, on the hob. The ale was poured in, made quite hot, but not allowed to boil, and then sugar and spice were added according to taste, some women having a special mode of making the brew. When ready, the hot ale was ladled into bowls,—the large earthenware ones now so rare. A white one, with blue decorations, was used in the parlour, a commoner one, of the yellowish earthenware kind, with rough blue or other coloured bands for ornamentation, being for the kitchen. These, nearly full of the steaming brew, were carried to the tables. Whoever then dropped in, and usually there were many, to see parlour or kitchen company, had to drink from these bowls, lifting the bowl to the lips with both hands, expressing a good seasonable wish, and taking a hearty drink. The visitors then partook of anything on the table they liked, and one and all were treated bountifully. Soon, as the company arrived, the fun increased in parlour and kitchen, particularly in the latter, as the womenkind went through the old-fashioned ceremony

85

ceremony under the mistletoe, which was hung aloft from a highly-decorated 'kissing-bunch.'

"All sorts of games and fun went on till about ten o'clock, as a rule, about which time the master, mistress, and family, with the rest of the parlour company, visited the kitchen. Then the steaming ale bowl was refilled, and all, beginning with the master and the mistress, in turn drank from the bowl. This over, the parlour company remained, and entered into the games for a time. There was always some one who could sing a suitable song ; and one, if song it can be called, was :

The Folks' Song.

When me an' my folks
Come to see you an' your folks,
Let you an' your folks
Treat me an' my folks
As kind, as me an' my folks
Treated you an' your folks,
When you an' your folks
Came to see me an' my folks,
Sure then ! never were such folks
Since folks were folks !

"This was sung several times over with the last two lines as a chorus. The proceedings in the kitchen closed with another general sup from the replenished bowl, the parlour folks returning to the parlour. During the evening the proceedings were varied by visits from Christmas singers and the mummers, all of whom were well entertained. Usually, if the weather was fit, the kitchen folks wound up the night with a stroll, dropping in to see friends at other houses. As a rule, soon after midnight the feastings were over, but most folks never thought of retiring till they heard the bands of singers in the distance singing the morning hymn, 'Christians, awake!'"

A very old custom was that of "wassailing" the fruit trees on Christmas eve, although it obtained on other days, such as New Year's day and Twelfth day. Herrick says :

Wassaile the Trees that they may beare
You many a Plum and many a Peare ;
For more or lesse fruits they will bring,
As you do give them Wassailing.

This

This custom of drinking to the trees and pouring forth libations to them differs according to the locality. In some parts of Devonshire it used to be customary for the farmer, with his family and friends, after partaking together of hot cakes and cider (the cakes being dipped in the liquor previous to being eaten), to proceed to the orchard, one of the party bearing hot cake and cider as an offering to the principal apple tree. The cake was formally deposited on the fork of the tree, and the cider thrown over it.

In the neighbourhood of the New Forest the following lines are sung at the wassailing of the trees :

> Apples and pears, with right good corn
> Come in plenty to every one ;
> Eat and drink good cake and hot ale,
> Give earth to drink, and she'll not fail.

Horsfield, who wrote of Sussex, speaks somewhat at length of this subject, and says that the wassail bowl was compounded of ale, sugar, nutmeg, and roasted apples, the latter called "lambs' wool." The wassail bowl is placed on a small round table, and each person present is furnished with a silver spoon to stir. They then walk round the table as they go, and stirring with the right hand, and every alternate person passes at the same time under the arm of his preceding neighbour. The wassailing (or "worsling," as it is termed in West Sussex) of the fruit trees is considered a matter of grave importance, and its omission is held to bring ill luck, if not the loss of all the next crop. Those who engage in the ceremony are called "howlers."

The farm labourers, or boys (says Horsfield), after the day's toil is ended, assemble in a group to wassail the apple trees, etc. The trumpeter of the party is furnished with a cow's horn, with which he makes sweet music. Thus equipped, they call on the farmer, and inquire, "please, sir, do you want your trees worsled?" they then proceed to the orchard, and encircling one of the largest and best-bearing trees, chant in a low voice a certain doggerel rhyme ; and this ended, all shout in chorus, with the exception of the trumpeter, who blows a loud blast. During the ceremony they rap the trees with their sticks. "Thus going from tree

87

tree to tree, or group to group, they wassail the whole orchard; this finished, they proceed to the house of the owner, and sing at his door a song common on the occasion. They are then admitted, and, placing themselves around the kitchen fire, enjoy the sparkling ale and the festivities of the season."

There are two wassail rhymes in Sussex:

> Stand fast, root; bear well, top;
> Pray the God send us a good howling crop.
> Every twig, apples big;
> Every bough, apples enow.
> Hats full, caps full,
> Full quarters, sacks full.
>   Holloa, boys, holloa! Hurrah!"

The other is:

> "Here's to thee, old apple tree;
> May'st thou bud, may'st thou blow,
> May'st thou bear apples enow!
> Hats full! Caps full!
> Bushel, bushel sacks full!
> And my pockets full, too!
>   Hurrah!

In the *Gentleman's Magazine* (January 1820, p. 33) mention is made of "an ancient superstitious custom obtaining at Tretyre, in Herefordshire, upon Christmas Eve. They make a cake, poke a stick through it, fasten it upon the horn of an ox, and say certain words, begging a good crop of corn for the master. The men and boys attending the oxen range themselves around. If the ox throws the cake behind it belongs to the men; if before, to the boys. They take with them a wooden bottle of cyder, and drink it, repeating the charm before mentioned."

There is a curious custom at Downside College, near Bath. On Christmas eve the scholars of this well-known institution proceed to the election of their king and other officers of his household, consisting of the mayor of the palace, etc. His reign lasts fourteen days, during which period there are many good feasts; a room in the college being fitted up in fine style, and used by his Majesty as his palace. At Oxford, too, in pre-Reformation time, at Merton

Merton College, they had a king of Christmas, or misrule; at St. John's he was styled lord, and at Trinity he was emperor!

There is a rather rough but pretty west country carol for Christmas eve, which is to be found in Davies Giddy, or Gilbert's *Ancient Christmas Carols, etc.*, and which, he says, was chanted in private houses on Christmas eve throughout the west of England up to the latter part of the last century.

The Lord at first did Adam make
  Out of the dust and clay,
And in his nostrils breathed life,
  E'en as the Scriptures say.
And then in Eden's Paradise
  He placed him to dwell,
That he, within it, should remain,
  To dress and keep it well.
    Now let good Christians all begin
    An holy life to live,
    And to rejoice and merry be,
    For this is Christmas Eve.

And then within the garden he
  Commanded was to stay,
And unto him in commandment
  These words the Lord did say:
"The fruit which in the garden grows
  To thee shall be for meat,
Except the tree in the midst thereof,
  Of which thou shalt not eat."
    Now let good Christians, etc.

"For in the day that thou shalt eat,
  Or to it then come nigh;
For if that thou doth eat thereof,
  Then surely thou shalt die."
But Adam he did take no heed
  Unto that only thing,
But did transgress God's holy law,
  And so was wrapt in sin.
    Now let good Christians, etc.

Now, mark the goodness of the Lord,
  Which He for mankind bore,
His mercy soon He did extend,
  Lost man for to restore;
And then, for to redeem our souls
  From death and hellish thrall,
He said His own dear Son should be
  The Saviour of us all.
    Now let good Christians, etc.

Which promise now is brought to
  pass,
Christians, believe it well;
And by the coming of God's dear
  Son
We are redeemed from thrall.
Then, if we truly do believe,
  And do the thing aright;
Then, by His merits, we, at last,
  Shall live in heaven bright.
    Now let good Christians, etc.

And now the Tide is nigh at hand
  In which our Saviour came;
Let us rejoice, and merry be,
  In keeping of the same.
Let's feed the poor and hungry souls,
  And such as do it crave;
Then, when we die, in heaven sure
  Our reward we shall have.
    Now let good Christians, etc.

Christmas eve is notable in the Roman Catholic Church for the unique fact that mass is celebrated at midnight.

I

I say, advisably, *is* celebrated, because, although Cardinal
Manning abolished public mass at that hour within the
diocese of Westminster about 1867, yet in conventual
establishments it is still kept up, and in every church three
masses are celebrated. The ancient, and, in fact, the modern
use, until interrupted by Cardinal Manning, was to celebrate
mass at midnight, at day-break, and at the third hour
(9 a.m.) This use is very old; for Thelesphorus, who was
Pope A.D. 127, decreed that three masses should be sung
in Festo Nativitatis, to denote that the birth of Christ
brought salvation to the fathers of three periods—viz. the
fathers before, under, and after the law.

Another Roman Catholic custom on Christmas eve
is the preparation of "the Manger," which in some places
is a very elaborate affair. The Christ is lying on straw
between the ox and ass, Mary and Joseph bending over
Him; the shepherds are kneeling in adoration, and the
angels, hovering above, are supposed to be singing the
gloria in excelsis. A writer in the *Catholic World* (vol. xxxiv.
p. 439) says:—"Christmas Dramas are said to owe their
origin to St. Francis of Assisi. Before his death he celebrated the sacred Birth-night in the woods, where a stable
had been prepared with an ox and an ass, and a crib for
an altar. A great number of people came down from the
mountains, singing joyful hymns and bearing torches in
their hands; for it was not fitting that a night that had
given light to the whole world, should be shrouded in
darkness. St. Francis, who loved to associate all nature
with his ministry, was filled with joy. He officiated at the
Mass as deacon. He sang the Gospel, and then preached
in a dramatic manner on the birth of Christ. When he
spoke of the Lamb of God, he was filled with a kind of
divine frenzy, and imitated the plaintive cry of the sacrificial
lamb; and, when he pronounced the sweet name of Jesus,
it was as if the taste of honey were on his lips. One soul
before the rural altar, that night, with purer eyes than the
rest, saw the Divine Babe, radiant with eternal beauty,
lying in the manger."

CHAPTER XII

Decorating with Evergreens—Its Origin and Antiquity—Mistletoe in Churches—The permissible Evergreens—The Holly—"Holly and Ivy"—"Here comes Holly"—"Ivy, chief of Trees"—"The Contest of the Ivy and the Holly"—Holly Folk-lore—Church Decorations—To be kept up till Candlemas day.

CHRISTMAS EVE is especially the time for decorating houses and churches with evergreens, a custom which seems to have come from heathen times; at least, no one seems to know when it commenced. Polydore Vergil[1] says :—"Trymming of the temples with hangynges, floures, boughes, and garlondes, was taken of the heathen people, whiche decked their idols and houses with such array." That it is an old custom in England to deck houses, churches, etc., at Christ-tide with evergreens is undoubted—the only question is, how old is it? Stow, in his *Survey*, says : "Against the Feast of Christmas, every man's house, as also their parish churches, were decked with holme, ivy, bayes, and whatsoever the season of the year afforded to be green. The Conduits and Standards in the streets were, likewise, garnished; among the which I read that, in the year 1444, by tempest of thunder and lightning, towards the morning of Candlemas day, at the Leadenhall in Cornhill, a standard of tree, being set up in the midst of the pavement, fast in the ground, nailed full of holme and ivie, for disport of Christmass to the people, was torne up and cast down by the malignant Spirit (as was thought), and the stones of the pavement all about were cast in the streets, and into divers houses, so that the people were sore aghast at the great tempests."

Stow,

[1] Langley's *Abridg.*, p. 100.

91

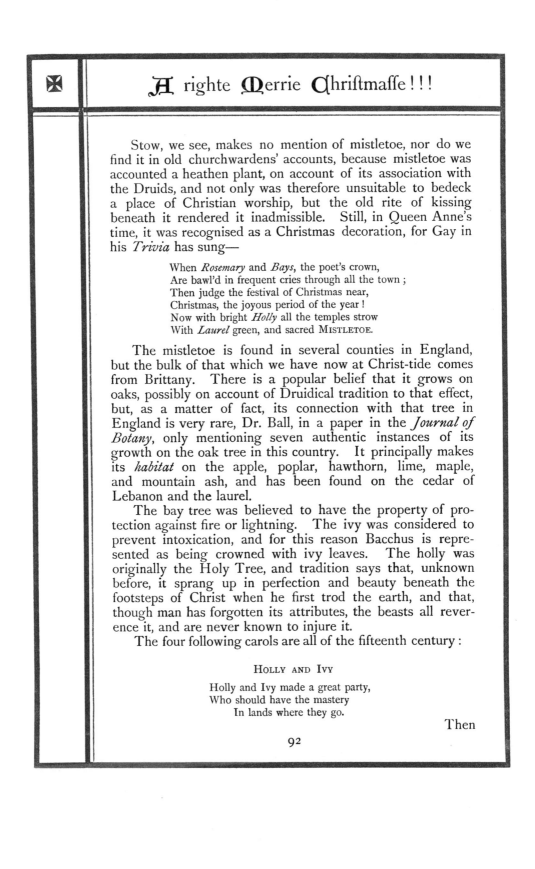

Stow, we see, makes no mention of mistletoe, nor do we find it in old churchwardens' accounts, because mistletoe was accounted a heathen plant, on account of its association with the Druids, and not only was therefore unsuitable to bedeck a place of Christian worship, but the old rite of kissing beneath it rendered it inadmissible. Still, in Queen Anne's time, it was recognised as a Christmas decoration, for Gay in his *Trivia* has sung—

> When *Rosemary* and *Bays*, the poet's crown,
> Are bawl'd in frequent cries through all the town ;
> Then judge the festival of Christmas near,
> Christmas, the joyous period of the year !
> Now with bright *Holly* all the temples strow
> With *Laurel* green, and sacred Mistletoe.

The mistletoe is found in several counties in England, but the bulk of that which we have now at Christ-tide comes from Brittany. There is a popular belief that it grows on oaks, possibly on account of Druidical tradition to that effect, but, as a matter of fact, its connection with that tree in England is very rare, Dr. Ball, in a paper in the *Journal of Botany*, only mentioning seven authentic instances of its growth on the oak tree in this country. It principally makes its *habitat* on the apple, poplar, hawthorn, lime, maple, and mountain ash, and has been found on the cedar of Lebanon and the laurel.

The bay tree was believed to have the property of protection against fire or lightning. The ivy was considered to prevent intoxication, and for this reason Bacchus is represented as being crowned with ivy leaves. The holly was originally the Holy Tree, and tradition says that, unknown before, it sprang up in perfection and beauty beneath the footsteps of Christ when he first trod the earth, and that, though man has forgotten its attributes, the beasts all reverence it, and are never known to injure it.

The four following carols are all of the fifteenth century :

HOLLY AND IVY

> Holly and Ivy made a great party,
> Who should have the mastery
> In lands where they go.

Then

Then spake Holly, "I am fierce and jolly,
I will have the mastery
In lands where we go."

Then spake Ivy, "I am loud and proud,
And I will have the mastery
In lands where we go."

Then spake Holly, and set him down on his knee,
"I pray thee, gentle Ivy, say[1] me no villany
In lands where we go."

HERE COMES HOLLY

Alleluia, Alleluia,
Alleluia, now sing we.
Here comes Holly, that is so gent,[2]
To please all men is his intent,
Alleluia.

But Lord and Lady of this Hall,
Whosoever against Holly call.
Alleluia.

Whosoever against Holly do cry,
In a lepe[3] he shall hang full high.
Alleluia.

Whosoever against Holly doth sing,
He may weep and hands wring.
Alleluia.

IVY, CHIEF OF TREES

The most worthy she is in town,
He that saith other, doth amiss;
And worthy to bear the crown;
Veni coronaberis.

Ivy is soft and meek of speech,
Against all bale she is bliss;
Well is he that may her reach,
Veni coronaberis.

Ivy

---

[1] Do.   [2] Pretty.   [3] A large basket.

Ivy is green with colour bright,
Of all trees best she is;
And that I prove well now be right,
Veni coronaberis.

Ivy beareth berries black.
God grant us all His bliss;
For there shall we nothing lack,
Veni coronaberis.

THE CONTEST OF THE IVY AND THE HOLLY

Nay, Ivy, nay, it shall not be, I wis,
Let Holly have the mastery as the manner is.

Holly standeth in the hall, fair to behold,
Ivy stands without the door; she is full sore a cold.
Nay, Ivy, nay, etc.

Holly and his merry men, they dancen and they sing;
Ivy and her maidens, they weepen and they wring.
Nay, Ivy, nay, etc.

Ivy hath a lybe, she caught it with the cold,
So may they all have, that with Ivy hold.
Nay, Ivy, nay, etc.

Holly hath berries, as red as any rose,
The foresters, the hunters, keep them from the does.
Nay, Ivy, nay, etc.

Ivy hath berries, as black as any sloe,
There comes the owl and eats them as she go.
Nay, Ivy, nay, etc.

Holly hath birds, a full fair flock,
The nightingale, the poppinjay, the gentle laverock.
Nay, Ivy, nay, etc.

Good Ivy, good Ivy, what birds hast thou?
None but the owlet that cries How! How!
Nay, Ivy, nay, etc.

It is just as well to be particular as to the quality of the
holly used in Christmas decorations; for on that depends
who

94

who will be the ruler of the house during the coming year—the wife or the husband. If the holly is smooth the wife will get the upper hand, but if it be prickly, then the husband will gain the supremacy. It is also unlucky to bring holly into the house before Christmas Eve. And, please, if you are doing at home any decorations for the church, be sure and make them on the ground floor, for it is specially unlucky to make anything intended for use in a church in an upper chamber.

The custom of church decoration may possibly have been suggested by a verse in the first lesson appointed to be read on Christmas eve — lx. Isaiah, 13. "The glory of Lebanon shall come unto thee, the fir tree, the pine tree, and the box together, to beautify the place of my sanctuary." Some years ago, at the commencement of the great Church revival, the Christmas decorations in churches were very elaborate, but they are now, as a rule, much quieter, and the only admissible evergreens are contained in the following distich—

> Holly and Ivy, Box and Bay,
> Put in the Church on Christmas day.

These decorations, both in church and in private houses, ought to be kept up until the 1st of February, Candlemas eve, when they should be burnt—a proceeding which set fire to the hall of Christ Church, Oxford, in 1719. Herrick gives the following :—

CEREMONIES FOR CANDLEMASSE EVE

> Down with the Rosemary and Bayes,
> Down with the Mistleto ;
> Instead of Holly, now upraise
> The greener Box (for show).

> The Holly, hitherto did sway ;
> Let Box now domineere ;
> Untill the dancing Easter day,
> Or Easter's Eve appeare.

> The youthfull Box, which now hath grace,
> Your houses to renew ;
> Grown old, surrender must his place,
> Unto the crisped Yew.

When

95

When Yew is out, then Birch comes in,
   And many Flowers beside ;
Both of a fresh and fragrant kinne
   To honour Whitsuntide.

Green Rushes then, and sweetest Bents,
   With cooler Oken boughs ;
Come in for comely ornaments,
   To readorn the house
Thus times do shift ; each thing his turn do's hold ;
New things succeed, as former things grow old.

And with Candlemas day ends all festivity connected
with Christ-tide.

End now the White-loafe, and the Pye,
And let all sports with Christmas dye.

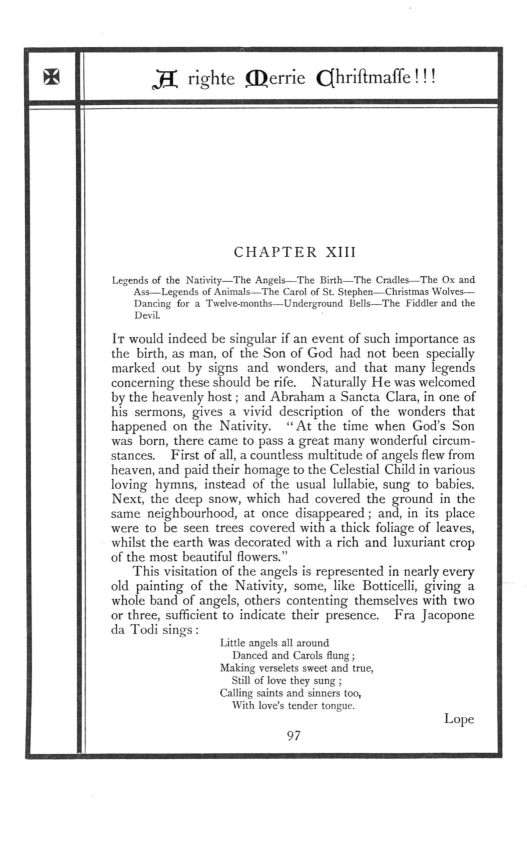

CHAPTER XIII

Legends of the Nativity—The Angels—The Birth—The Cradles—The Ox and Ass—Legends of Animals—The Carol of St. Stephen—Christmas Wolves—Dancing for a Twelve-months—Underground Bells—The Fiddler and the Devil.

IT would indeed be singular if an event of such importance as the birth, as man, of the Son of God had not been specially marked out by signs and wonders, and that many legends concerning these should be rife. Naturally He was welcomed by the heavenly host; and Abraham a Sancta Clara, in one of his sermons, gives a vivid description of the wonders that happened on the Nativity. "At the time when God's Son was born, there came to pass a great many wonderful circumstances. First of all, a countless multitude of angels flew from heaven, and paid their homage to the Celestial Child in various loving hymns, instead of the usual lullabie, sung to babies. Next, the deep snow, which had covered the ground in the same neighbourhood, at once disappeared; and, in its place were to be seen trees covered with a thick foliage of leaves, whilst the earth was decorated with a rich and luxuriant crop of the most beautiful flowers."

This visitation of the angels is represented in nearly every old painting of the Nativity, some, like Botticelli, giving a whole band of angels, others contenting themselves with two or three, sufficient to indicate their presence. Fra Jacopone da Todi sings:

> Little angels all around
>   Danced and Carols flung;
> Making verselets sweet and true,
>   Still of love they sung;
> Calling saints and sinners too,
>   With love's tender tongue.

Lope

97

Lope de Vega makes Our Lady caution the angels as they come through the palm trees—

Holy angels, and blest,
Through these palms as ye sweep,
Hold their branches at rest,
For my Babe is asleep.

And ye, Bethlehem palm-trees,
As stormy winds rush
In tempest and fury,
Your angry noise hush ;—

Move gently, move gently,
Restrain your wild sweep ;
Hold your branches at rest,
My Babe is asleep.

Mrs. Jameson[1] says that "one legend relates that Joseph went to seek a midwife, and met a woman coming down from the mountains, with whom he returned to the stable. But, when they entered, it was filled with light greater than the sun at noonday ; and, as the light decreased, and they were able to open their eyes, they beheld Mary sitting there with her Infant at her bosom. And the Hebrew woman, being amazed, said : 'Can this be true ?' and Mary answered, 'It is true ; as there is no child like unto my son, so there is no woman like unto his mother.'"

Le Bon,[2] speaking of the cradle of Jesus, says : "According to tradition, the stone cradle contained one of wood. That of stone still exists at Bethlehem, not in its primitive state, but decorated with white marble, and enriched with magnificent draperies. The wooden one was, in the seventh century, at the time of the Mahometan Invasion in the East, transported to Rome, then become the new Jerusalem, the Bethlehem of a new people. It there reposes in the superb basilica of Santa Maria Maggiore, where it is guarded by the eternal city with more affection than the Ark of the Covenant, and with more respect than the cottage of Romulus. Centuries have not been able to enfeeble the veneration and the love
with

[1] *Legends of the Madonna*, p. 205. [2] *Fleurs de Catholicisme*, vol. iii. p. 236.

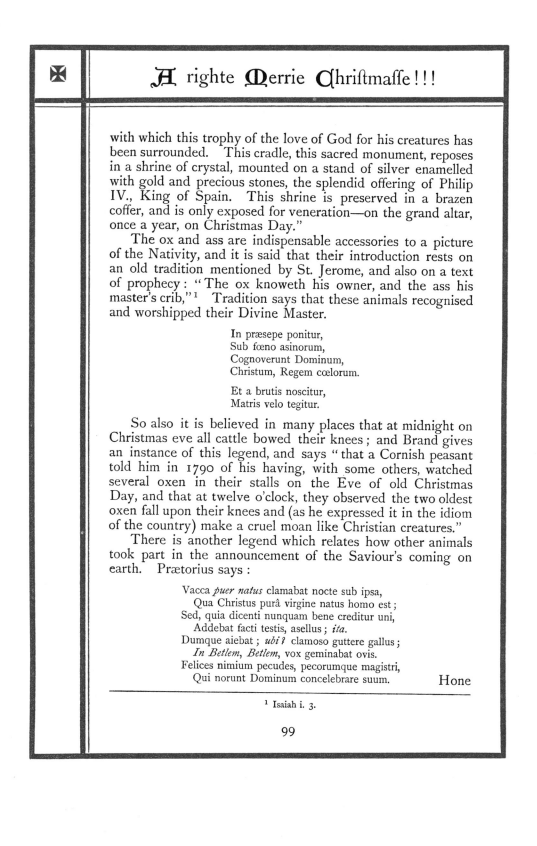

with which this trophy of the love of God for his creatures has been surrounded. This cradle, this sacred monument, reposes in a shrine of crystal, mounted on a stand of silver enamelled with gold and precious stones, the splendid offering of Philip IV., King of Spain. This shrine is preserved in a brazen coffer, and is only exposed for veneration—on the grand altar, once a year, on Christmas Day."

The ox and ass are indispensable accessories to a picture of the Nativity, and it is said that their introduction rests on an old tradition mentioned by St. Jerome, and also on a text of prophecy: "The ox knoweth his owner, and the ass his master's crib,"[1] Tradition says that these animals recognised and worshipped their Divine Master.

> In præsepe ponitur,
> Sub fœno asinorum,
> Cognoverunt Dominum,
> Christum, Regem cœlorum.
>
> Et a brutis noscitur,
> Matris velo tegitur.

So also it is believed in many places that at midnight on Christmas eve all cattle bowed their knees; and Brand gives an instance of this legend, and says "that a Cornish peasant told him in 1790 of his having, with some others, watched several oxen in their stalls on the Eve of old Christmas Day, and that at twelve o'clock, they observed the two oldest oxen fall upon their knees and (as he expressed it in the idiom of the country) make a cruel moan like Christian creatures."

There is another legend which relates how other animals took part in the announcement of the Saviour's coming on earth. Prætorius says:

> Vacca *puer natus* clamabat nocte sub ipsa,
> Qua Christus purâ virgine natus homo est;
> Sed, quia dicenti nunquam bene creditur uni,
> Addebat facti testis, asellus; *ita*.
> Dumque aiebat; *ubi?* clamoso guttere gallus;
> *In Betlem, Betlem*, vox geminabat ovis.
> Felices nimium pecudes, pecorumque magistri,
> Qui norunt Dominum concelebrare suum.   Hone

---

[1] Isaiah i. 3.

Hone describes a curious sheet of carols printed in London in 1701. "It is headed 'CHRISTUS NATUS EST; *Christ is born*,' with a wood-cut 10 inches high by 8½ inches wide, representing the stable of Bethlehem; Christ in the crib, watched by the Virgin and Joseph; shepherds kneeling, angels attending; a man playing on the bagpipes; a woman with a basket of fruit on her head; a sheep bleating, and an ox lowing on the ground; a raven croaking, and a crow cawing, on the hay rack; a cock crowing above them; and angels singing in the sky. The animals have labels from their mouths bearing Latin inscriptions. Down the side of the wood-cut is the following account and explanation :—'A religious man inventing the concerts of both birds and beasts drawn in the picture of our Saviour's birth, doth thus express them : The cock croweth, *Christus natus est*—Christ is born. The raven asked *Quando ?*—When ? The crow replied, *Hac nocte*—this night. The ox crieth out, *Ubi ? Ubi ?*—Where ? Where ? The sheep bleateth out *Bethlehem*. A voice from heaven sounded, *Gloria in Excelsis*—Glory be on high !'"

Another pictorial representation of this legend is mentioned by the Rev. Dr. John Mason Neale in *The Unseen World* (p. 27). An example which, in modern times, would be considered ludicrous, of the manner in which our ancestors made external Nature bear witness to our Lord, occurs in what is called the Prior's Chamber in the small Augustinian house of Shulbrede, in the parish of Linchmere, in Sussex. On the wall is a fresco of the Nativity ; and certain animals are made to give their testimony to that event in words which somewhat resemble, or may be supposed to resemble, their natural sounds. A cock, in the act of crowing, stands at the top, and a label, issuing from his mouth, bears the words, *Christus natus est*. A duck inquires, *Quando ? Quando ?* A raven hoarsely answers, *In hac nocte*. A cow asks, *Ubi ? Ubi ?* And a lamb bleats out *Bethlehem*."

This idea that beasts were endowed with human speech on Christmas night was very widespread, as the following legend well instances, it being common both to Switzerland and Suabia. One Christmas night, in order to test the truth of this legend, a peasant crept slyly upon that solemn and holy night into the stable, where his oxen were quietly chewing

ing the hay set before them. An instant after the peasant had hidden himself, one of the oxen said to another "We are going to have a hard and heavy task to do this week." "How is that? the harvest is got in and we have drawn home all the winter fuel." "That is so," was the reply, "but we shall have to drag a coffin to the churchyard, for our poor master will most certainly die this week." The peasant shrieked, and fell back, senseless, was taken home, and the ox's prophecy was duly fulfilled.

It is also thought that the cocks crow all night at Christmas, and Bourne says, anent this belief, that it was about the time of cock crowing when our Saviour was born, and the heavenly host had then descended to sing the first Christmas carol to the poor shepherds in the fields of Bethlehem.

Shakespeare mentions this popular tradition in Hamlet, act i. sc. i.:—

> Some say, that ever 'gainst that season comes
> Wherein our Saviour's birth is celebrated,
> The bird of dawning singeth all night long :
> And then, they say, no spirit dares stir abroad ;
> The nights are wholesome ; then no planets strike,
> No fairy takes, nor witch hath power to charm,
> So hallow'd and so gracious is the time.

But there is yet another legend of cock-crowing which is found in a carol for St. Stephen's Day, temp. Henry VI.:—

Saint Stephen was a clerk
  In King Herod his hall,
And served him of bread and cloth,
  As ever King befall.

Stephen out of kitchen came
  With boar his head on hand,
He saw a star was fair and bright
  Over Bethlem stand.

He cast adown the boar his head,
  And went into the hall.
"I forsake thee, King Herod,
  And thy works all.

"I forsake thee, King Herod,
  And thy works all,
There is a Child in Bethlem born,
  Is better than we all."

"What aileth thee, Stephen,
  What is thee befall?
Lacketh thee either meat or drink,
  In King Herod his hall?"

"Lacketh me neither meat nor drink,
  In King Herod his hall ;
There is a Child in Bethlem born,
  Is better than we all."

               "What

" What aileth thee, Stephen,
  Art thou wode,[1] or ginnest to brede [2]
Lacketh thee either gold or fee,
  Or any rich weed ? " [3]

" Lacketh me neither gold nor fee,
  Nor none rich weed,
There is a child in Bethlem born
  Shall help us at our need."

" That is all so sooth, Stephen,
  All so sooth, I wis,
As this capon crow shall,
  That lyeth here in my dish."

That word was not so soon said,
  That word in that hall,
The Capon crew, *Christus natus est !*
  Among the lords, all.

Riseth up my tormentors,
  By two, and all by one,
And leadeth Stephen out of this town
  And stoneth him with stone.

Tooken they Stephen
  And stoned him in the way,
And therefore is his even,
  On Christ his own day.

There are several minor legends of animals and Christ-tide—for instance, at this time the bees are said to hum the Old Hundredth Psalm, but this is mild to what Olaus Magnus tells us *Of the Fiercenesse of Men, who by Charms are turned into Wolves :*—" In the Feast of Christ's Nativity, in the night, at a certain place, that they are resolved upon amongst themselves, there is gathered together such a huge multitude of Wolves changed from men, that dwell in divers places, which afterwards, the same night, doth so rage with wonderfull fiercenesse, both against mankind, and other creatures that are not fierce by nature, that the Inhabitants of that country suffer more hurt from them than ever they do from the true natural Wolves. For, as it is proved, they sit upon the houses of men that are in the Woods, with wonderfull fiercenesse, and labour to break down the doors, whereby they may destroy both men and other creatures that remain there.

" They go into the Beer-Cellars, and there they drink out some Tuns of Beer or Mede, and they heap al the empty vessels one upon another in the midst of the Cellar, and so leave them ; wherin they differ from the natural and true Wolves. But the place, where, by chance they stayed that night, the Inhabitants of those Countries think to be prophetical ; Because, if any ill successe befall a Man in that place ; as if his Cart overturn, and he be thrown down in the Snow, they are fully persuaded that man must die that year, as they have,

---

[1] Mad.   [2] Beginnest to upbraid.   [3] Dress.

have, for many years, proved it by experience. Between *Lituania, Samogetia* and *Curonia*, there is a certain wall left, of a Castle that was thrown down; to this, at a set time, some thousands of them come together, that each of them may try his nimblenesse in leaping. He that cannot leap over this wall, as commonly the fat ones cannot, are beaten with whips by their Captains."

There is a story told of another Magnus, only in this case it was a Saint of that name. On Christmas eve, in the year 1012, a party of about thirty-three young men and women were merrily dancing in the churchyard of a certain church, dedicated to St. Magnus. A priest was at his devotions inside the church, and was so much disturbed by their merriment that he sent to them, asking them to desist for a while. But of this they took no heed, although the message was more than once repeated. Thereupon, waxing indignant, the holy man prayed his patron saint, St. Magnus, to visit the offenders with condign punishment. His prayer was heard, and the result was that the festive crew could not leave off dancing. For twelve whole months they continued dancing; night and day, winter and summer, through sunshine or storm, they had to prance. They knew no weariness, they needed no rest, nor did their clothes or boots wear out; but they wore away the surface of the earth so much that at the end of the twelvemonths they were in a hole up to their middles. The legend goes on to say, that on the expiration or their Terpsichorean punishment they slept continuously for three days and nights.

There are some curious legends of underground bells which sound only at Christmas. A writer in *Notes and Queries* (5 series, ii. 509) says—" Near Raleigh, Notts, there is a valley said to have been caused by an earthquake several hundred years ago, which swallowed up a whole village, together with the Church. Formerly, it was a custom of the people to assemble in this valley every Christmas Day morning to listen to the ringing of the bells of the Church beneath them. This, it was positively stated, might be heard by placing the ear to the ground, and hearkening attentively. As late as 1827 it was usual on this morning for old men and women to tell their children and young friends to go to the valley,

valley, stoop down, and hear the bells ring merrily. The villagers heard the ringing of the bells of a neighbouring church, the sound of which was communicated by the surface of the ground. A similar belief exists, or did, a short time ago, at Preston, Lancashire."

This legend is not peculiar to England, for there is the same told of a place in the Netherlands, named Been, near Zoutleeuw, now engulphed in the ocean. It was a lovely and a stately city, but foul with sin, when our Lord descended to earth upon a Christmas night to visit it. All the houses were flaming with lights, and filled with luxury and debauchery; and, as our Lord, in the guise of a beggar, passed from door to door, there was not found a single person who would afford Him the slightest relief. Then, in His wrath, He spoke one word, and the waves of the sea rushed over the wicked city, and it was never seen more; but the place where it was immersed is known by the sound of the church bells coming up through the waters on a Christmas night.

In spite of Shakespeare's dictum that "no spirit dares stir abroad," the rule would not seem to obtain in the Isle of Man —for there is a legend there, how a fiddler, having agreed with a stranger to play, during the twelve days of Christmas, to whatever company he should bring him, was astonished at seeing his new master vanish into the earth as soon as the bargain had been made. Terrified at the thought of having agreed to work for such a mysterious personage, he quickly resorted to the clergyman, who ordered him to fulfil his engagement, but to play nothing but psalms. Accordingly, as soon as Christ-tide arrived, the weird stranger made his appearance, and beckoned the fiddler to a spot where some company was assembled. On reaching his destination, he at once struck up a psalm tune, which so enraged his audience that they instantly vanished, but not without so violently bruising him that it was with difficulty that he reached home to tell his novel Christmas experience.

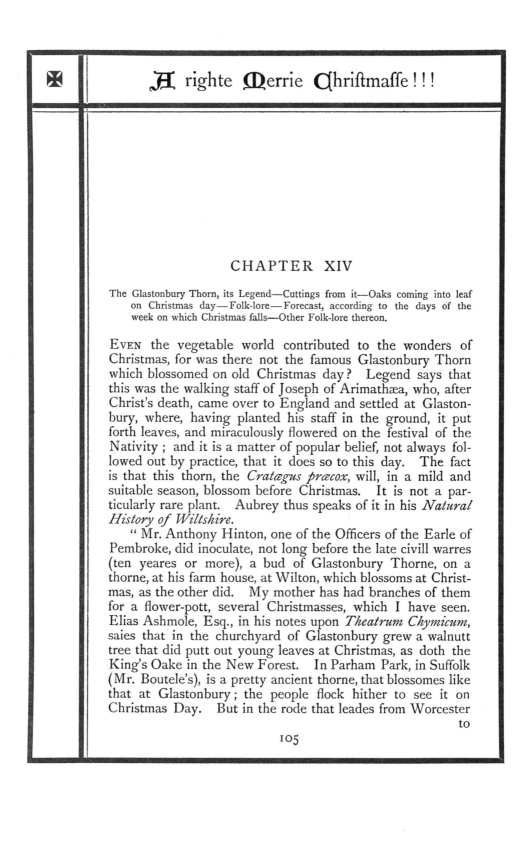

CHAPTER XIV

The Glastonbury Thorn, its Legend—Cuttings from it—Oaks coming into leaf on Christmas day—Folk-lore—Forecast, according to the days of the week on which Christmas falls—Other Folk-lore thereon.

Even the vegetable world contributed to the wonders of Christmas, for was there not the famous Glastonbury Thorn which blossomed on old Christmas day? Legend says that this was the walking staff of Joseph of Arimathæa, who, after Christ's death, came over to England and settled at Glastonbury, where, having planted his staff in the ground, it put forth leaves, and miraculously flowered on the festival of the Nativity ; and it is a matter of popular belief, not always followed out by practice, that it does so to this day. The fact is that this thorn, the *Cratægus præcox*, will, in a mild and suitable season, blossom before Christmas. It is not a particularly rare plant. Aubrey thus speaks of it in his *Natural History of Wiltshire.*

" Mr. Anthony Hinton, one of the Officers of the Earle of Pembroke, did inoculate, not long before the late civill warres (ten yeares or more), a bud of Glastonbury Thorne, on a thorne, at his farm house, at Wilton, which blossoms at Christmas, as the other did. My mother has had branches of them for a flower-pott, several Christmasses, which I have seen. Elias Ashmole, Esq., in his notes upon *Theatrum Chymicum,* saies that in the churchyard of Glastonbury grew a walnutt tree that did putt out young leaves at Christmas, as doth the King's Oake in the New Forest. In Parham Park, in Suffolk (Mr. Boutele's), is a pretty ancient thorne, that blossomes like that at Glastonbury ; the people flock hither to see it on Christmas Day. But in the rode that leades from Worcester to

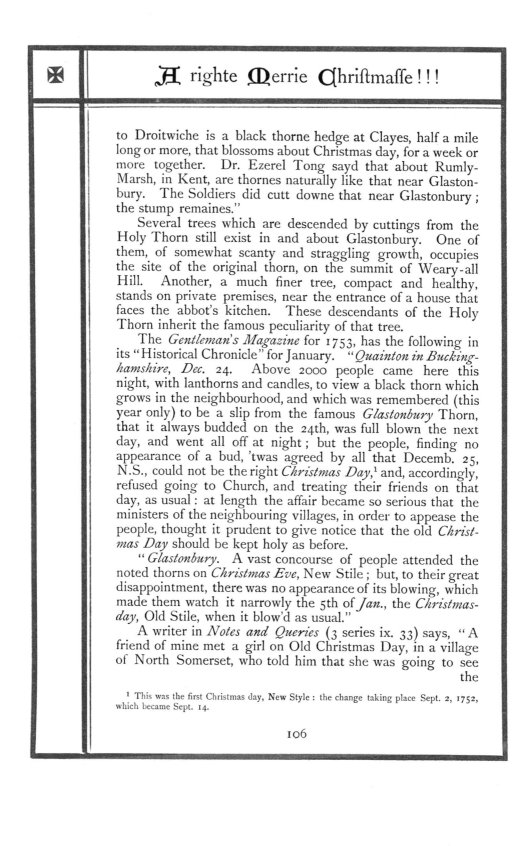

to Droitwiche is a black thorne hedge at Clayes, half a mile long or more, that blossoms about Christmas day, for a week or more together. Dr. Ezerel Tong sayd that about Rumly-Marsh, in Kent, are thornes naturally like that near Glastonbury. The Soldiers did cutt downe that near Glastonbury; the stump remaines."

Several trees which are descended by cuttings from the Holy Thorn still exist in and about Glastonbury. One of them, of somewhat scanty and straggling growth, occupies the site of the original thorn, on the summit of Weary-all Hill. Another, a much finer tree, compact and healthy, stands on private premises, near the entrance of a house that faces the abbot's kitchen. These descendants of the Holy Thorn inherit the famous peculiarity of that tree.

The *Gentleman's Magazine* for 1753, has the following in its "Historical Chronicle" for January. *"Quainton in Buckinghamshire, Dec.* 24. Above 2000 people came here this night, with lanthorns and candles, to view a black thorn which grows in the neighbourhood, and which was remembered (this year only) to be a slip from the famous *Glastonbury* Thorn, that it always budded on the 24th, was full blown the next day, and went all off at night; but the people, finding no appearance of a bud, 'twas agreed by all that Decemb. 25, N.S., could not be the right *Christmas Day*,[1] and, accordingly, refused going to Church, and treating their friends on that day, as usual: at length the affair became so serious that the ministers of the neighbouring villages, in order to appease the people, thought it prudent to give notice that the old *Christmas Day* should be kept holy as before.

"Glastonbury. A vast concourse of people attended the noted thorns on *Christmas Eve*, New Stile; but, to their great disappointment, there was no appearance of its blowing, which made them watch it narrowly the 5th of *Jan.*, the *Christmas-day*, Old Stile, when it blow'd as usual."

A writer in *Notes and Queries* (3 series ix. 33) says, "A friend of mine met a girl on Old Christmas Day, in a village of North Somerset, who told him that she was going to see the

[1] This was the first Christmas day, **New Style**: the change taking place Sept. 2, 1752, which became Sept. 14.

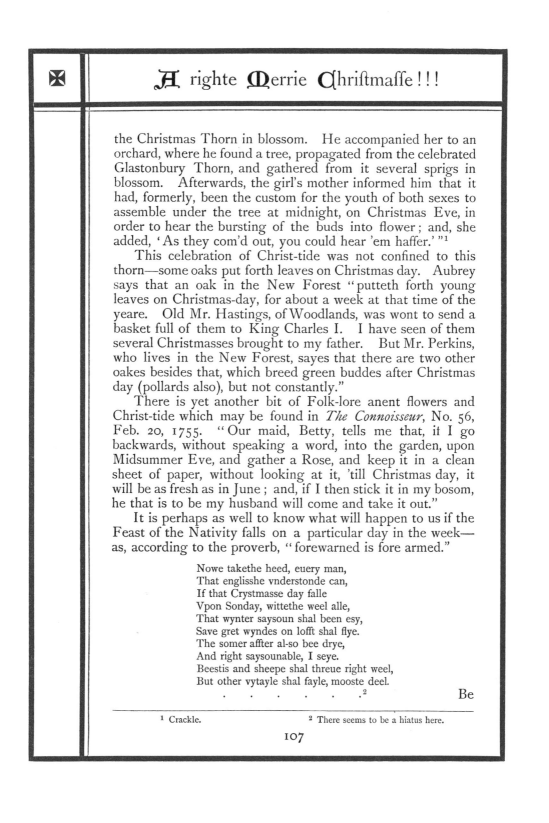

the Christmas Thorn in blossom. He accompanied her to an orchard, where he found a tree, propagated from the celebrated Glastonbury Thorn, and gathered from it several sprigs in blossom. Afterwards, the girl's mother informed him that it had, formerly, been the custom for the youth of both sexes to assemble under the tree at midnight, on Christmas Eve, in order to hear the bursting of the buds into flower; and, she added, 'As they com'd out, you could hear 'em haffer.' "[1]

This celebration of Christ-tide was not confined to this thorn—some oaks put forth leaves on Christmas day. Aubrey says that an oak in the New Forest "putteth forth young leaves on Christmas-day, for about a week at that time of the yeare. Old Mr. Hastings, of Woodlands, was wont to send a basket full of them to King Charles I. I have seen of them several Christmasses brought to my father. But Mr. Perkins, who lives in the New Forest, sayes that there are two other oakes besides that, which breed green buddes after Christmas day (pollards also), but not constantly."

There is yet another bit of Folk-lore anent flowers and Christ-tide which may be found in *The Connoisseur*, No. 56, Feb. 20, 1755. "Our maid, Betty, tells me that, if I go backwards, without speaking a word, into the garden, upon Midsummer Eve, and gather a Rose, and keep it in a clean sheet of paper, without looking at it, 'till Christmas day, it will be as fresh as in June; and, if I then stick it in my bosom, he that is to be my husband will come and take it out."

It is perhaps as well to know what will happen to us if the Feast of the Nativity falls on a particular day in the week— as, according to the proverb, "forewarned is fore armed."

> Nowe takethe heed, euery man,
> That englisshe vnderstonde can,
> If that Crystmasse day falle
> Vpon Sonday, wittethe weel alle,
> That wynter saysoun shal been esy,
> Save gret wyndes on lofft shal flye.
> The somer affter al-so bee drye,
> And right saysounable, I seye.
> Beestis and sheepe shal threue right weel,
> But other vytayle shal fayle, mooste deel.
> .   .   .   .   .   .[2]   Be

---

[1] Crackle.   [2] There seems to be a hiatus here.

Be kynde shal, with-outen lees,
Alle landes thanne shal haue pees.
But offt-tymes, for synne that is doone,
Grace is wyth-drawen from many oone
And goode tyme alle thinges for to do ;
But who-so feelethe, is sone for-do.
What chylde that day is borne,
Gret and ryche he shal be of Corne.

If Cristmasse day on Monday bee,
Gret wynter that yeer shal ghee see,
And ful of wynde lowde and scille ;[1]
But the somer, truwly to telle,
Shal bee sterne with wynde also,
Ful of tempeste eeke ther-too ;
And vitayles shal soo multeplye,
And gret moryne of bestes shal hye.
They that bee borne, with-outen weene,
Shoulle be strong men and kene.

If Crystmasse day on Tuysday be,
Wymmen shal dye gret plentee.
That wynter shal shewe gret merveylle
Shippes shal bee in gret parayle ;
That yeer shal kynges and lordes bee sleyne,
In lande, of werre gret woone,[2] certayne.
A drye somer shal be that yeere ;
Alle that been borne that day in-feere,
They been stronge and coveytous,
But theyre ende shal be petous ;[3]
They shal dye with swerd or knyff.
If thou stele ought, hit leesethe thy lyfe ;
But if thou falle seeke, certayne,
Thou shalt tourne to lyf ageyne.

If that the Cristmasse day
Falle vpon a Weddensday,
That yeere shal be hardee and strong,
And many huge wyndes amonge.
The somer goode and mury shal be,
And that yeere shal be plentee.
Yonge folkes shal dye alsoo ;
Shippes in the see, tempest and woo.

What

---

[1] Shrill.   [2] Abundance.   [3] Piteous.

What chylde that day is borne is his
Fortune to be doughty and wys,
Discrete al-so and sleeghe of deede,
To fynde feel [1] folkes mete and weede. [2]

If Cristmasse day on therusday bee,
A wonder wynter yee shoule see,
Of wyndes, and of weders wicke, [3]
Tempestes eeke many and thicke.
The somer shal bee strong and drye,
Corne and beestes shal multeplye,
Ther as the lande is goode of tilthe;
But kynges and lordes shal dye by filthe
What chylde that day eborne bee,
He shal no dowte Right weel ethee, [4]
Of deedes that been good and stable.
Of speeche ful wyse and Raysonable.
Who-so that day bee thefft aboute,
He shall bee shent, [5] with-outen doute;
But if seeknesse that day thee felle,
Hit may not long with thee dwelle.

If Cristmasse day on fryday be,
The frost of wynter harde shal be,
The frost, snowe and the floode;
But at the eende hit shal bee goode.
The somer goode and feyre alsoo,
Folke in eerthe shal haue gret woo.
Wymmen with chylde, beestes and corne,
Shal multeplye, and noon be lorne. [6]
The children that been borne that day,
Shoule longe lyve, and lechcherous ay.

If Cristmasse day on saturday falle,
That wynter wee most dreeden alle.
Hit shal bee ful of foule tempest,
That hit shal slee bothe man and beest.
Fruytes and corne shal fayle, gret woone,
And eelde folk dye many oon.
What woman that of chylde travayle,
They shoule bee boothe in gret parayle.
And children that been borne that day,
With June half yeere shal dy, no nay.

The

---

[1] Many.   [2] Clothing.   [3] Wicked, foul.
[4] Thrive.   [5] Brought to confusion.   [6] Lost.

The *Shepherd's Kalendar* says: "If the sun shines clear and bright on Christmas day, it promises a peaceful year, free from clamours and strife, and foretells much plenty to ensue; but if the wind blows stormy towards sunset, it betokens sickness in the spring and autumn quarters."

Another authority, *Husband-man's Practice*, warns us that "when Christmas day cometh while the moon waxeth, it shall be a very good year, and the nearer it cometh to the new moon, the better shall that year be. If it cometh when the moon decreaseth, it shall be a hard year, and the nearer the latter end thereof it cometh, the worse and harder shall the year be."

The same book says: "The wise and cunning masters in Astrology have found that men may see and mark the weather of the holy Christmas night, how the whole year after shall be in his working and doing, and they shall speak on this wise:

"When on the Christmas night and evening it is very fair and clear weather, and is without wind and rain, then it is a token that this year will be plenty of wine and fruite.

"But if the contrariwise, foul weather and windy, so shall it be very scant of wine and fruite.

"But if the wind arise at the rising of the sun, then it betokeneth great dearth among beasts and cattle this year.

"But if the wind arise at the going down of the same, then it signifieth death to come among kings and other great lords.'

CHAPTER XV

Withholding Light—"Wesley Bob"—Wassail Carol—Presents in Church—
Morris Dancers — "First Foot" — Red-haired Men — Lamprey Pie —
"Hodening"—Its Possible Origin—The "Mari Lhoyd."

THERE was a curious tradition in the north of England,
which is practically done away with in these days of lucifer
matches. In the old days of tinder boxes, if any one failed
to get a light, it was of no use his going round to the neighbours to get one, for even his dearest friends would refuse
him, it being considered *most unlucky* to allow any light to
leave the house between Christmas eve and New Year's day,
both inclusive. No reason has been found for this singular
and somewhat churlish custom.

Another north country custom, especially at Leeds, was
for the children to go from house to house carrying a "Wessel
(or Wesley) bob," a kind of bower made of evergreens, inside
which were placed a couple of dolls, representing the Virgin
and Infant Christ. This was covered with a cloth until they
came to a house door, when it was uncovered. At Hudders-
field, a "wessel bob" was carried about, gorgeously ornamented with apples, oranges, and ribbons, and when they
reached a house door they sung the following carol :

Here we come a wassailing
 Among the leaves so green,
Here we come a wandering
 So fair to be seen.

Chorus.

For it is in Christmas time
 Strangers travel far and near,
So God bless you, and send you a
 happy New Year.

We are not daily beggars,
 That beg from door to door,
But we are neighbours' children,
 Whom you have seen before.

Call up the butler of this house,
 Put on his golden ring,
Let him bring us a glass of beer,
 And the better we shall sing.
         We

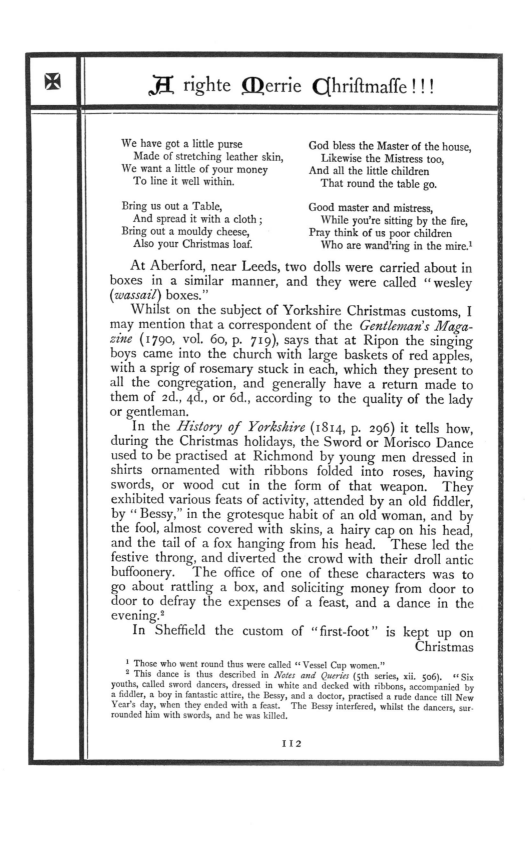

We have got a little purse
  Made of stretching leather skin,
We want a little of your money
  To line it well within.

Bring us out a Table,
  And spread it with a cloth;
Bring out a mouldy cheese,
  Also your Christmas loaf.

God bless the Master of the house,
  Likewise the Mistress too,
And all the little children
  That round the table go.

Good master and mistress,
  While you're sitting by the fire,
Pray think of us poor children
  Who are wand'ring in the mire.[1]

At Aberford, near Leeds, two dolls were carried about in boxes in a similar manner, and they were called "wesley (*wassail*) boxes."

Whilst on the subject of Yorkshire Christmas customs, I may mention that a correspondent of the *Gentleman's Magazine* (1790, vol. 60, p. 719), says that at Ripon the singing boys came into the church with large baskets of red apples, with a sprig of rosemary stuck in each, which they present to all the congregation, and generally have a return made to them of 2d., 4d., or 6d., according to the quality of the lady or gentleman.

In the *History of Yorkshire* (1814, p. 296) it tells how, during the Christmas holidays, the Sword or Morisco Dance used to be practised at Richmond by young men dressed in shirts ornamented with ribbons folded into roses, having swords, or wood cut in the form of that weapon. They exhibited various feats of activity, attended by an old fiddler, by "Bessy," in the grotesque habit of an old woman, and by the fool, almost covered with skins, a hairy cap on his head, and the tail of a fox hanging from his head. These led the festive throng, and diverted the crowd with their droll antic buffoonery. The office of one of these characters was to go about rattling a box, and soliciting money from door to door to defray the expenses of a feast, and a dance in the evening.[2]

In Sheffield the custom of "first-foot" is kept up on Christmas

---

[1] Those who went round thus were called "Vessel Cup women."

[2] This dance is thus described in *Notes and Queries* (5th series, xii. 506). "Six youths, called sword dancers, dressed in white and decked with ribbons, accompanied by a fiddler, a boy in fantastic attire, the Bessy, and a doctor, practised a rude dance till New Year's day, when they ended with a feast. The Bessy interfered, whilst the dancers, surrounded him with swords, and he was killed.

Christmas day and New Year's day, but there is no distinction as to complexion or colour of hair of the male who first enters the house.

A correspondent in *Notes and Queries* (3rd series, i. 223), writes: "The object of desire is that the first person who enters a house on the morning of Christmas day or that of New Year's day, should have black or dark hair. Many make arrangements by special invitation that some man or boy of dark hair, and otherwise approved, should present himself at an early hour to wish the compliments of the season, and the door is not opened to let any one else in until the arrival of the favoured person. He is regaled with spice cake and cheese, and with ale or spirits, as the case may be. All the 'ill luck'—that is, the untoward circumstances of the year, would be ascribed to the accident of a person with light hair having been the first to enter a dwelling on the mornings referred to. I have known instances where such persons, innocently presenting themselves, have met with anything but a Christmas welcome. The great object of dread is a red-haired man or boy (women or girls of any coloured hair or complexion are not admissible as the first visitors at all), and all light shades are objectionable.

"I have not been able to trace the origin of the custom, nor do I remember having read any explanation of its meaning. I once heard an aged woman, who was a most stern observer of all customs of the neighbourhood, especially those which had an air of mystery or a superstition attached to them, attempt to connect the observance with the disciple who sold the Saviour. In her mind all the observances of Christmas were associated with the birth or death of Christ, and she made no distinction whatever between the events which attended the Nativity, and those which preceded and followed the Crucifixion. She told me that Judas had red hair, and it was in vain to argue with her that he had no connection whatever with the events which our Christmas solemnities and festivities were intended to commemorate. It satisfied her mind, and that was enough. After many inquiries, I was not able to obtain any answer more reasonable."

More

113

More than twenty-two years after the above, another cor-respondent writing on the subject to the same periodical (6th series, x. 482) says (speaking of Yorkshire): "The first person to enter the house on a Christmas morning must be a male, and the first thing brought in must be green. Some folks used to lay a bunch of holly on the doorstep on Christ-mas Eve, so as to be ready. Some say you must not admit a *strange* woman on Christmas day; but I have heard of one old gentleman near York who would never permit *any* woman to enter his house on a Christmas Day."

It was formerly the custom of the city of Gloucester to present a lamprey pie to the king at Christmas. This cus-tom was kept up until early in this century, when it fell into desuetude. It was revived in 1893, not at Christmas, but in May, when a beautiful pie, with finely moulded paste, and enamelled silver skewers, which also served as spoons, was presented to Her Majesty.

There was, or is, a curious custom in Kent at Christ-tide called "Hodening," the best account of which that I have seen is in the *Church Times* of January 23, 1891: "Hoden-ing was observed on Christmas Eve at Walmer in 1886, which was the last time I spent the festival there," writes one antiquary. Another writes: "When I was a lad, about forty-five years since, it was always the custom, on Christmas Eve, with the male farm servants from every farm in our parish of Hoath (Borough of Reculver), and neighbouring parishes of Herne and Chislet, to go round in the evening from house to house with the hoodining horse, which consisted of the imitation of a horse's head made of wood, life size, fixed on a stick about the length of a broom handle, the lower jaw of the head was made to open with hinges, a hole was made through the roof of the mouth, then another through the forehead, coming out by the throat; through this was passed a cord attached to the lower jaw, which, when pulled by the cord at the throat, caused it to close and open; on the lower jaw large-headed hobnails were driven in to form the teeth. The strongest of the lads was selected for the horse; he stooped, and made as long a back as he could, supporting himself by the stick carrying the head; then he was covered with a horsecloth, and one of his com-panions

panions mounted his back. The horse had a bridle and reins. Then commenced the kicking, rearing, jumping, etc., and the banging together of the teeth. As soon as the doors were opened the 'horse' would pull his string incessantly, and the noise made can be better imagined than described. I confess that, in my very young days, I was horrified at the approach of the hoodining horse, but, as I grew older, I used to go round with them. I was at Hoath on Thursday last, and asked if the custom was still kept up. It appears it is now three or four years since it has taken place. I never heard of it in the Isle of Thanet. There was no singing going on with the hoodining horse, and the party was strictly confined to the young men who went with the horses on the farms. I have seen some of the wooden heads carved out quite hollow in the throat part, and two holes bored through the forehead to form the eyes. The lad who played the horse would hold a lighted candle in the hollow, and you can imagine how horrible it was to any one who opened the door to see such a thing close to his eyes. Carollers in those days were called hoodiners in the parishes I have named."

And the following communication is interesting and valuable : " Some such custom prevailed in the seventh century. In the *Penitential* of Archbishop Theodore (d. 690) penances are ordained for 'any who, on the Kalends of January, clothe themselves with the skins of cattle and carry heads of animals.' The practice is condemned as being *dæmoniacum* (see Kemble's *Saxons*, vol. i., p. 525). The custom would, therefore, seem to be of pagan origin, and the date is practically synchronous with Christmas, when, according to the rites of Scandinavian mythology, one of the three great annual festivals commenced. At the sacrifices which formed part of these festivals, the horse was a frequent victim in the offerings to Odin for martial success, just as in the offerings to Frey for a fruitful year the hog was the chosen animal. I venture, therefore, to suggest that *hodening* (or probably *Odening*) is a relic of the Scandinavian mythology of our forefathers."

Brand says : " It has been satisfactorily shown that the *Mari Lhoyd*, or horse's skull decked with ribbons, which

used

used to be carried about at Christmas in Wales, was not exclusively a Welsh custom, but was known and practised in the border counties. It was undoubtedly a form of the old English Hobby Horse, one universally prevalent as a popular sport, and conducted, as the readers of Strutt, Douce, and others are already well aware, with all kinds of grotesque and whimsical mummery."

CHAPTER XVI

Curious Gambling Customs in Church—Boon granted—Sheaf of Corn for the Birds—Crowning of the Cock—"The Lord Mayor of Pennyless Cove "— "Letting in Yule "—Guisards—Christmas in the Highlands—Christmas in Shetland—Christmas in Ireland.

IN 1570 was published "The Popish Kingdome, or, Reigne of Antichrist, written in Latin Verse by Thomas Naogeorgus (Kirchmayer) and englished by Barnabe Googe," and in it we have some curious Christmas customs and folk-lore.

Then comes the day wherein the Lorde
　did bring his birth to passe ;
Whereas at midnight up they rise,
　and every man to Masse.
This time so holy counted is,
　that divers earnestly
Do thinke the waters all to wine
　are chaunged sodainly ;
In that same houre that Christ himselfe
　was borne, and came to light,
And unto water streight againe
　transformde and altred quight.
There are beside that mindfully
　the money still do watch,
That first to aultar commes, which then
　they privily do snatch.
The priestes, least other should it have,
　takes oft the same away,
Whereby they thinke, throughout the yeare
　to have good lucke in play,
And not to lose : then straight at game
　till day-light do they strive,
To make some present proofe how well
　their hallowde pence wil thrive.

Three

117

Three Masses every priest doth sing
  upon that solemne day,
With offrings unto every one,
  that so the more may play.
This done, a woodden child in clowtes
  is on the aultar set,
About the which both boyes and gyrles
  do daunce and trymly jet,
And Carrols sing in prayse of Christ,
  and, for to helpe them heare,
The organs aunswere every verse
  with sweete and solemne cheere.
The priestes doe rore aloude ; and round
  about the parentes stande,
To see the sport, and with their voyce
  do helpe them and their hande.

Another old Christmas belief may be found in the *Golden Legend*, printed by Wynkyn de Worde, where it is said, "that what persone beynge in clene lyfe desyre on thys daye (*Christmas*) a boone of God: as ferre as it is ryghtfull and good for hym, our lorde at reuerence of thys blessid and hye feste of his natiuite wol graunt it to hym."

Most English Christmas customs, save the Christmas Tree, cards, and the stocking hung up to receive gifts, are old, but one of the prettiest modern ones that I know of was started by the Rev. J. Kenworthy, Rector of Ackworth, in Yorkshire, about forty years since, of hanging a sheaf of corn outside the church porch, on Christmas eve, for the special benefit of the birds. It seems a pity that it is not universally practised in rural parishes.

To be spoken of in the past tense also are, I fear, the Christ-tide customs of Wales—the *Mari Lhoyd*, or *Lwyd*, answering to the Kentish *Hodening*, and the *Pulgen*, or the Crowning of the Cock, which was a simple religious ceremony. About three o'clock on Christmas morning the Welsh in many parts used to assemble in church, and, after prayers and a sermon, continue there singing psalms and hymns with great devotion till it was daylight; and if, through age or infirmity, any were disabled from attending, they never failed having prayers at home and carols on our Saviour's nativity.

At Tenby it was customary at four o'clock on Christmas morning

morning for the young men of the town to escort the rector with lighted torches from his residence to the church. Sometimes also, before or after Christmas day, the fishermen of Tenby dressed up one of their number, whom they called the "Lord Mayor of Pennyless Cove," with a covering of evergreens and a mask over his face; they would then carry him about, seated in a chair, with flags flying, and a couple of violins playing before him. Before every house the "Lord Mayor" would address the occupants, wishing them a merry Christmas and a happy New Year. If his good wishes were responded to with money his followers gave three cheers, the masquer would himself give thanks, and the crowd again cheered.

In Scotland, Christ-tide is not observed as much as in England, the Scotch reserving all their festive energy for the New Year. Yet, in some parts of Scotland, he who first opens the door on Yule day is esteemed more fortunate during the coming year than the remainder of the family, because he "lets in Yule." And Yule is treated as a real person, as some people set a table or chair, covered with a clean cloth, in the doorway, and set upon it bread and cheese for Yule. It is common also to have a table covered in the house from morning till night with bread and drink upon it, that every one who calls may take a portion, and it is considered particularly inauspicious if any one comes into a house and leaves it without doing so. However many be the callers during the day, all must partake of the good cheer.

In Chambers's *Popular Rhymes* (ed. 1870, p. 169), it is said that the doings of the guisards (masquers) form a conspicuous feature in the New Year proceedings throughout Scotland. The evenings on which these persons are understood to be privileged to appear are those of Christmas, Hogmanay, New Year's day, and Handsel Monday. Dressed in quaint and fantastic attire, they sing a selection of songs which have been practised by them some weeks before. There were important doings, however—one of a theatrical character. There is one rude and grotesque drama (called Galatian) which they are accustomed to perform on each of the four above-mentioned nights; and which, in various fragments or versions,

exists

119

exists in every part of Lowland Scotland.   The performers, who are never less than three, but sometimes as many as six, having dressed themselves, proceed in a band from house to house, generally contenting themselves with the kitchen as an arena, whither, in mansions presided over by the spirit of good humour, the whole family will resort to witness the scene of mirth.

Grant, in his *Popular Superstitions of the Highlands*, says that as soon as the brightening glow of the eastern sky warns the anxious housemaid of the approach of Christmas day, she rises, full of anxiety at the prospect of her morning labours. The meal, which was steeped in the *sowans bowie* a fortnight ago to make the *Prechdacdan sour*, or *sour scones*, is the first object of her attention.   The gridiron is put on the fire, and the sour scones are soon followed by hard cakes, soft cakes, buttered cakes, bannocks, and *pannich perm*.   The baking being once over, the sowans pot succeeds the gridiron, full of new sowans, which are to be given to the family, agreeably to custom, this day in their beds.   The sowans are boiled into the consistency of molasses, when the *lagan-le-vrich*, or yeast bread, to distinguish it from boiled sowans, is ready.   It is then poured into as many bickers as there are individuals to partake of it, and presently served to the whole, both old and young.   As soon as each despatches his bicker, he jumps out of bed—the elder branches to examine the ominous signs of the day, and the younger to enter into its amusements.

Flocking to the swing—a favourite amusement on this occasion, the youngest of the family gets the first " shouder," and the next oldest to him, in regular succession.   In order to add more to the spirit of the exercise, it is a common practice with the person in the swing, and the person appointed to swing him, to enter into a very warm and humorous altercation.   As the swung person approaches the swinger, he exclaims, " *Ei mi tu chal*"—" I'll eat your kail."   To this the swinger replies, with a violent shove, " *Cha ni u mu chal*"—"You shan't eat my kail."   These threats and repulses are sometimes carried to such a height as to break down or capsize the threatener, which generally puts an end to the quarrel.

As the day advances those minor amusements are ter-minated

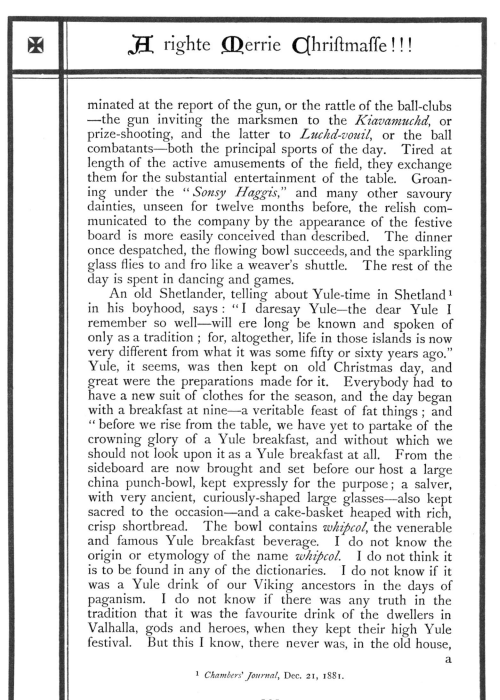
minated at the report of the gun, or the rattle of the ball-clubs
—the gun inviting the marksmen to the *Kiavamuchd*, or
prize-shooting, and the latter to *Luchd-vouil*, or the ball
combatants—both the principal sports of the day. Tired at
length of the active amusements of the field, they exchange
them for the substantial entertainment of the table. Groan-
ing under the "*Sonsy Haggis*," and many other savoury
dainties, unseen for twelve months before, the relish communicated to the company by the appearance of the festive
board is more easily conceived than described. The dinner
once despatched, the flowing bowl succeeds, and the sparkling
glass flies to and fro like a weaver's shuttle. The rest of the
day is spent in dancing and games.

An old Shetlander, telling about Yule-time in Shetland[1]
in his boyhood, says: "I daresay Yule—the dear Yule I
remember so well—will ere long be known and spoken of
only as a tradition; for, altogether, life in those islands is now
very different from what it was some fifty or sixty years ago."
Yule, it seems, was then kept on old Christmas day, and
great were the preparations made for it. Everybody had to
have a new suit of clothes for the season, and the day began
with a breakfast at nine—a veritable feast of fat things; and
" before we rise from the table, we have yet to partake of the
crowning glory of a Yule breakfast, and without which we
should not look upon it as a Yule breakfast at all. From the
sideboard are now brought and set before our host a large
china punch-bowl, kept expressly for the purpose; a salver,
with very ancient, curiously-shaped large glasses—also kept
sacred to the occasion—and a cake-basket heaped with rich,
crisp shortbread. The bowl contains *whipcol*, the venerable
and famous Yule breakfast beverage. I do not know the
origin or etymology of the name *whipcol*. I do not think it
is to be found in any of the dictionaries. I do not know if it
was a Yule drink of our Viking ancestors in the days of
paganism. I do not know if there was any truth in the
tradition that it was the favourite drink of the dwellers in
Valhalla, gods and heroes, when they kept their high Yule
festival. But this I know, there never was, in the old house,

a

[1] *Chambers' Journal*, Dec. 21, 1881.

a Yule breakfast without it. It had come down to us from time immemorial, and was indissolubly connected with Yule morning. That is all I am able to say about it, except that I am able to give the constituents of this luscious beverage, which is not to be confounded with egg-flip. The yelks of a dozen fresh eggs are whisked for about half an hour with about a pound of sifted loaf sugar; nearly half a pint of old rum is added, and then a pint of rich, sweet cream. A bumper of this, tossed off to many happy returns of Yule day, together with a large square of shortbread, always rounded up our Yule breakfast."

Football was the only game played at, and at this they continued till 3 P.M., when they sat down to a dinner which entirely eclipsed the breakfast. After tea, there was dancing to the music of a fiddler until eleven, when a substantial supper was partaken of, then several glasses of potent punch, before retiring to rest. For a whole week this feasting and football playing was kept up, and wonderful must have been the constitutions of the Shetlanders who could stand it.

In Catholic Ireland, as opposed to Presbyterian Scotland, we might expect a better observance of Christ-tide; and the best account I can find of Christmas customs in Ireland is to be met with in *Notes and Queries* (3rd series, viii. 495).

" Many of what are called ' the good old customs ' are not now observed in the rural districts of Ireland; and I have heard ignorant old men attribute the falling off to the introduction of railways, the improvement of agricultural operations, and cattle shows! Amongst some of the customs that I remember in the south-east of Ireland were the following :

" A week or two before Christmas landed proprietors would have slaughtered fine fat bullocks, the greater portion of which would be distributed to the poor; and farmers holding from ten acres of land upwards, were sure to kill a good fat pig, fed up for the purpose, for the household ; but the poorer neighbours were also certain of receiving some portions as presents. When the hay was made up in the farm yards, which was generally about the time that apples became ripe, quantities of the fruit would be put in the hayricks, and left there till Christmas. The apples thus received a fine flavour, no doubt from the aroma of the new-mown hay. In localities
of

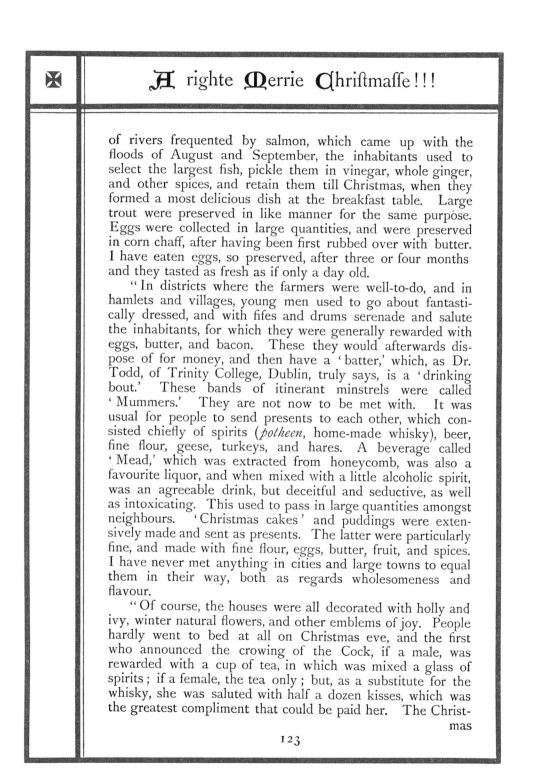

of rivers frequented by salmon, which came up with the floods of August and September, the inhabitants used to select the largest fish, pickle them in vinegar, whole ginger, and other spices, and retain them till Christmas, when they formed a most delicious dish at the breakfast table. Large trout were preserved in like manner for the same purpose. Eggs were collected in large quantities, and were preserved in corn chaff, after having been first rubbed over with butter. I have eaten eggs, so preserved, after three or four months and they tasted as fresh as if only a day old.

"In districts where the farmers were well-to-do, and in hamlets and villages, young men used to go about fantastically dressed, and with fifes and drums serenade and salute the inhabitants, for which they were generally rewarded with eggs, butter, and bacon. These they would afterwards dispose of for money, and then have a 'batter,' which, as Dr. Todd, of Trinity College, Dublin, truly says, is a 'drinking bout.' These bands of itinerant minstrels were called 'Mummers.' They are not now to be met with. It was usual for people to send presents to each other, which consisted chiefly of spirits (*potheen*, home-made whisky), beer, fine flour, geese, turkeys, and hares. A beverage called 'Mead,' which was extracted from honeycomb, was also a favourite liquor, and when mixed with a little alcoholic spirit, was an agreeable drink, but deceitful and seductive, as well as intoxicating. This used to pass in large quantities amongst neighbours. 'Christmas cakes' and puddings were extensively made and sent as presents. The latter were particularly fine, and made with fine flour, eggs, butter, fruit, and spices. I have never met anything in cities and large towns to equal them in their way, both as regards wholesomeness and flavour.

"Of course, the houses were all decorated with holly and ivy, winter natural flowers, and other emblems of joy. People hardly went to bed at all on Christmas eve, and the first who announced the crowing of the Cock, if a male, was rewarded with a cup of tea, in which was mixed a glass of spirits; if a female, the tea only; but, as a substitute for the whisky, she was saluted with half a dozen kisses, which was the greatest compliment that could be paid her. The Christmas

mas block for the fire, or Yule log, was indispensable.   The
last place in which I saw it was the hall of Lord Ward's
mansion, near Downpatrick, in Ireland ; and although it was
early in the forenoon, his lordship (then a young man) insisted
on my tasting a glass of whisky, not to break the custom of
the country, or the hall.   He did the same himself."

CHAPTER XVII

Ordinance against out-door Revelry—Marriage of a Lord of Misrule—Mummers and Mumming—Country Mummers—Early Play—Two modern Plays.

THESE Christmas revelries were sometimes carried to excess, and needed curbing with the strong hand of the law, an early instance of which we find in Letter Book I. of the Corporation of the City of London, fol. 223, 6 Henry V., A.D. 1418.

" The Mair and Aldermen chargen on þe kynges byhalf, and þis Cite, þat no manere persone, of what astate, degre, or condicoun þat euere he be, duryng þis holy tyme of Christemes be so hardy in eny wyse to walk by nyght in eny manere mommyng, pleyes, enterludes, or eny oþer disgisynges with eny feynyd berdis,[1] peyntid visers, diffourmyd or colourid visages in eny wyse, up peyne of enprisonement of her bodyes and makyng fyne after þe discrecioun of þe Mair and Aldremen ; ontake[2] þat hit be leful to eche persone for to be honestly mery as he can, within his owne hous dwellyng. And more ouere þei charge on þe Kynges byhalf, and þe Cite, þat eche honest persone, dwellyng in eny hye strete or lane of þis Citee, hang out of her house eche night, duryng þis solempne Feste, a lanterne with a candell þer in, to brenne[3] as long as hit may endure, up[4] peyne to pay ivd, to þe chaumbre at eche tyme þat hit faillith."

And to cite another case, much later in date, the Commissioners for Causes Ecclesiastical kept strict watch on some of the Christmas revellers of 1637. They had before them one Saunders, from Lincolnshire, for carrying revelry too far. Saunders and others, at Blatherwick, had appointed a Lord
of

[1] False beards.   [2] Except that it shall be.   [3] Burn.   [4] Upon pain of paying.

of Misrule over their festivities. This was perfectly lawful, and could not be gainsaid. But they had resolved that he should have a lady, or Christmas wife; and probably there would have been no harm in that, if they had not carried the matter too far. They, however, brought in as bride one Elizabeth Pitto, daughter of the hog-herd of the town. Saunders received her, disguised as a parson, wearing a shirt or smock for a surplice. He then married the Lord of Misrule to the hog-herd's daughter, reading the whole of the marriage service from the Book of Common Prayer. All the after ceremonies and customs then in use were observed, and the affair was carried to its utmost extent. The parties had time to repent at leisure in prison.

The old English disport of mumming at Christmas is of great antiquity—so great that its origin is lost. Fosbroke, in his *Encyclopædia of Antiquities* (ed. 1843, ii. 668), says, under the heading "Mummers: These were amusements derived from the Saturnalia, and so called from the Danish *mumme*, or Dutch *momme*—disguise in a mask. Christmas was the grand scene of mumming, and some mummers were disguised as bears, others like unicorns, bringing presents. Those who could not procure masks rubbed their faces with soot, or painted them. In the Christmas mummings the chief aim was to surprise by the oddity of the masks, and singularity and splendour of the dresses. Everything was out of nature and propriety. They were often attended with an exhibition of gorgeous machinery.[1] It was an old custom also to have mummeries on Twelfth night. They were the common holiday amusements of young people of both sexes; but by 6 Edward III. the mummers, or masqueraders, were ordered to be whipped out of London."

The original mumming was in dumb show, and was sometimes of considerable proportions, *vide* one in 1348, where there were "eighty tunics of buckram, forty-two visors, and a great variety of other whimsical dresses were provided for the disguising at court at the Feast of Christmas." A most magnificent mummery or disguising was exhibited by the citizens of London in 1377, for the amusement

---

[1] Fosbroke here seems to have mixed up masquers and mummers.

126

amusement of Richard, Prince of Wales, in which no fewer than 130 persons were disguised; which, with that in 1401, I have already described. Philip Stubbes, the Puritan, says: "In 1440, one captain John Gladman, a man ever true and faithful to God and the King, and constantly sportive, made public disport with his neighbours at Christmas. He traversed the town on a horse as gaily caparisoned as himself, preceded by the twelve months, each dressed in character. After him crept the pale attenuated figure of Lent, clothed in herring skins, and mounted on a sorry horse, whose harness was covered with oyster shells. A train, fantastically garbed, followed. Some were clothed as bears, apes, and wolves; others were tricked out in armour; a number appeared as harridans, with blackened faces and tattered clothes, and all kept up a promiscuous fight. Last of all marched several carts, whereon a number of fellows, dressed as old fools, sat upon nests, and pretended to hatch young fools."

We still have our mummers in very many a country village; but the sport is now confined to the village boys, who, either masked or with painted faces, ribbons, and other finery (I have known them tricked out with paper streamers, obtained from a neighbouring paper mill), act a play (!), and, of course, ask for money at its conclusion. By some, it is considered that this play originated in the commemoration of the doughty deeds of the Crusaders.

The earliest of these plays that I can find is in a fifteenth century MS.—*temp.* Edward IV.—and the characters are the nine worthies:

Ector de Troye.	Thow Achylles in bataly me slow,
	Of my worthynes men speken I now.
Alisander.	And in romaunce often am I leyt,
	As conqueror gret thow I seyt.
Julius Cæsar.	Thow my cenatoures me slow in cŏllory,
	Fele londes byfore by conquest wan I.
Josue.	In holy Chyrche ʒe mowen here and rede,
	Of my worthynes and of my dede.
Dauit.	After yᵗ slayn was Golyas,
	By me the sawter than made was.
Judas Macabeus.	Of my wurthynesse ʒyf ʒe wyll wete,
	Secke the byble, for ther it is wrete.

Arthour.

127

Arthour.	The round tabyll I sette wᵗ Knyghtes strong,
	Zyt shall I come aȝen, thow it be long.
Charles.	With me dwellyd Rouland Olyvere,
	In all my conquest fer and nere.
Godefry de Boleyn.	And I was Kyng of Jherusalem,
	The crowne of thorn I wan fro hem."

Of the comparatively modern play acted by the mummers space only enables me to give two examples, although I could give many more. The first is the simplest, and only requires three principal actors, and this is still played in Oxfordshire.[1]

A Knight enters with his sword drawn, and says :

> Room, room, make room, brave gallants all,
> For me and my brave company !
> Where's the man that dares bid me stand ?
> I'll cut him down with my bold hand !

St. George.	Here's the man that dares bid you stand ;
	He defies your courageous hand !
The Knight.	Then mind your eye, to guard the blow,
	And shield your face, and heart also.

(St George gets wounded in the combat, and falls.)

> Doctor, Doctor, come here and see,
> St. George is wounded in the knee ;
> Doctor, Doctor, play well your part.
> St. George is wounded in the heart !

(The Doctor enters.)

> I am a Doctor, and a Doctor good,
> And with my hand I'll stop the blood.

The Knight.	What can you cure, Doctor ?
The Doctor.	I can cure coughs, colds, fevers, gout,
	Both pains within and aches without ;
	I will bleed him in the thumb.
St. George.	O ! will you so ? then I'll get up and run !

Some

---

[1] *Notes and Queries,* 6th series xii. 489.

Enter COLONEL SPRING.

Holloa! behold me, here am I!
I'll have thee now prepare,
And by this arm thou'lt surely die,
I'll have thee this night, beware.
So, see, what bloody works thou'st made,
Thou art a butcher, sir, by trade.
I'll kill, as thou did'st kill my brother,
For one good turn deserves another.

(*They fight*, St. George *kills the* Colonel.)

ST. PATRICK.

Stay thy hand, St. George, and slay no more; for I feel for the wives and families of those men thou hast slain.

ST. GEORGE.

So am I sorry. I'll freely give any sum of money to a doctor to restore them again. I have heard talk of a mill to grind old men young, but I never heard of a doctor to bring dead men to life again.

ST. PATRICK.

There's an Irish doctor, a townsman of mine, who lived next door to St. Patrick, he can perform wonders. Shall I call him, St. George?

ST. GEORGE.

With all my heart. Please to walk in, Mr. Martin Dennis. It's an ill wind that blows no good work for the doctor. If you will set these men on

Enter DOCTOR.

their pins, I'll give thee a hundred pound, and here is the money.

DOCTOR.

So I will, my worthy knight, and then I shall not want for whiskey for one twelvemonth to come. I am sure, the first man I saw beheaded, I put his head on the wrong way. I put his mouth where his poll ought to be, and he's exhibited in a wondering nature.

ST. GEORGE.

Very good answer, Doctor. Tell me the rest of your miracles, and raise those warriors.

DOCTOR

DOCTOR.

I can cure love-sick maidens, jealous husbands, squalling wives, brandy-drinking dames, with one touch of my triple liquid, or one sly dose of my Jerusalem balsam, and that will make an old crippled dame dance the hornpipe, or an old woman of seventy years of age conceive and bear a twin. And now to convince you all of my exertions,—Rise, Captain Bluster, Gracious King, General Valentine, and Colonel Spring! Rise, and go to your father!

(On the application of the medicine they all rise and retire.)

Enter OLD BET.

Here comes dame Dorothy,
A handsome young woman, good morning to ye.
I am rather fat, but not very tall,
I'll do my best endeavour to please you all.
My husband, he is to work, and soon he will return,
And something for our supper bring,
And, perhaps, some wood to burn.
Oh! here he comes!

Enter JAN, *or* OLD FATHER CHRISTMAS.

Well! Jan.

OLD FATHER CHRISTMAS.

Oh! Dorothy.

OLD BET.

What have you been doing all this long day, Jan?

OLD FATHER CHRISTMAS.

I have been a-hunting, Bet.

OLD BET.

The devil! a hunting is it? Is that the way to support a wife? Well, what have you catched to-day, Jan?

OLD FATHER CHRISTMAS.

A fine jack hare, and I intend to have him a-fried for supper; and here is some wood to dress him.

OLD BET.

Fried! no, Jan, I'll roast it nice.

OLD

134

OLD FATHER CHRISTMAS.

I say, I'll have it fried.

OLD BET.

Was there ever such a foolish dish!

OLD FATHER CHRISTMAS.

No matter for that. I'll have it a-done; and if you don't do as I do bid, I'll hit you in the head.

OLD BET.

You may do as you like for all I do care,
I'll never fry a dry jack hare.

OLD FATHER CHRISTMAS.

Oh! you won't, wooll'ee?

(He strikes her and she falls.)

Oh! what have I done! I have murdered my wife!
The joy of my heart, and the pride of my life.
And out to the gaol I quickly shall be sent.
In a passion I did it, and no malice meant.
Is there a doctor that can restore?
Fifty pounds I'll give him, or twice fifty more.

(Some one speaks.)

Oh! yes, Uncle Jan, there is a doctor just below, and for God's sake let him just come in. Walk in, Doctor.

Enter DOCTOR.

OLD FATHER CHRISTMAS.

Are you a doctor?

DOCTOR.

Yes, I am a doctor—a doctor of good fame. I have travelled through Europe, Asia, Africa, and America, and by long practice and experience I have learned the best of cures for most disorders instant (*incident?*) to the human body; find nothing difficult in restoring a limb, or mortification, or an arm being cut off by a sword, or a head being struck off by a cannon-ball, if application have not been delayed till it is too late.

OLD FATHER CHRISTMAS.

You are the very man, I plainly see,
That can restore my poor old wife to me.
Pray tell me thy lowest fee.

DOCTOR

DOCTOR.

A hundred guineas, I'll have to restore thy wife,
'Tis no wonder that you could not bring the dead to life.

OLD FATHER CHRISTMAS.

That's a large sum of money for a dead wife!

DOCTOR.

Small sum of money to save a man from the gallows. Pray what big
stick is that you have in your hand?

OLD FATHER CHRISTMAS.

That is my hunting pole.

DOCTOR.

Put aside your hunting pole, and get some assistance to help up your wife.

(Old Bet *is raised up to life again.*)

Fal, dal, lal! fal, dal, lal! my wife's alive!

Enter SERVANT MAN *who sings.*

Well met, my brother dear!
All on the highway
Sall and I were walking along,
So I pray, come tell to me
What calling you might be.
I'll have you for some serving man.

OLD FATHER CHRISTMAS.

I'll give thee many thanks,
And I'll quit thee as soon as I can;
Vain did I know
Where thee could do so or no,
For to the pleasure of a servant man.

SERVANT MAN.

Some servants of pleasure
Will pass time out of measure,
With our hares and hounds
They will make the hills and valleys sound
That's a pleasure for some servant man.

OLD

OLD FATHER CHRISTMAS.

My pleasure is more than for to see my oxen grow fat,
And see them prove well in their kind,
A good rick of hay, and a good stack of corn to fill up my barn,
That's a pleasure of a good honest husband man.

SERVANT MAN.

Next to church they will go with their livery fine and gay,
With their cocked-up hat, and gold lace all round,
And their shirt so white as milk,
And stitched so fine as silk,
That's a habit for a servant man.

OLD FATHER CHRISTMAS.

Don't tell I about thee silks and garments that's not fit to travel the bushes.
Let I have on my old leather coat,
And in my purse a groat,
And there, that's a habit for a good old husband man.

SERVANT MAN.

Some servant men doth eat
The very best of meat,
A cock, goose, capon, and swan ;
After lords and ladies dine,
We'll drink strong beer, ale, and wine ;
That's a diet for some servant man.

OLD FATHER CHRISTMAS.

Don't tell I of the cock, goose, or capon, nor swan ; let I have a good rusty piece of bacon, pickled pork, in the house, and a hard crust of bread and cheese once now and then ; that's a diet for a good old honest husband man.

So we needs must confess
That your calling is the best,
And we will give you the uppermost hand ;
So no more we won't delay,
But we will pray both night and day,
God bless the honest husband man. Amen.

[*Exeunt* OMNES.]

CHAPTER XVIII

A Christmas jest—Ben Jonson's Masque of Christmas—Milton's Masque of Comus—Queen Elizabeth and the Masters of Defence.

THIS is rather sorry stuff; but then in purely rural places, untouched by that great civiliser, the railroad, a little wit goes a great way, as we may see by the following story told in Pasquil's "Jests," 1604. "There was some time an old knight, who, being disposed to make himself merry on a Christmas time, sent for many of his tenants and poore neighbours, with their wives to dinner; when, having made meat to be set on the table, he would suffer no man to drinke till he that was master over his wife should sing a carrol; great niceness there was who should be the musician. Yet with much adoe, looking one upon another, after a dry hemme or two, a dreaming companion drew out as much as he durst towards an ill-fashioned ditty. When, having made an end, to the great comfort of the beholders, at last it came to the women's table, when, likewise, commandment was given that there should no drinkes be touched till she that was master over her husband had sung a Christmas carroll, whereupon they fell all to such a singing that there never was heard such a catterwauling piece of musicke. Whereat the knight laughed so heartily that it did him halfe as much good as a corner of his Christmas pie."

Of Masques I have already written, in describing Royal Christ-tides, but there is one, a notice of which must not be omitted, Ben Jonson's Masque of Christmas, as it was presented at Court 1616. The *dramatis personæ* are :—

CHRISTMAS,

138

CHRISTMAS, attired in round hose, long stockings, a closed doublet, a high-crowned hat, with a brooch, a long thin beard, a truncheon, little ruffs, white shoes, his scarfs and garters tied cross, and his drum beaten before him.

HIS SONS AND DAUGHTERS (ten in number) led in, in a string, by CUPID, who is attired in a flat cap, and a prentice's coat, with wings at his shoulders.

MISRULE, in a velvet cap, with a sprig, a short cloak, great yellow ruff, his torch-bearer bearing a rope, a cheese, and a basket.

CAROL, a long tawney coat, with a red cap, and a flute at his girdle, his torch-bearer carrying a song-book open.

MINCED PIE, like a fine cook's wife, drest neat; her man carrying a pie, dish, and spoons.

GAMBOL, like a tumbler, with a hoop and bells; his torch-bearer arm'd with a colt staff and a binding staff.

POST AND PAIR, with a pair-royal of aces in his hat; his garment all done over with pairs and purs; his squire carrying a box, cards, and counters.

NEW YEAR'S GIFT, in a blue coat, serving man like, with an orange, and a sprig of rosemary gilt, on his head, his hat full of brooches, with a collar of gingerbread; his torch-bearer carrying a march pane with a bottle of wine on either arm.

MUMMING, in a masquing pied suit, with a vizard; his torch-bearer carrying the box, and ringing it.

WASSEL, like a neat sempster and songster; her page bearing a brown bowl, drest with ribands, and rosemary, before her.

OFFERING, in a short gown, with a porter's staff in his hand, a wyth borne before him, and a bason, by his torch-bearer.

BABY CAKE (*Twelfth cake*), dressed like a boy, in a fine long coat, biggin bib, muckender, and a little dagger; his usher bearing a great cake, with a bean and a pease.

After

After some dialogue, Christmas introduces his family in the following song :—

> Now, their intent, is above to present,
>   With all the appurtenances,
> A right Christmas, as, of old, it was,
>   To be gathered out of the dances.
>
> Which they do bring, and afore the king,
>   The queen, and prince, as it were now
> Drawn here by love ; who over and above,
>   Doth draw himself in the geer too.

[*Here the drum and fife sounds, and they march about once. In the second coming up*, Christmas *proceeds to his* Song.]

> Hum drum, sauce for a coney ;
>   No more of your martial music ;
> Even for the sake o' the next new stake,
>   For there I do mean to use it.
>
> And now to ye, who in place are to see
>   With roll and farthingale hoopèd ;
> I pray you know, though he want his bow,
>   By the wings, that this is CUPID.
>
> He might go back, for to cry *What you lack ?*
>   But that were not so witty :
> His cap and coat are enough to note,
>   That he is the Love o' the City.
>
> And he leads on, though he now be gone,
>   For that was only his rule :
> But now comes in, Tom of Bosom's-Inn,
>   And he presenteth MIS-RULE.
>
> Which you may know, by the very show,
>   Albeit you never ask it :
> For there you may see, what his ensigns be,
>   The rope, the cheese, and the basket.
>
> This CAROL plays, and has been in his days
>   A chirping boy, and a kill-pot.
> Kit cobler it is, I'm a father of his,
>   And he dwells in the lane called Fill-pot.

But,

But, who is this?   O, my daughter Cis,
    MINCED PIE; with her do not dally
On pain o' your life; she's an honest cook's wife,
    And comes out of Scalding-alley.

Next in the trace, comes GAMBOL in place;
    And to make my tale the shorter,
My son Hercules, tane out of Distaff lane,
    But an active man and a porter.

Now, POST AND PAIR, old Christmas's heir,
    Doth make and a gingling sally;
And wot you who, 'tis one of my two
    Sons, card makers in Pur-alley.

Next, in a trice, with his box and his dice,
    Mac' pipin my son, but younger,
Brings MUMMING in; and the knave will win
    For he is a costermonger.

But NEW YEAR'S GIFT, of himself makes shift
    To tell you what his name is;
With orange on head, and his gingerbread,
    Clem Waspe of Honey lane 'tis.

This, I you tell, is our jolly WASSEL,
    And for Twelfth night more meet too;
She works by the ell, and her name is Nell,
    And she dwells in Threadneedle street too.

Then OFFERING, he, with his dish and his tree,
    That in every great house keepeth,
Is by my son, young Little-worth, done,
    And in Penny-rich street he sleepeth.

Last BABY CAKE, that an end doth make
    Of Christmas merry, merry vein-a,
Is child Rowlan, and a straight young man,
    Though he comes out of Crooked lane-a.

There should have been, and a dozen, I ween,
    But I could find but one more
Child of Christmas, and a LOG it was,
    When I had them all gone o'er.

I prayed him, in a tune so trim,
    That he would make one to prance it:
And I myself would have been the twelfth,
    O! but LOG was too heavy to dance it.

Nor

Nor must we forget a Masque by Milton, "Comus, a Masque, at Ludlow Castle, 1634," in which appeared the Lord Brockley, Mr. Thomas Egerton, his brother, and the Lady Alice Egerton.

But all Christmas sports were not so gentle as was the Masque, as the following account of the Virgin Queen's amusements shows us. Amongst the original letters preserved by the descendants of Sir John Kytson, of Hengrave Hall, is one addressed by Christopher Playter to Mr. Kytson, in 1572, which contains the following: "At Chris-time here were certayne ma^rs of defence, that did challenge all comers at all weapons, as long sworde, staff, sword and buckler, rapier with the dagger: and here was many broken heads, and one of the ma^rs of defence dyed upon the hurt which he received on his head. The challenge was before the quenes Matie, who seemes to have pleasure therein; for when some of them would have sollen a broken pate, her Majesty bade him not to be ashamed to put off his cap, and the blood was spied to run about his face. There was also at the corte new plays, w^h lasted almost all night. The name of the play was huff, suff, and ruff, with other masks both of ladies and gents."

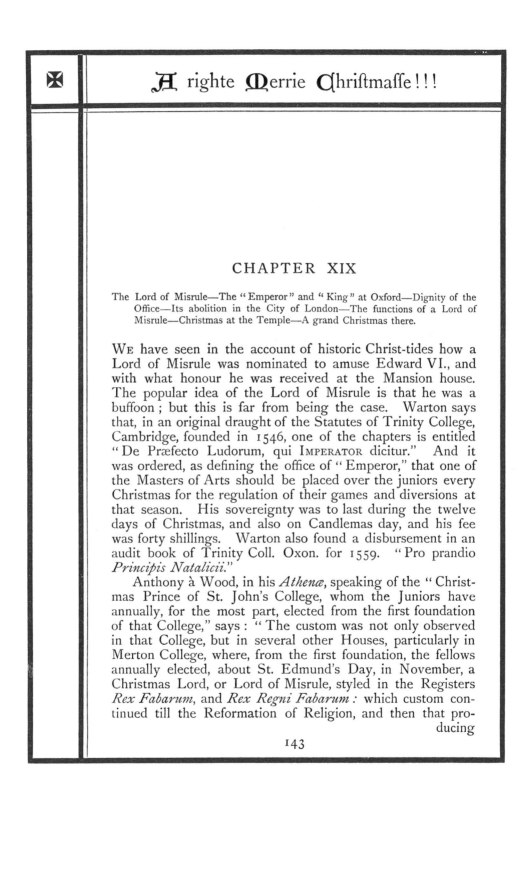

CHAPTER XIX

The Lord of Misrule—The "Emperor" and "King" at Oxford—Dignity of the Office—Its abolition in the City of London—The functions of a Lord of Misrule—Christmas at the Temple—A grand Christmas there.

WE have seen in the account of historic Christ-tides how a Lord of Misrule was nominated to amuse Edward VI., and with what honour he was received at the Mansion house. The popular idea of the Lord of Misrule is that he was a buffoon ; but this is far from being the case. Warton says that, in an original draught of the Statutes of Trinity College, Cambridge, founded in 1546, one of the chapters is entitled "De Præfecto Ludorum, qui IMPERATOR dicitur." And it was ordered, as defining the office of "Emperor," that one of the Masters of Arts should be placed over the juniors every Christmas for the regulation of their games and diversions at that season. His sovereignty was to last during the twelve days of Christmas, and also on Candlemas day, and his fee was forty shillings. Warton also found a disbursement in an audit book of Trinity Coll. Oxon. for 1559. "Pro prandio *Principis Natalicii.*"

Anthony à Wood, in his *Athenæ,* speaking of the "Christmas Prince of St. John's College, whom the Juniors have annually, for the most part, elected from the first foundation of that College," says : " The custom was not only observed in that College, but in several other Houses, particularly in Merton College, where, from the first foundation, the fellows annually elected, about St. Edmund's Day, in November, a Christmas Lord, or Lord of Misrule, styled in the Registers *Rex Fabarum,* and *Rex Regni Fabarum :* which custom continued till the Reformation of Religion, and then that producing

143

ducing Puritanism, and Puritanism Presbytery, the possession of it looked upon such laudable and ingenious customs as popish, diabolical, and anti-Christian."

The office was one of dignity, as we may see by Henry Machyn's diary, 1551-52 : "The iiij day of Januarii was made a grett skaffold in chepe, hard by the crosse, agaynst the kynges lord of myssrule cummyng from Grenwyche and (he) landyd at Toure warff, and with hym yonge knyghts and gentyllmen a gret nombur on hosse bake sum in gownes and cotes and chaynes abowt ther nekes, and on the Toure hyll ther they went in order, furst a standard of yelow and grene sylke with Saint George, and then gounes and skuybes (squibs) and trompets and bagespypes, and drousselars and flutes, and then a gret company all in yelow and gren, and docturs declaryng my lord grett, and then the mores danse, dansyng with a tabret," etc.

But so popular were these Lords of Misrule that every nobleman and person of position had one. Henry Percy, fifth Earl of Northumberland, had one certainly in 1512, whose fee was 30s. Nor did Sir Thomas More, when attached to the household of Cardinal Morton, object to "stepp in among the players." That they were usual adjuncts to great houses is evidenced by an extract from Churchyard's *Lamentacion of Freyndshypp*, a ballad printed about 1565 :—

> Men are so used these dayes wyth wordes,
> They take them but for jestes and boordes,
> That *Christmas Lordes* were wont to speke.

Stow tells us that, by an Act of Common Council, 12, Philip and Mary, for retrenching expenses, among other things it was ordered that the Lord Mayor or Sheriffs shall not keep any Lord of Misrule in any of their houses. But it still seems to have been customary for Sheriffs, at least, to have them, for Richard Evelyn, Esq. (father of the diarist), who kept his Shrievalty of Surrey and Sussex in 1634, in a most splendid manner, did not forego his Lord of Misrule, as the following shows :—

"Articles made and appoynted by the Right Wo[ll] Richard Evelyn Esq., High Sheriffe and Deputie Leave-
tenaunt

144

tenaunt to the Kinge's Matie for the Counties of Surrey and Sussex.

IMPRIMIS. I give free leave to Owen Flood my Trumpeter, gent. to be Lo^d of Misrule of all good Orders during the twelve dayes. And also I give free leave to the said Owen Flood to comand all and every person whatsoev^r, as well servants as others, to be at his comand whensoev^r he shall sound his Trumpett or Musick, and to do him good service as though I were present my selfe at their perills.

"His Lo^pp commaunds every person or persons whatsoev^r to appeare at the Hall at seaven of the Clocke in the morninge, to be at prayers, and afterwards to be at his Lo^pps commaunds, upon paine of punishment, accordinge as his Lo^pp shall thinke fitt.

"If any person shall sware any oath w^thin the precinct of the . . . shall suffer punishment at his Lo^pps pleasure.

"If any man shall come into the Hall, and sett at dinner or supper more than once, he shall endure punishment at his Lo^pps pleasure.

"If any man shal bee drunke, or drinke more than is fitt, or offer to sleepe during the time abovesaid, or do not drinke up his bowle of beere, but flings away his snuffe (that is to say) the second draught, he shall drinke two, and afterwards be excluded.

"If any man shall quarrell, or give any ill language to any person duringe the abovesaid twelve dayes w^thin the gates or precinct thereof, he is in danger of his Lo^pps displeasure.

"If any person shall come into the kitchen whiles meate is a dressinge, to molest the cookes, he shall suffer the rigor of his Lo^pps law.

"If any man shall kisse any maid, widdow or wife, except to bid welcome or farewell, w^thout his Lo^pps consent, he shall have punishment as his Lo^pp shall thinke convenient.

"The last article : I give full power and authoritie to his Lo^pp to breake up all lockes, bolts, barres, doores, and latches, and to flinge up all doores out of hendges to come at those whoe presume to disobey his Lo^pps commaunds.

"God save the King."

These

145

These somewhat whimsical articles of agreement were evidently intended to prevent mirth relapsing into licence, which, unfortunately, was too often the case, especially with the Lord of Misrule or Prince of Love, who directed the revels of the law students. Gerard Legh, in *The Accidens of Armory*, 1562, says that Christmas was inaugurated with " the shot of double cannon, in so great a number, and so terrible, that it darkened the whole air," and meeting " an honest citizen, clothed in a long garment," he asked him its meaning, " who friendly answered, ' It is,' quoth he, ' a warning to the Constable Marshall of the Inner Temple to prepare the dinner.'"

Sir William Dugdale, in *Origines Juridiciales* (ed. 1666, p. 163, etc.), gives us the following account of a grand Christmas in the Inner Temple, "extracted out of the Accompts of the House" :—

" First, it hath been the duty of the Steward to provide five fat Brawns, Vessells, Wood, and other necessaries belonging to the Kitchin: As also all manner of Spices, Flesh, Fowl, and other Cates for the Kitchin.

" The Office of the Chief Butler to provide a rich Cupboard of Plate, Silver and Parcel gilt ; Seaven dozen of Silver and gilt Spoons ; Twelve fair Salt-cellars, likewise Silver and gilt ; Twenty Candlesticks of the like.

" Twelve fine large Table Cloths of Damask and Diaper. Twenty dozen of Napkins suitable, at the least. Three dozen of fair large Towells ; whereof the Gentlemen Servers and Butlers of the House to have, every of them, one at meal times, during their attendance. Likewise to provide Carving Knives: Twenty dozen of white Cups and green Potts ; a Carving Table ; Torches ; Bread ; Beer, and Ale. And the chief of the Butlers was to give attendance on the highest Table in the Hall, with Wine, Ale, and Beer ; and all the other Butlers to attend at the other Tables in like sort.

" The Cupboard of Plate is to remain in the Hall on *Christmass* day, *St. Stephan's* day, and *New Year's* day. Upon the Banquetting night it was removed into the Buttry ; which, in all respects, was very laudably performed.

" The Office of the Constable Marshall to provide for his imployment, a fair gilt compleat Harneys, with a nest of Fethers

146

Fethers in the Helm; a fair Poleaxe to bear in his hand, to be chevalrously ordered on *Christmass* day, and other days, as, afterwards, is shewed : touching the ordering and setling of all which ceremonies, during the said *grand Christmass*, a solempn consultation was held at their Parliament in this House, in form following :—

"First, at the Parliament kept in their Parliament Chamber of this House, on the even at night of *St. Thomas* the Apostle, Officers are to attend, according as they had been, long before that time, at a former Parliament named and elected to undergo several offices for this time of solempnity, honour, and pleasure : Of which Officers, these are the most eminent; namely the *Steward, Marshall, Constable Marshall, Butler,* and *Master of the Game.* These Officers are made known, and elected in *Trinity Term* next before ; and to have knowledg thereof by Letters, if in the Country, to the end that they may prepare themselves against *All Hallow-tide ;* that, if such nominated Officers happen to fail, others may then be chosen in their rooms. The other Officers are appointed at other times neerer *Christmass* day.

"If the Steward, or any of the said Officers named in *Trinity Term*, refuse, or fail, he, or they, were fined, every one, at the discretion of the Bench ; and the Officers aforenamed agreed upon. And at such a Parliament, if it be fully resolved to proceed with such a *grand Christmass*, then the two youngest Butlers must light two Torches, and go before the Bench to the Upper end of the Hall ; who, being set down, the ancientest Bencher delivereth a Speech, briefly to the whole society of gentlemen then present, touching their Consent, as afore ; which ended, the eldest Butler is to publish all the Officers names, appointed in Parliament ; and then in token of joy and good liking, the Bench and Company pass beneath the Harth, and sing a Carol, and so to Boyer (drink).

"The *Marshall* at Dinner is to place at the highest Table's end, and next to the Library, all *Christmas Eve.* on one side thereof, the most ancient persons in the Company present : the Dean of the Chapell next to him ; then an Antient, or Bencher, beneath him. At the other end of the Table, the Server, Cup-bearer and Carver. At the upper end of the Bench Table, the King's Serjeant and

147

and Chief Butler: and, when the Steward hath served in, and set on the Table, the first Mess, then he, also, is to sit down.

"Also, at the upper end of the other Table, on the other side of the Hall, are to be placed the three Masters of the Revells; and at the lower end of the Bench Table, are to sit, the King's Attorney, the Ranger of the Forest, and the Master of the Game. And, at the lower end of the Table, on the other side of the Hall, the fourth Master of the Revells, the Common Sergeant, and Constable Marshall. And, at the upper end of the Utter Barister's Table, the Marshall sitteth, when he hath served in the first Mess: The Clark of the Kitchin, also, and the Clark of the Sowce-tub, when they have done their offices in the Kitchin, sit down. And, at the upper end of the Clark's Table, the Lieutenant of the Tower, and the attendant to the Buttry are placed.

"At these two Tables last rehersed, the persons there, may sit on both sides of the Table: but, of the other three Tables, all are to sit upon one side. And then, the Butlers, or Christmas servants, are first to cover the Tables with fair linnen Table-Cloths; and furnish them with Salt-cellars, Napkins and Trenchers, and a Silver Spoon. And then, the Butlers of the House must place at the Salt-cellar, at every the said first three highest Tables, a stock of Trenchers, and Bread: and, at the other Tables, Bread only, without Trenchers.

"At the first Course the Minstrells must sound their Instruments, and go before; and the Steward and Marshall are, next, to follow together; and, after them, the Gentlemen Server; and, then, cometh the meat. Those three Officers are to make, altogether, three solempn Curtesies, at three several times, between the Skreen and the upper Table; beginning with the first, at the end of the Bencher's table; the second at the midst; and the third at the other end; and then, standing by, the Server performeth his Office.

"When the first Table is set and served, the Steward's Table is next to be served. After him, the Master's table of the Revells; then that of the Master of the Game, the High Constable - Marshall: Then the Lieutenant of the Tower;

Tower; then the Utter Barister's table; and lastly, the Clerk's table. All which time the Musick must stand right above the Harthside, with the noise of their Musick, their faces direct towards the highest Table: and, that done, to return into the Buttry, with their Musick sounding.

"At the second course, every Table is to be served, as at the first Course, in every respect, which performed, the Servitors and Musicians are to resort to the place assigned them to dine at; which is the Valect's, or Yeoman's Table, beneath the Skreen. Dinner ended, the Musicians prepare to sing a Song, at the highest Table; which ceremony accomplished, then the Officers are to address themselves, every one in his office, to avoid the Tables in fair and decent manner, they beginning at the Clerk's Table; thence proceed to the next; and thence to all the others, till the highest Table be solempnly avoided.

"Then, after a little repose, the persons at the highest Table arise, and prepare to Revells: in which time, the Butlers and other Servitors with them, are to dine in the Library.

"At both the dores in the Hall, are Porters to view the Comers in and out at meal times: To each of them is allowed a Cast of Bread and a Candle nightly, after Supper.

"At night, before Supper, are Revells and Dancing; and so also after Supper, during the twelve days of Christmass. The antientest Master of the Revells is, after Dinner and Supper, to sing a Caroll, or Song; and command other Gentlemen then there present, to sing with him and the Company, and so it is very decently performed.

"A Repast at Dinner is viii$^{d.}$

"Service in the Church ended, the Gentlemen presently repair into the Hall, to Breakfast, with *Christmass day.* Brawn, Mustard, and Malmsey.

"At Dinner, the Butler appointed for the *grand Christmass*, is to see the Tables covered and furnished: and the ordinary Butlers of the House are decently to set Bread, Napkins, and Trenchers in good form, at every Table; with Spoones and Knives.

"At the first Course is served in, a fair and large Bore's head, upon a Silver Platter, with Minstralsye. Two Gentlemen

149

men in Gownes are to attend at Supper, and to bear two fair Torches of Wax, next before the Musicians and Trumpeters, and stand above the Fire with the Musick, till the first Course be served in, through the Hall. Which performed, they, with the Musick, are to return to the Buttry. The like course is to be observed in all things, during the time of Christmass. The like at Supper.

"At Service time this Evening, the two youngest Butlers are to bear Torches in the Genealogia. A Repast at Dinner is xii^d. which Strangers of worth are admitted to take in the Hall; and such are to be placed at the discretion of the Marshall.

"The Butler appointed for Christmass is to see the Tables covered, and furnished with Salt- *St. Stephan's* cellars, Napkins, Bread, Trenchers and Spoones. *;day.* Young gentlemen of the House are to attend and serve till the latter Dinner, and then dine themselves.

"This day, the Server, Carver and Cup - bearer are to serve, as afore. After the first Course served in, the Constable Marshall cometh into the Hall, arrayed with a fair, rich, compleat Harneys, white and bright, and gilt; with a Nest of Fethers of all Colours upon his Crest or Helm, and a gilt Poleaxe in his hand: to whom is associate the Lieutenant of the Tower, armed with a fair white Armour, a Nest of Fethers in his Helm, and a like Poleaxe in his hand; and with them sixteen Trumpetters; four Drums and Fifes going in rank before them: and, with them, attendeth four men in white Harneys, from the middle upwards, and Halberds in their hands, bearing on their shoulders the Tower; which persons, with the Drums, Trumpets and Musick, go three times about the Fire. Then the Constable Marshall, after two or three Curtesies made, kneeleth down before the Lord Chancellor; behind him the Lieutenant; and they kneeling, the Constable Marshall pronounceth an Oration of a quarter of an hour's length, thereby declaring the purpose of his coming; and that his purpose is, to be admitted into his Lordship's service.

"The Lord Chancellor saith, He will take farther advice thereon.

" Then

"Then the Constable Marshall, standing up, in submissive manner, delivereth his naked Sword to the Steward, who giveth it to the Lord Chancellour: and, thereupon, the Lord Chancellour willeth the Marshall to place the Constable Marshall in his Seat; and so he doth, with the Lieutenant, also, in his Seat or Place. During this ceremony, the Tower is placed beneath the fire.

"Then cometh in the Master of the Game apparalled in green Velvet: and the Ranger of the Forest also, in a green suit of Satten; bearing in his hand a green Bow, and divers Arrows; with, either of them, a Hunting Horn about their Necks; blowing together three blasts of Venery, they pace round about the fire three times. Then the Master of the Game maketh three Curtesies, as aforesaid; and kneeleth down before the Lord Chancellour, declaring the cause of his coming, and desireth to be admitted into his service, &c. All this time, the Ranger of the Forest standeth directly behind him. Then the Master of the Game standeth up.

"This ceremony also performed, a Huntsman cometh into the Hall, with a Fox and a Purse-net; with a Cat, both bound at the end of a staff; and, with them, nine or ten Couple of Hounds, with the blowing of Hunting Hornes. And the Fox and Cat are, by the Hounds, set upon, and killed beneath the Fire. This sport finished, the Marshall placeth them in their several appointed places.

"Then proceedeth the second Course; which done, and served out, the Common Serjeant delivereth a plausible Speech to the Lord Chancellour, and his Company, at the highest Table, how necessary a thing it is to have Officers at this present; the Constable Marshall, and Master of the Game, for the better honour and reputation of the Common-Wealth; and wisheth them to be received, &c.

"Then the King's Serjeant at Law declareth and inferreth the necessity; which heard, the Lord Chancellour desireth respite of farther advice. Then the antientist of the Masters of the Revells singeth a Song, with assistance of others there present.

"At Supper, the Hall is to be served with all solempnity, as upon Christmass day, both the first and second Course
to

to the highest Table. Supper ended, the Constable Marshall presenteth himself with Drums afore him, mounted upon a Scaffold, borne by four men; and goeth three times round about the Harthe, crying out aloud, *A Lord, A Lord*, &c. Then he descendeth and goeth to dance, &c., and, after, he calleth his Court, every one by name, one by one, in this Manner :—

Sir Francis Flatterer, of FOWLESHURST, in the County of BUCKINGHAM.

Sir Randle Backbite, of RASCALL HALL, in the County of RAKE HELL.

Sir Morgan Mumchance, of MUCH MONKERY, in the County of MAD MOPERY.

Sir Bartholomew Baldbreech, of BUTTOCKSBURY, in the County of BREKE NECK.

"This done, the Lord of Misrule addresseth himself to the Banquet: which ended with some Minstralsye, mirth and dancing, every man departeth to rest.

"At every Mess is a pot of Wine allowed. Every Repast is vi^{d.}

"About Seaven of the Clock in the Morning, the Lord of Misrule is abroad, and, if he lack any *St. John's day.* Officer or Attendant, he repaireth to their Chambers, and compelleth them to attend in person upon him after Service in the Church, to breakfast, with Brawn, Mustard and Malmsey. After Breakfast ended, his Lordship's power is in suspence, untill his personal presence at night; and then his power is most potent.

"At Dinner and Supper is observed the Diet and service performed on *St. Stephan's* day. After the second Course served in, the King's Serjeant, Oratour like, declareth the disorder of the Constable Marshall, and of the Common Serjeant; which complaint is answered by the Common Serjeant, who defendeth himself and the Constable Marshall with words of great efficacy: Hereto the King's Serjeant replyeth. They rejoyn &c., and whoso is found faulty, committed to the Tower &c.

"If any Officer be absent at Dinner or Supper Times; if it be complained of, he that sitteth in his place is adjudged to have like punishment, as the Officer should have had, being

152

being present : and then, withall, he is enjoyned to supply the Office of the true absent Officer, in all points. If any offendor escape from the Lieutenant, into the Buttery, and bring into the Hall a Manchet upon the point of a knife, he is pardoned. For the Buttry, in that case, is a Sanctuary. After Cheese served to the Table, not any is commanded to sing.

"In the Morning, as afore, on Monday, the Hall is served ; saving that the Server, Carver and Cup bearer do not attend any service. Also like Ceremony at Supper. *Childermass day.*

"In the Morning no Breakfast at all ; but like service as afore is mentioned, both at Dinner and Supper. *Wednesday.*

"At Breakfast, Brawn, Mustard and Malmsey. At Dinner, Roast Beef, Venison - Pasties, with like solempnities as afore. And at Supper, Mutton and Hens roasted. *Thursday.*

"In the Morning, Breakfast, as formerly. At Dinner like solempnity as on Christmass Eve. *New Year's day.*

" *The Banquetting Night.*

"It is proper to the Butler's Office to give warning to every House of Court, of this Banquet ; to the end that they, and the Innes of Chancery be invited thereto, to see a Play and Mask. The Hall is to be furnished with Scaffolds to sit on, for Ladies to behold the Sports, on each side. Which ended, the Ladies are to be brought into the Library, unto the Banquet there ; and a Table is to be covered and furnished with all Banquetting Dishes, for the Lord Chancellour, in the Hall ; where he is to call to him the Ancients of other Houses, as many as may be on the one side of the Table. The Banquet is to be served in, by Gentlemen of the House.

"The Marshall and Steward are to come before the Lord Chancellour's Mess. The Butlers for Christmas must serve Wine ; and the Butlers of the House, Beer and Ale &c. When the Banquet is ended, then cometh into the Hall,

Hall, the Constable Marshall, fairly mounted on his Mule; and deviseth some sport, for passing away the rest of the night.

"At Breakfast, Brawn, Mustard and Malmsey, after Morning Prayer ended: And, at Dinner, *Twelf Day.* the Hall is to be served as upon *St. John's* Day."

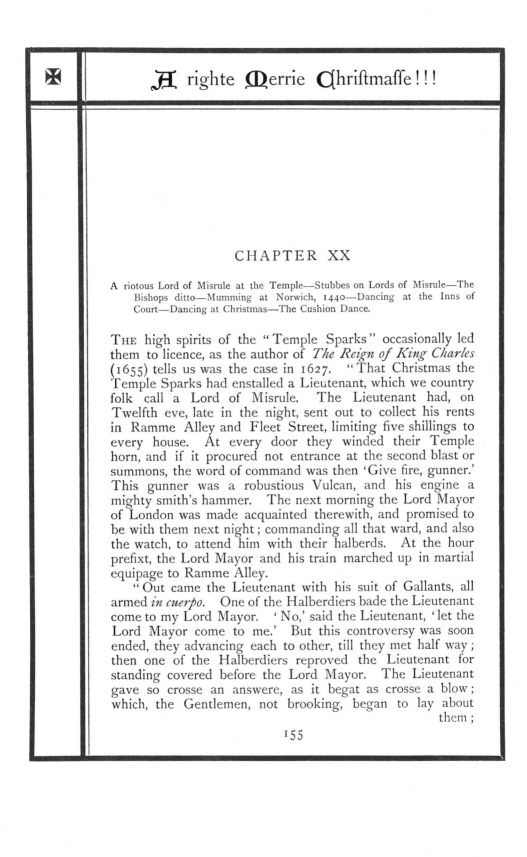
CHAPTER XX

A riotous Lord of Misrule at the Temple—Stubbes on Lords of Misrule—The
Bishops ditto—Mumming at Norwich, 1440—Dancing at the Inns of
Court—Dancing at Christmas—The Cushion Dance.

THE high spirits of the "Temple Sparks" occasionally led
them to licence, as the author of *The Reign of King Charles*
(1655) tells us was the case in 1627. "That Christmas the
Temple Sparks had enstalled a Lieutenant, which we country
folk call a Lord of Misrule. The Lieutenant had, on
Twelfth eve, late in the night, sent out to collect his rents
in Ramme Alley and Fleet Street, limiting five shillings to
every house. At every door they winded their Temple
horn, and if it procured not entrance at the second blast or
summons, the word of command was then 'Give fire, gunner.'
This gunner was a robustious Vulcan, and his engine a
mighty smith's hammer. The next morning the Lord Mayor
of London was made acquainted therewith, and promised to
be with them next night; commanding all that ward, and also
the watch, to attend him with their halberds. At the hour
prefixt, the Lord Mayor and his train marched up in martial
equipage to Ramme Alley.

"Out came the Lieutenant with his suit of Gallants, all
armed *in cuerpo*. One of the Halberdiers bade the Lieutenant
come to my Lord Mayor. 'No,' said the Lieutenant, 'let the
Lord Mayor come to me.' But this controversy was soon
ended, they advancing each to other, till they met half way;
then one of the Halberdiers reproved the Lieutenant for
standing covered before the Lord Mayor. The Lieutenant
gave so crosse an answere, as it begat as crosse a blow;
which, the Gentlemen, not brooking, began to lay about
them;

155

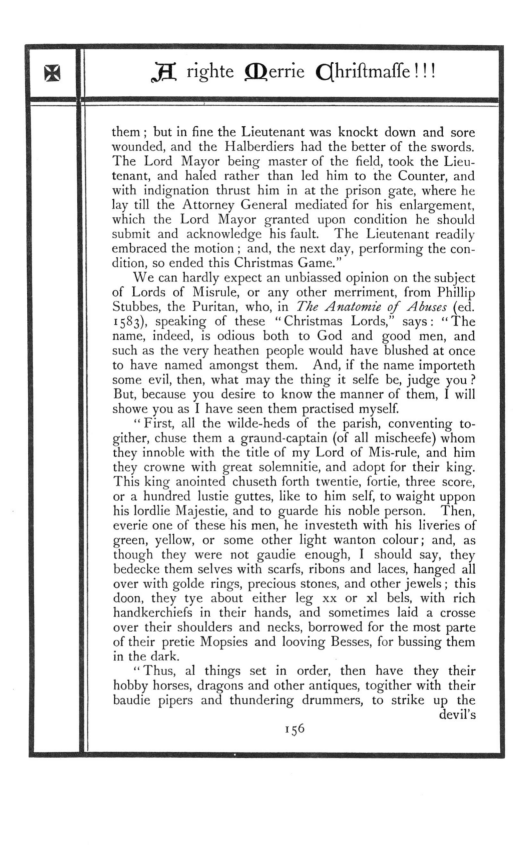

them ; but in fine the Lieutenant was knockt down and sore
wounded, and the Halberdiers had the better of the swords.
The Lord Mayor being master of the field, took the Lieutenant, and haled rather than led him to the Counter, and
with indignation thrust him in at the prison gate, where he
lay till the Attorney General mediated for his enlargement,
which the Lord Mayor granted upon condition he should
submit and acknowledge his fault. The Lieutenant readily
embraced the motion ; and, the next day, performing the condition, so ended this Christmas Game."

We can hardly expect an unbiassed opinion on the subject
of Lords of Misrule, or any other merriment, from Phillip
Stubbes, the Puritan, who, in *The Anatomie of Abuses* (ed.
1583), speaking of these "Christmas Lords," says : "The
name, indeed, is odious both to God and good men, and
such as the very heathen people would have blushed at once
to have named amongst them. And, if the name importeth
some evil, then, what may the thing it selfe be, judge you ?
But, because you desire to know the manner of them, I will
showe you as I have seen them practised myself.

"First, all the wilde-heds of the parish, conventing togither, chuse them a graund-captain (of all mischeefe) whom
they innoble with the title of my Lord of Mis-rule, and him
they crowne with great solemnitie, and adopt for their king.
This king anointed chuseth forth twentie, fortie, three score,
or a hundred lustie guttes, like to him self, to waight uppon
his lordlie Majestie, and to guarde his noble person. Then,
everie one of these his men, he investeth with his liveries of
green, yellow, or some other light wanton colour; and, as
though they were not gaudie enough, I should say, they
bedecke them selves with scarfs, ribons and laces, hanged all
over with golde rings, precious stones, and other jewels ; this
doon, they tye about either leg xx or xl bels, with rich
handkerchiefs in their hands, and sometimes laid a crosse
over their shoulders and necks, borrowed for the most parte
of their pretie Mopsies and looving Besses, for bussing them
in the dark.

"Thus, al things set in order, then have they their
hobby horses, dragons and other antiques, togither with their
baudie pipers and thundering drummers, to strike up the
devil's

devil's daunce withall. Then marche these heathen company towards the church and church yard, their pipers piping, their drummers thundring, their stumps dauncing, their bels jyngling, their handkerchefs swinging about their heds like madmen, their hobbie horses and other monsters skirmishing amongst the route ; and in this sorte they go to the church (I say), and into the church (though the minister be at praier, or preaching), dancing and swinging their handkercheifs over their heds in the church, like devils incarnate, with such a confuse noise, that no man can hear his own voice. Then, the foolish people, they looke, they stare, they laugh, they fleer, and mount upon fourmes and pewes, to see these goodly pageants solemnized in this sort. Then, after this, about the church they goe againe and again, and so foorth into the churchyard, where they have commonly their sommer haules, their bowers, arbors, and banqueting houses set up, wherin they feast, banquet and daunce al that day, and (peradventure) all the night too. And thus these terrestriall furies spend the Sabaoth day.

" They have, also, certain papers, wherein is painted some babblerie or other, of imagery woork, and these they call My Lord of Misrule's badges : these they give to every one that wil give money for them, to maintaine them in their heathenrie, devilrie, whordome, drunkennes, pride, and what not. And who will not be buxom to them, and give them money for these their devilish cognizances, they are mocked and flouted at not a little. And, so assotted are some, that they not only give them monie, to maintain their abhomination withall, but also weare their badges and cognizances in their hats and caps openly. But let them take heede ; for these are the badges, seales, brands, and cognizances of the devil, whereby he knoweth his servants and clyents from the children of God ; and so long as they weare them, *Sub vexillo diaboli militant contra Dominum et legem suam :* they fight under the banner and standerd of the Devil against Christ Jesus, and all his lawes. Another sorte of fantasticall fooles bring to these hel-hounds (the Lord of Mis-rule and his complices) some bread, some good ale, some new cheese, some olde, some custards and fine Cakes ; some one thing, some another ; but, if they knew that as often as they bring anything to the
maintenance

maintenance of these execrable pastimes, they offer sacrifice
to the devil and Sathanas, they would repent and withdraw
their hands, which God graunt they may!"

Although Stubbes wrote with exceeding bitterness and
party bias, he had some warrant for his diatribe. In the
Injunctions of Parkhurst, Bishop of Norwich[1] (1569), he says:
"Item, that no person or persons calling themselves lords of
misrule in the Christmas tyme, or other vnreuerent persons at
any other tyme, presume to come into the church vnreuerently
playing their lewd partes, with scoffing, iesting, or rebaldry
talke, and, if any such haue alredy offended herein, to present
them and their names to the ordinary."

Grindal, Archbishop of York, in his *Injunctions* (1571) also
says: "Item, that the Minister and Churchwardens shall not
suffer any lordes of misrule, or sommer lordes or ladies, or any
disguised persons or others, in Christmas or . . . at rish bear-
ings, or any other times to come vnreuerently into any Church,
or Chapell, or Churchyarde, and there daunce . . . namely, in
the time of diuine service, or of anie sermon." And so say
Overton, Bishop of Lichfield (1584); Bancroft, Bishop of
London (1601); and Howson, Bishop of Oxford (1619).

Merely to show how general throughout England were
these Rulers of Christmas Festivities, I will give one more
example, taken from the *Records of Norwich*, re what happened there at Christ-tide 1440. "John Hadman,[2] a wealthy
citizen, made disport with his neighbours and friends, and
was crowned King of Christmas. He rode in state through
the City, dressed forth in silks and tinsel, and preceded by
twelve persons habited as the twelve months of the year.
After King Christmas followed Lent, clothed in white garments, trimmed with herring skins, on horseback, the horse
being decorated with trappings of oyster shells, being indi-
cative that sadness and a holy time should follow Christmas
revelling. In this way they rode through the City, accompanied by numbers in various grotesque dresses, making
disport and merriment; some clothed in armour, others,
dressed as devils, chased the people, and sorely affrighted the
women

---

[1] *Second Report of Ritual Comm.*, from which the examples following are also taken.
[2] Probably the John Gladman spoken of by Stubbes (see p. 127).

women and children; others wearing skin dresses, and counterfeiting bears, wolves, lions, and other animals, and endeavouring to imitate the animals they represented, in roaring and raving, alarming the cowardly, and appalling the stoutest hearts."

Naturally, among the pastimes of this festive season dancing was not the least. And it was reckoned as a diversion for staid people. We know how—

> The grave Lord Keeper led the braules,
> The mace and seals before him.

It was a practice for the bar to dance before the Judges at Lincoln's Inn at Christmas, and in James I.'s time the under barristers were, by decimation, put out of Commons, because they did not dance, as was their wont, according to the ancient custom of the Society.[1] This practice is also mentioned in a book published about 1730, called *Round About our Coal Fire*, etc. "The dancing and singing of the Benchers in the great Inns of Court at Christmas is, in some sort, founded upon interest, for they hold, as I am informed, some priviledge by dancing about the fire in the middle of their Hall, and singing the song of *Round About our Coal Fire*." In the prologue to the same book we have the following song :—

O you merry, merry Souls,
　Christmas is a coming,
We shall have flowing bowls,
　Dancing, piping, drumming.

Delicate minced pies,
　To feast every virgin,
Capon and goose likewise,
　Brawn, and a dish of sturgeon.

Then, for your Christmas box,
　Sweet plumb cakes and money,
Delicate Holland smocks,
　Kisses sweet as honey.

Hey for the Christmas Ball,
　Where we shall be jolly,
Coupling short and tall,
　Kate, Dick, Ralph, and Molly.

Then to the hop we'll go,
　Where we'll jig and caper,
Cuckolds all a-row,
　Will shall pay the scraper.

Hodge shall dance with Prue,
　Keeping time with kisses,
We'll have a jovial crew
　Of sweet smirking Misses.

We still keep up the custom of dancing at Christ-tide, and no Christmas party is complete without it; but of all the
old

[1] Dugdale's *Orig. Jurid.* cap. 64.

old tunes, such as *Sellinger's Rounds*, the one mentioned in the above song, with many others, but one remains to us, and that is peculiar to this season—*Sir Roger de Coverly*.

Notes and Queries, 19th December 1885, gives an account of a very curious dance. "One of the most popular indoor games at Christmas time was, in Derbyshire, that of the 'Cushion Dance,' which was performed at most of the village gatherings and farm-house parties during the Christmas holidays upwards of forty years ago. The following is an account of the dance as it was known amongst the farmer's sons and daughters and the domestics, all of whom were on a pretty fair equality, very different from what prevails in farm-houses of to-day. The dance was performed with boisterous fun, quite unlike the game as played in higher circles, where the conditions and rules of procedure were of a more refined order.

"The company were seated round the room, a fiddler occupying a raised seat in a corner. When all were ready, two of the young men left the room, returning presently, one carrying a large square cushion, the other an ordinary drinking horn, china bowl, or silver tankard, according to the possessions of the family. The one carrying the cushion locked the door, putting the key in his pocket. Both gentlemen then went to the fiddler's corner, and, after the cushion-bearer had put a coin in the vessel carried by the other, the fiddler struck up a lively tune, to which the young men began to dance round the room, singing or reciting to the music :—

> "'Frinkum, frankum is a fine song,
> An' we will dance it all along;
> All along and round about
> Till we find the pretty maid out.'

After making the circuit of the room, they halted on reaching the fiddler's corner, and the cushion-bearer, still to the music of the fiddle, sang or recited :—

> "'Our song it will no further go!'

" *The Fiddler*—

> "'Pray, kind sir, why say you so?'

" *The Cushion-Bearer*—

> "'Because Jane Sandars won't come to.

" *The*

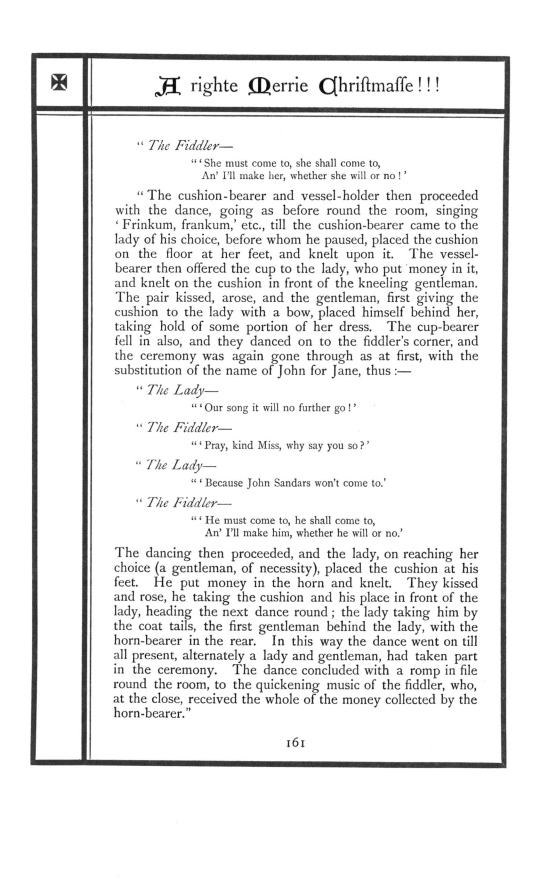

"*The Fiddler—*

"'She must come to, she shall come to,
An' I'll make her, whether she will or no!'

" The cushion-bearer and vessel-holder then proceeded with the dance, going as before round the room, singing 'Frinkum, frankum,' etc., till the cushion-bearer came to the lady of his choice, before whom he paused, placed the cushion on the floor at her feet, and knelt upon it. The vessel-bearer then offered the cup to the lady, who put money in it, and knelt on the cushion in front of the kneeling gentleman. The pair kissed, arose, and the gentleman, first giving the cushion to the lady with a bow, placed himself behind her, taking hold of some portion of her dress. The cup-bearer fell in also, and they danced on to the fiddler's corner, and the ceremony was again gone through as at first, with the substitution of the name of John for Jane, thus :—

"*The Lady—*

"'Our song it will no further go!'

"*The Fiddler—*

"'Pray, kind Miss, why say you so?'

"*The Lady—*

"'Because John Sandars won't come to.'

"*The Fiddler—*

"'He must come to, he shall come to,
An' I'll make him, whether he will or no.'

The dancing then proceeded, and the lady, on reaching her choice (a gentleman, of necessity), placed the cushion at his feet. He put money in the horn and knelt. They kissed and rose, he taking the cushion and his place in front of the lady, heading the next dance round ; the lady taking him by the coat tails, the first gentleman behind the lady, with the horn-bearer in the rear. In this way the dance went on till all present, alternately a lady and gentleman, had taken part in the ceremony. The dance concluded with a romp in file round the room, to the quickening music of the fiddler, who, at the close, received the whole of the money collected by the horn-bearer."

161

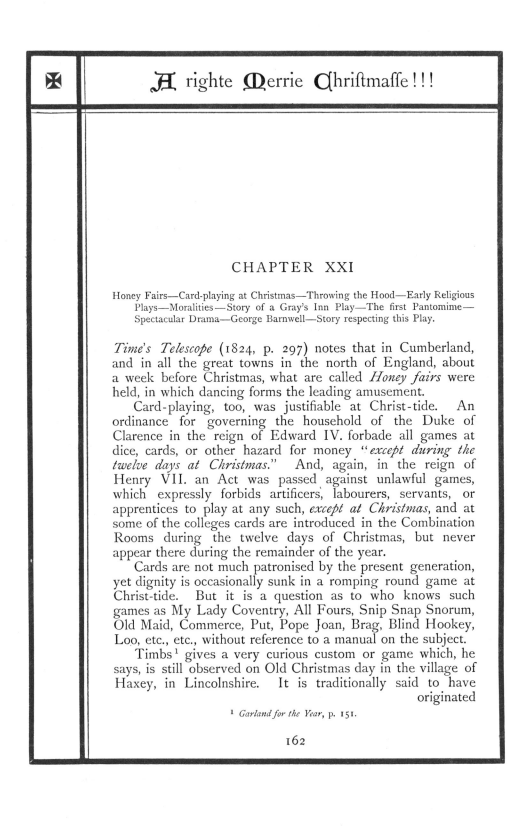
CHAPTER XXI

Honey Fairs—Card-playing at Christmas—Throwing the Hood—Early Religious
Plays—Moralities—Story of a Gray's Inn Play—The first Pantomime—
Spectacular Drama—George Barnwell—Story respecting this Play.

Time's Telescope (1824, p. 297) notes that in Cumberland,
and in all the great towns in the north of England, about
a week before Christmas, what are called *Honey fairs* were
held, in which dancing forms the leading amusement.

Card-playing, too, was justifiable at Christ-tide. An
ordinance for governing the household of the Duke of
Clarence in the reign of Edward IV. forbade all games at
dice, cards, or other hazard for money "*except during the
twelve days at Christmas.*" And, again, in the reign of
Henry VII. an Act was passed against unlawful games,
which expressly forbids artificers, labourers, servants, or
apprentices to play at any such, *except at Christmas*, and at
some of the colleges cards are introduced in the Combination
Rooms during the twelve days of Christmas, but never
appear there during the remainder of the year.

Cards are not much patronised by the present generation,
yet dignity is occasionally sunk in a romping round game at
Christ-tide. But it is a question as to who knows such
games as My Lady Coventry, All Fours, Snip Snap Snorum,
Old Maid, Commerce, Put, Pope Joan, Brag, Blind Hookey,
Loo, etc., etc., without reference to a manual on the subject.

Timbs[1] gives a very curious custom or game which, he
says, is still observed on Old Christmas day in the village of
Haxey, in Lincolnshire. It is traditionally said to have
originated

---

[1] *Garland for the Year*, p. 151.

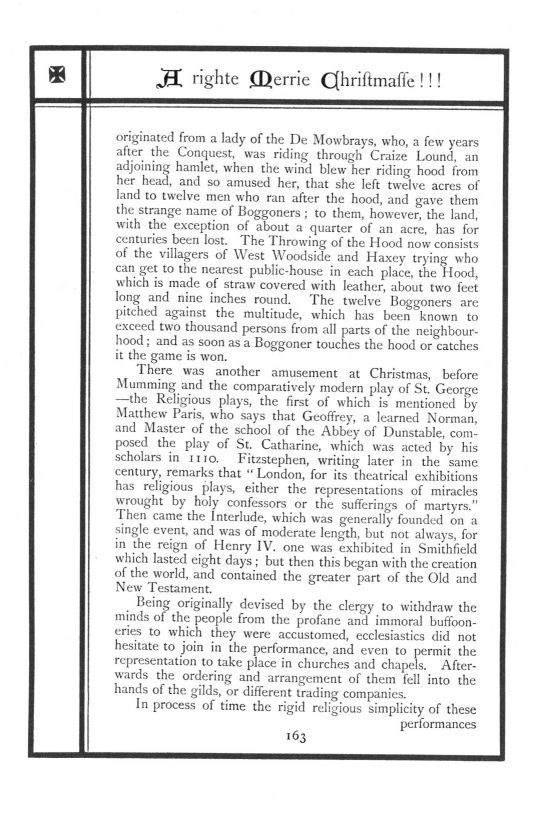
originated from a lady of the De Mowbrays, who, a few years after the Conquest, was riding through Craize Lound, an adjoining hamlet, when the wind blew her riding hood from her head, and so amused her, that she left twelve acres of land to twelve men who ran after the hood, and gave them the strange name of Boggoners ; to them, however, the land, with the exception of about a quarter of an acre, has for centuries been lost. The Throwing of the Hood now consists of the villagers of West Woodside and Haxey trying who can get to the nearest public-house in each place, the Hood, which is made of straw covered with leather, about two feet long and nine inches round. The twelve Boggoners are pitched against the multitude, which has been known to exceed two thousand persons from all parts of the neighbour-hood ; and as soon as a Boggoner touches the hood or catches it the game is won.

There was another amusement at Christmas, before Mumming and the comparatively modern play of St. George —the Religious plays, the first of which is mentioned by Matthew Paris, who says that Geoffrey, a learned Norman, and Master of the school of the Abbey of Dunstable, com-posed the play of St. Catharine, which was acted by his scholars in 1110. Fitzstephen, writing later in the same century, remarks that " London, for its theatrical exhibitions has religious plays, either the representations of miracles wrought by holy confessors or the sufferings of martyrs." Then came the Interlude, which was generally founded on a single event, and was of moderate length, but not always, for in the reign of Henry IV. one was exhibited in Smithfield which lasted eight days ; but then this began with the creation of the world, and contained the greater part of the Old and New Testament.

Being originally devised by the clergy to withdraw the minds of the people from the profane and immoral buffoon-eries to which they were accustomed, ecclesiastics did not hesitate to join in the performance, and even to permit the representation to take place in churches and chapels. After-wards the ordering and arrangement of them fell into the hands of the gilds, or different trading companies.

In process of time the rigid religious simplicity of these performances

performances was broken in upon, and the devil and a circle
of infernal associates were introduced to relieve the performance, and to excite laughter by all sorts of strange noises and
antics. By and by, abstract personifications, such as Truth,
Justice, Mercy, etc., found their way into these plays, and
they then became moral plays, or "Moralities." These were
in their highest vogue in the reigns of Henries VII. and VIII.,
and Holinshed tells a story of one played at Christ-tide
1526-27.

"This Christmasse was a goodlie disguising plaied at
Graies In, which was compiled for the most part by maister
John Roo, sergeant at the law manie yeares past, and long
before the cardinall had any authoritie. The effect of the
plaie was that lord gouernance was ruled by dissipation and
negligence, by whose misgouernance and evill order ladie
publike weale was put from gouernance; which caused rumor
populi, inwarde grudge and disdaine of wanton souereignetie
to rise, with a great multitude, to expell negligence and dissipation, and to restore publike weale againe to hir estate,
which was so doone.

"This plaie was so set foorth with riche and costlie
apparell, with strange devises of Maskes and morrishes, that
it was highlie praised of all men, sauing of the cardinall,
which imagined that the play had been devised of him, and
in a great furie sent for the said maister Roo, and took from
him his coife, and sent him to the Fleet; and after, he sent
for the yoong gentlemen that plaied in the plaie, and them
highlie rebuked and threatned, and sent one of them, called
Thomas Moile, of Kent, to the Fleet; but by means of
friends, maister Roo and he were deliuered at last. This
plaie sore displeased the cardinall, and yet it was neuer meant
to him, as you haue heard. Wherfore manie wise men
grudged to see him take it so hartilie, and euer the cardinall
said that the king was highlie displeased with it, and spake
nothing of himselfe."

J. P. Collier, in his *Annals of the Stage* (ed. 1879, pp.
68, 69), gives an account of two Interludes played before
royalty at Richmond, Christ-tide 1514-15, which he found in
a paper folded up in a roll in the Chapter House. "The
Interlud was callyd the tryumpe of Love and Bewte, and yt
was

was wryten and presented by Mayster Cornyshe and oothers of the Chappell of our soverayne lorde the Kynge, and the chyldern of the sayd Chapell. In the same, Venus and Bewte dyd tryumpe over al ther enemys, and tamyd a salvadge man and a lyon, that was made very rare and naturall, so as the Kynge was gretly plesyd therwyth, and gracyously gaf Mayster Cornysshe a ryche rewarde owt of his owne hand, to be dyvyded with the rest of his felows. Venus did synge a songe with Beawte, which was lykyd of al that harde yt, every staffe endyng after this sorte—

"Bowe you downe, and doo your dutye
To Venus and the goddes Bewty :
We tryumpe hye over all,
Kyngs attend when we doo call.

Inglyshe, and the oothers of the Kynges pleyers, after pleyed an Interluyt, whiche was wryten by Mayster Midwell, but yt was so long, yt was not lykyd : yt was of the fyndyng of Troth, who was caryed away by ygnoraunce and ypocresy. The foolys part was the best, but the kyng departyd befor the end to hys chambre."

Of Christ-tide Masques I have already written, and after they fell into desuetude there was nothing theatrical absolutely peculiar to Christmas until Rich, in 1717, introduced the comic pantomime at his theatre in Lincoln's Inn Fields, where, on 26th December of that year, he produced *Harlequin Executed*. Davies says : "To retrieve the credit of his theatre, Rich created a species of dramatic composition, unknown to this, and I believe to any other country, which he called a pantomime ; it consisted of two parts—one serious, and the other comic. By the help of gay scenes, fine habits, grand dances, appropriate music, and other decorations, he exhibited a story from Ovid's *Metamorphoses*, or some other fabulous writer. Between the pauses, or acts, of this serious, representation he interwove a comic fable ; consisting chiefly of the courtship of Harlequin and Columbine, with a variety of surprizing adventures and tricks, which were produced by the magic wand of Harlequin ; such as the sudden transformation of palaces and temples to huts and cottages, of men and women into wheelbarrows and joint stools, of trees turned
into

165

into houses, colonades to beds of tulips, and mechanics' shops into serpents and ostriches." From 1717 until 1761, the date of his death, he brought out a succession of pantomimes, all of which were eminently successful, and ran at least forty or fifty nights each. That the pantomime, very slightly altered from Rich's first conception, still is attractive, speaks for itself.

No other style of entertainment for Christ-tide was ever so popular. Garrick tried spectacular drama, and failed. Walpole, writing to Lady Ossory, 30th December 1772, says : "Garrick has brought out what he calls a *Christmas tale*, adorned with the most beautiful scenes, next to those in the Opera at Paradise, designed by Loutherbourg. They have much ado to save the piece from being sent to the Devil. It is believed to be Garrick's own, and a new proof that it is possible to be the best actor and the worst author in the world, as Shakspeare was just the contrary." Some of us are old enough to remember with delight Planché's extravaganzas, *The King of the Peacocks*, etc., which were so beautifully put on the stage of the Lyceum Theatre by Madame Vestris, but I do not think they were a financial success, and they have never been repeated by other managers.

Up to a very recent date a stock piece at the minor theatres on Boxing Night was the tragedy of *The London Merchant ; or, The History of George Barnwell*, acted at Drury Lane in 1731, which was so successful that the Queen sent for the MS. to read it, and Hone (*Every-Day Book*, ii. 1651) remarks as a notable circumstance that "the representation of this tragedy was omitted in the Christmas holidays of 1819 at both the theatres for the first time."

It was considered a highly moral play, and was acted for the particular benefit of apprentices, to deter them from the crime of theft, and from keeping company with bad women. David Ross, the actor, wrote in 1787 the following letter to a friend :—

"In the year 1752, during the Christmas holidays, I played George Barnwell, and the late Mrs. Pritchard played Millwood. Doctor Barrowby, physician to St. Bartholomew's Hospital, told me he was sent for by a young gentleman in Great St. Helen's, apprentice to a very capital merchant. He

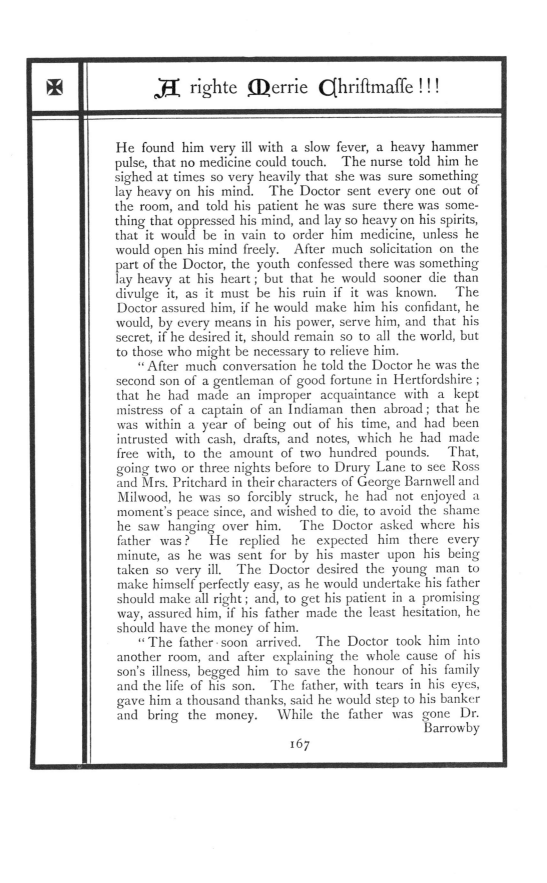

He found him very ill with a slow fever, a heavy hammer pulse, that no medicine could touch. The nurse told him he sighed at times so very heavily that she was sure something lay heavy on his mind. The Doctor sent every one out of the room, and told his patient he was sure there was something that oppressed his mind, and lay so heavy on his spirits, that it would be in vain to order him medicine, unless he would open his mind freely. After much solicitation on the part of the Doctor, the youth confessed there was something lay heavy at his heart; but that he would sooner die than divulge it, as it must be his ruin if it was known. The Doctor assured him, if he would make him his confidant, he would, by every means in his power, serve him, and that his secret, if he desired it, should remain so to all the world, but to those who might be necessary to relieve him.

"After much conversation he told the Doctor he was the second son of a gentleman of good fortune in Hertfordshire; that he had made an improper acquaintance with a kept mistress of a captain of an Indiaman then abroad; that he was within a year of being out of his time, and had been intrusted with cash, drafts, and notes, which he had made free with, to the amount of two hundred pounds. That, going two or three nights before to Drury Lane to see Ross and Mrs. Pritchard in their characters of George Barnwell and Milwood, he was so forcibly struck, he had not enjoyed a moment's peace since, and wished to die, to avoid the shame he saw hanging over him. The Doctor asked where his father was? He replied he expected him there every minute, as he was sent for by his master upon his being taken so very ill. The Doctor desired the young man to make himself perfectly easy, as he would undertake his father should make all right; and, to get his patient in a promising way, assured him, if his father made the least hesitation, he should have the money of him.

"The father soon arrived. The Doctor took him into another room, and after explaining the whole cause of his son's illness, begged him to save the honour of his family and the life of his son. The father, with tears in his eyes, gave him a thousand thanks, said he would step to his banker and bring the money. While the father was gone Dr. Barrowby

167

Barrowby went to his patient, and told him everything would be settled in a few minutes to his ease and satisfaction ; that his father was gone to his banker for the money, and would soon return with peace and forgiveness, and never mention or even think of it more. What is very extraordinary, the Doctor told me that, in a few minutes after he communicated this news to his patient, upon feeling of his pulse, without the help of any medicine, he was quite another creature. The father returned with notes to the amount of £200, which he put into his son's hands. They wept, kissed, embraced. The son soon recovered, and lived to be a very eminent merchant.

" Dr. Barrowby never told me the name ; but the story he mentioned often in the green-room of Drury Lane Theatre ; and after telling it one night when I was standing by, he said to me, ' You have done some good in your profession—more, perhaps, than many a clergyman who preached last Sunday,' for the patient told the Doctor the play raised such horror and contrition in his soul that he would, if it would please God to raise a friend to extricate him out of that distress, dedicate the rest of his life to religion and virtue. Though I never knew his name or saw him, to my knowledge, I had, for nine or ten years, at my benefit a note sealed up, with ten guineas, and these words—' *A tribute of gratitude from one who was highly obliged, and saved from ruin, by seeing Mr. Ross's performance of Barnwell.*'"

CHAPTER XXII

Profusion of Food at Christ-tide—Old English Fare—Hospitality—Proclamations
for People to spend Christ-tide at their Country Places—Roast Beef—
Boar's Head—Boar's Head Carol—Custom at Queen's Coll. Oxon.—
Brawn—Christmas Pie—Goose Pie—Plum Pudding—Plum Porridge—
Anecdotes of Plum Pudding—Large one—Mince Pies—Hackin—Folk-
lore—Gifts at Christ-tide—Yule Doughs—Cop-a-loaf—Snap-dragon.

IF any exception can be taken to Christ-tide in England, it is
to the enormous amount of flesh, fowl, etc., consumed. To a
sensitive mind, the butchers' shops, gorged with the flesh of
fat beeves, or the poulterers, with their hetacombs of turkeys,
are repulsive, to say the least. It is the remains of a coarse
barbarism, which shows but little signs of dying out. Profusion of food at this season is traditional, and has been
handed down from generation to generation. A Christmas
dinner must, if possible, be every one's portion, down to the
pauper in the workhouse, and even the prisoner in the gaol.
Tusser, who, though he could write—

> At Christmas we banket, the riche with the poore,
> Who then (but the miser) but openeth his doore.
> At Christmas, of Christ, many Carols we sing ;
> And give many gifts, for the joy of that King,

could also sing of " Christmas husbandly fare "—

> Good husband and huswife, now chiefly be glad,
> Things handsome to have, as they ought to be had.
> They both do provide against Christmas do come,
> To welcome their neighbor, good chere to have some.
> Good bread and good drinke, a good fier in the hall,
> Brawne, pudding, and souse, and good mustard withall.
> Biefe, Mutton, and Porke, shred pies of the best,
> Pig, veale, goose, and capon, and Turkey well drest.

Cheese,

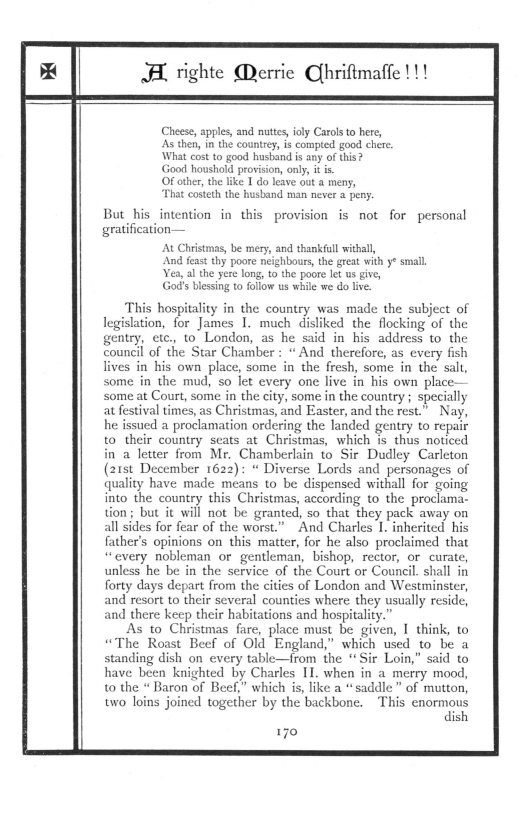

Cheese, apples, and nuttes, ioly Carols to here,
As then, in the countrey, is compted good chere.
What cost to good husband is any of this?
Good houshold provision, only, it is.
Of other, the like I do leave out a meny,
That costeth the husband man never a peny.

But his intention in this provision is not for personal gratification—

At Christmas, be mery, and thankfull withall,
And feast thy poore neighbours, the great with yᵉ small.
Yea, al the yere long, to the poore let us give,
God's blessing to follow us while we do live.

This hospitality in the country was made the subject of legislation, for James I. much disliked the flocking of the gentry, etc., to London, as he said in his address to the council of the Star Chamber: "And therefore, as every fish lives in his own place, some in the fresh, some in the salt, some in the mud, so let every one live in his own place—some at Court, some in the city, some in the country; specially at festival times, as Christmas, and Easter, and the rest." Nay, he issued a proclamation ordering the landed gentry to repair to their country seats at Christmas, which is thus noticed in a letter from Mr. Chamberlain to Sir Dudley Carleton (21st December 1622): "Diverse Lords and personages of quality have made means to be dispensed withall for going into the country this Christmas, according to the proclamation; but it will not be granted, so that they pack away on all sides for fear of the worst." And Charles I. inherited his father's opinions on this matter, for he also proclaimed that "every nobleman or gentleman, bishop, rector, or curate, unless he be in the service of the Court or Council. shall in forty days depart from the cities of London and Westminster, and resort to their several counties where they usually reside, and there keep their habitations and hospitality."

As to Christmas fare, place must be given, I think, to "The Roast Beef of Old England," which used to be a standing dish on every table—from the "Sir Loin," said to have been knighted by Charles II. when in a merry mood, to the "Baron of Beef," which is, like a "saddle" of mutton, two loins joined together by the backbone. This enormous dish

170

dish is not within the range of ordinary mortals; but the Queen always keeps up the custom of having one wherever she may be, at Windsor, or Osborne. Beef may be said to be the staple flesh of England, and is procurable by every one except the very poorest, whilst it is not given to all to obtain the lordly boar's head, which used to be an indispensable adjunct to the Christmas feast. One thing is, that wild boars only exist in England either in zoological gardens or in a few parks—notably Windsor—in a semi-domesticated state. The bringing in the boar's head was conducted with great ceremony, as Holinshed tells us that in 1170, when Henry I. had his son crowned as joint-ruler with himself, " Upon the daie of coronation King Henrie, the father, served his sonne at the table, as server, bringing up the bore's head with trumpets before it, according to the maner."

In "Christmasse carolles, newely enprinted at Londō, in the fletestrete at the Sygne of the Sonne, by Wynkyn de Worde. The Yere of our lorde M.D.XXI.," is the following, which, from its being "newely enprinted," must have been older than the date given :—

> A carol bringyng in the bores heed.
> Caput apri differo [1]
> Reddens laudes domino.
> The bores heed in hande bring I,
> With garlands gay and rosemary.
> I praye you all synge merely
> Qui estis in conuiuio.
> The bores heed I understande
> Is the chefe serbyce in this lande
> Loke where euer it be fande [2]
> Serbite cum cantico.
> Be gladde lordes bothe more and lasse, [3]
> For this hath ordeyned our stewarde
> To chere you all this Christmasse
> The bores heed with mustarde.
> Finis.

The custom of ceremoniously ntroducing the boar's head at Christ-tide was, at one time, of general use among the nobility,

[1] Defero.   [2] Found.   [3] Great and small.

171

nobility, and still obtains at Queen's College, Oxford ; and its *raison d'être* is said to be that at some remote time a student of this College was walking in the neighbouring forest of Shotover (*Chateau vert*), and whilst reading Aristotle was attacked by a wild boar. Unarmed, he did not know how to defend himself ; but as the beast rushed on him with open mouth he rammed the Aristotle down its throat, exclaiming, "*Græcum est,*" which ended the boar's existence. Some little ceremony is still used when it is brought in ; the head is decorated, as saith the carol, and it is borne into the hall on the shoulders of two College servants, followed by members of the College and the choir. The carol, which is a modification of the above, is generally sung by a Fellow, assisted by the choir, and the boar's head is solemnly deposited before the Provost, who, after helping those sitting at the high table, sends it round to all the other tables.

Dr. King, in his *Art of Cookery*, gives the following recipe for dishing up a boar's head :—

> Then if you would send up the Brawner's head,
> Sweet rosemary and bays around it spread ;
> His foaming tusks let some large pippin grace,
> Or midst these thundering spears an orange place.
> Sauce, like himself, offensive to its foes,
> The roguish mustard, dangerous to the nose.
> Sack, and the well-spic'd Hippocras the wine,
> Wassail the bowl with ancient ribbons fine,
> Porridge with plums, and turkies with the chine.

Of the boar's head was made *brawn*, which, when well made, is good indeed ; and this was another Christmas dish. Sandys says : " The French do not seem to have been so well acquainted with brawn ; for on the capture of Calais by them they found a large quantity, which they guessed to be some dainty, and tried every means of preparing it ; in vain did they roast it, bake it, boil it ; it was impracticable and impenetrable to their culinary arts. Its merits, however, being at length discovered, ' Ha!' said the monks, ' what delightful fish!' and immediately added it to their stock of fast day viands. The Jews, again, could not believe it was procured from that impure beast, the hog, and included in their list of clean animals."

Then

Then there was a dish, "the Christmas pie," which must have been very peculiar, if we can trust Henri Misson, who was in England in the latter end of the seventeenth century. Says he: " Every Family against *Christmass* makes a famous Pye, which they call *Christmass* Pye : It is a great Nostrum the composition of this Pasty ; it is a most learned Mixture of Neats - tongues, Chicken, Eggs, Sugar, Raisins, Lemon and Orange Peel, various kinds of Spicery, etc." Can this be the pie of which Herrick sang ?—

> Come, guard this night the Christmas pie,
> That the thiefe, though ne'r so slie,
> With his flesh hooks don't come nie
>> To catch it ;
> From him, who all alone sits there,
> Having his eyes still in his eare,
> And a deale of nightly feare,
>> To watch it.

Fletcher, in his poem *Christmas Day*,[1] thus describes the pie :—

> Christmas? give me my beads ; the word implies
> A plot, by its ingredients, beef and pyes.
> The cloyster'd steaks, with salt and pepper, lye
> Like Nunnes with patches in a monastrie.
> Prophaneness in a conclave? Nay, much more
> Idolatrie in crust ! Babylon's whore
> Rak'd from the grave, and bak'd by hanches, then
> Serv'd up in *coffins* to unholy men ;
> Defil'd with superstition like the Gentiles
> Of old, that worship'd onions, roots, and lentils.

The *Grub Street Journal* of 27th December 1733 has an essay on Christmas Pye ; but it is only a political satire, and not worth quoting here. There was once a famous Christmas pie which obtained the following notice in the *Newcastle Chronicle*, 6th January 1770 : "Monday last, was brought from Howick to Berwick, to be shipp'd for London, for sir Hen. Grey, bart., a pie, the contents whereof are as follows : viz. 2 bushels of flour, 20 lbs. of butter, 4 geese, 2 turkies, 2 rabbits, 4 wild ducks, 2 woodcocks, 6 snipes, and 4 partridges,

2

---

[1] *Ex Otio Negotium*, etc., ed. 1656, p. 114.

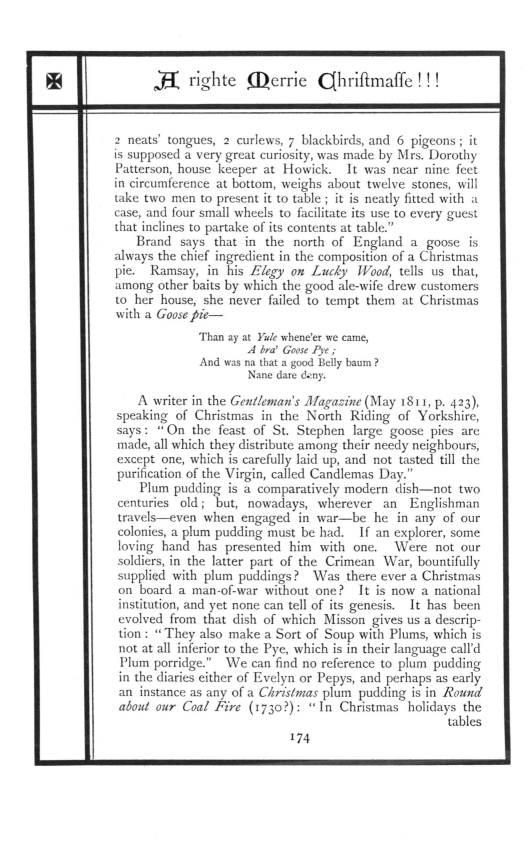

2 neats' tongues, 2 curlews, 7 blackbirds, and 6 pigeons; it is supposed a very great curiosity, was made by Mrs. Dorothy Patterson, house keeper at Howick. It was near nine feet in circumference at bottom, weighs about twelve stones, will take two men to present it to table; it is neatly fitted with a case, and four small wheels to facilitate its use to every guest that inclines to partake of its contents at table."

Brand says that in the north of England a goose is always the chief ingredient in the composition of a Christmas pie. Ramsay, in his *Elegy on Lucky Wood*, tells us that, among other baits by which the good ale-wife drew customers to her house, she never failed to tempt them at Christmas with a *Goose pie*—

> Than ay at *Yule* whene'er we came,
> *A bra' Goose Pye ;*
> And was na that a good Belly baum?
> Nane dare deny.

A writer in the *Gentleman's Magazine* (May 1811, p. 423), speaking of Christmas in the North Riding of Yorkshire, says: "On the feast of St. Stephen large goose pies are made, all which they distribute among their needy neighbours, except one, which is carefully laid up, and not tasted till the purification of the Virgin, called Candlemas Day."

Plum pudding is a comparatively modern dish—not two centuries old; but, nowadays, wherever an Englishman travels—even when engaged in war—be he in any of our colonies, a plum pudding must be had. If an explorer, some loving hand has presented him with one. Were not our soldiers, in the latter part of the Crimean War, bountifully supplied with plum puddings? Was there ever a Christmas on board a man-of-war without one? It is now a national institution, and yet none can tell of its genesis. It has been evolved from that dish of which Misson gives us a description: "They also make a Sort of Soup with Plums, which is not at all inferior to the Pye, which is in their language call'd Plum porridge." We can find no reference to plum pudding in the diaries either of Evelyn or Pepys, and perhaps as early an instance as any of a *Christmas* plum pudding is in *Round about our Coal Fire* (1730?): "In Christmas holidays the tables

174

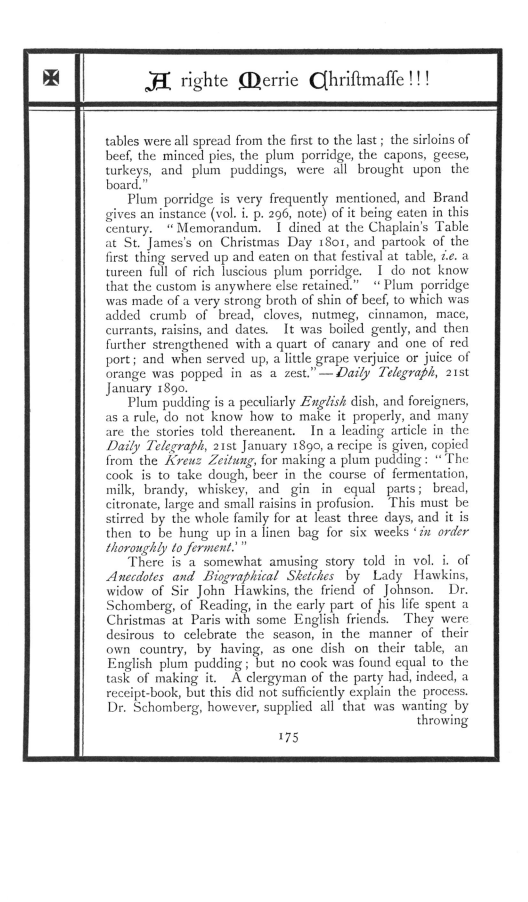

tables were all spread from the first to the last ; the sirloins of beef, the minced pies, the plum porridge, the capons, geese, turkeys, and plum puddings, were all brought upon the board."

Plum porridge is very frequently mentioned, and Brand gives an instance (vol. i. p. 296, note) of it being eaten in this century. "Memorandum. I dined at the Chaplain's Table at St. James's on Christmas Day 1801, and partook of the first thing served up and eaten on that festival at table, *i.e.* a tureen full of rich luscious plum porridge. I do not know that the custom is anywhere else retained." "Plum porridge was made of a very strong broth of shin of beef, to which was added crumb of bread, cloves, nutmeg, cinnamon, mace, currants, raisins, and dates. It was boiled gently, and then further strengthened with a quart of canary and one of red port ; and when served up, a little grape verjuice or juice of orange was popped in as a zest."—*Daily Telegraph*, 21st January 1890.

Plum pudding is a peculiarly *English* dish, and foreigners, as a rule, do not know how to make it properly, and many are the stories told thereanent. In a leading article in the *Daily Telegraph*, 21st January 1890, a recipe is given, copied from the *Kreuz Zeitung*, for making a plum pudding : "The cook is to take dough, beer in the course of fermentation, milk, brandy, whiskey, and gin in equal parts ; bread, citronate, large and small raisins in profusion. This must be stirred by the whole family for at least three days, and it is then to be hung up in a linen bag for six weeks '*in order thoroughly to ferment.*'"

There is a somewhat amusing story told in vol. i. of *Anecdotes and Biographical Sketches* by Lady Hawkins, widow of Sir John Hawkins, the friend of Johnson. Dr. Schomberg, of Reading, in the early part of his life spent a Christmas at Paris with some English friends. They were desirous to celebrate the season, in the manner of their own country, by having, as one dish on their table, an English plum pudding ; but no cook was found equal to the task of making it. A clergyman of the party had, indeed, a receipt-book, but this did not sufficiently explain the process. Dr. Schomberg, however, supplied all that was wanting by throwing

throwing the recipe into the form of a prescription, and sending it to an apothecary to be made up. To prevent any chance of error, he directed that it should be boiled in a cloth, and sent home in the same cloth. At the specified hour it arrived, borne by the apothecary's assistant, and preceded by the apothecary himself, dressed according to the professional formality of the time, with a sword. Seeing, on his entry into the apartment, instead of signs of sickness, a table well filled, and surrounded by very merry faces, he perceived that he was made a party to a joke that turned on himself, and indignantly laid his hand on his sword ; but an invitation to taste his own cookery appeased him, and all was well.

There is a good plum pudding story told of Lord Macartney when he was on his embassy to China, and wished to give gratification to a distinguished mandarin. He gave instructions to his Chinese *chef*, and, no doubt, they were carried out most conscientiously, but it came to table in a soup tureen, for my Lord *had forgotten all about the cloth.*

I cannot verify the following, nor do I know when it occurred. At Paignton Fair, near Exeter, a plum pudding of vast dimensions was drawn through the town amid great rejoicings. No wonder that a brewer's copper was needed for the boiling, seeing that the pudding contained 400 lbs. of flour, 170 lbs. of beef suet, 140 lbs. of raisins, and 240 eggs. This eight hundred pounder or so required continuous boiling from Saturday morning till the following Tuesday evening. It was finally placed on a car decorated with ribbons and evergreens, drawn through the streets by eight oxen, cut up, and distributed to the poor.

Every housewife has her own pet recipe for her Christmas pudding, of undoubted antiquity, none being later than that left as a precious legacy by grandmamma. Some housewives put a thimble, a ring, a piece of money, and a button, which will influence the future destinies of the recipients. It is good that every person in the family should take some part in its manufacture, even if only to stir it ; and it should be brought to table hoarily sprinkled with powdered sugar, with a fine piece of berried holly stuck in it, and surrounded on all sides by blazing spirits.

Mince pie, as we have seen in Ben Jonson's masque, is

one

176

one of the daughters of Father Christmas, but the mince pie of his day was not the same as ours; they were made of meat, and were called *minched* pies, or *shrid* pies. The meat might be either beef or mutton, but it was chopped fine, and mixed with plums and sugar. It is doubtful whether it was much known before the time of Elizabeth, although Shakespeare knew it well; but with poetic licence he makes it as known at the siege of Troy (*Troilus and Cressida*, Act i. sc. 2).

"*Pandarus*—Is not birth, beauty, good shape, discourse, manhood, learning, gentleness, virtue, youth, liberality, and such like, the spice and salt that season a man?

"*Cressida*—Ay, a minced man; and then to be baked with no date [1] in the pie,—for then the man's date's out."

Gradually the meat was left out, and more sweets introduced, until the product resulted in the modern mince pie, in which, however, some housewives still introduce a little chopped meat. There is no luck for the wight who does not eat a mince pie at Christmas. If he eat one, he is sure of one happy month; but if he wants a happy twelve months, he should eat one on each of the twelve days of Christmas.

There was another form of eating the minced or shrid meat, in the form of a great sausage, called "the hackin," so called from to *hack*, or chop; and this, by custom, must be boiled before daybreak, or else the cook must pay the penalty of being taken by the arms by two young men, and by them run round the market-place till she is ashamed of her laziness.

A writer in *Notes and Queries* (5 ser. x. 514) gives a very peculiar superstition prevalent in Derbyshire: "A neighbour had killed his Christmas pig, and his wife, to show her respect, brought me a goodly plate of what is known as 'pig's fry.' The dish was delivered covered with a snowy cloth, with the strict injunction, 'Don't wash the plate, please!' Having asked why the plate was to be returned unwashed, the reply was made, 'If *you* wash the plate upon which the fry was brought to you, the pig won't take the salt.'"

A very pretty custom obtained, as we learn by the records

[1] Dates were an ingredient in most kinds of pastry. See *All's Well that Ends Well*, Act i. sc. 1—"Your date is better in your pie and your porridge than in your cheek."

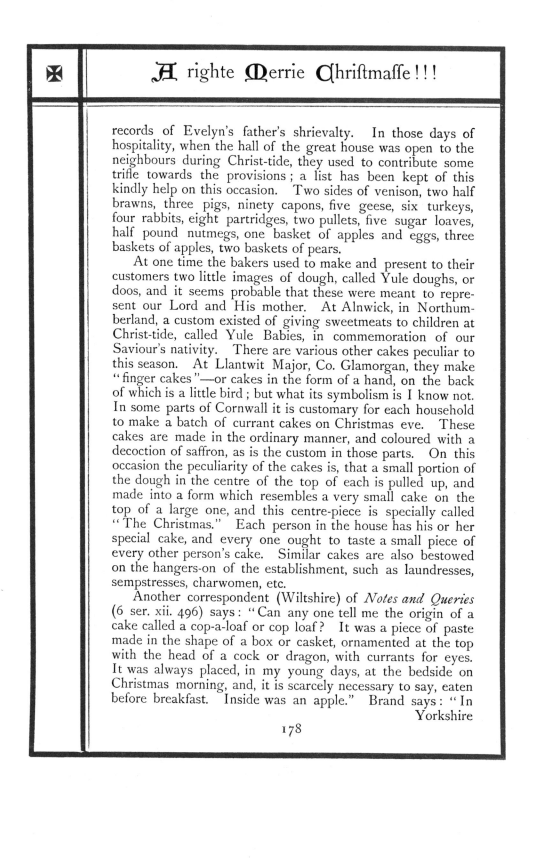

records of Evelyn's father's shrievalty. In those days of hospitality, when the hall of the great house was open to the neighbours during Christ-tide, they used to contribute some trifle towards the provisions ; a list has been kept of this kindly help on this occasion. Two sides of venison, two half brawns, three pigs, ninety capons, five geese, six turkeys, four rabbits, eight partridges, two pullets, five sugar loaves, half pound nutmegs, one basket of apples and eggs, three baskets of apples, two baskets of pears.

At one time the bakers used to make and present to their customers two little images of dough, called Yule doughs, or doos, and it seems probable that these were meant to represent our Lord and His mother. At Alnwick, in Northumberland, a custom existed of giving sweetmeats to children at Christ-tide, called Yule Babies, in commemoration of our Saviour's nativity. There are various other cakes peculiar to this season. At Llantwit Major, Co. Glamorgan, they make "finger cakes"—or cakes in the form of a hand, on the back of which is a little bird ; but what its symbolism is I know not. In some parts of Cornwall it is customary for each household to make a batch of currant cakes on Christmas eve. These cakes are made in the ordinary manner, and coloured with a decoction of saffron, as is the custom in those parts. On this occasion the peculiarity of the cakes is, that a small portion of the dough in the centre of the top of each is pulled up, and made into a form which resembles a very small cake on the top of a large one, and this centre-piece is specially called "The Christmas." Each person in the house has his or her special cake, and every one ought to taste a small piece of every other person's cake. Similar cakes are also bestowed on the hangers-on of the establishment, such as laundresses, sempstresses, charwomen, etc.

Another correspondent (Wiltshire) of *Notes and Queries* (6 ser. xii. 496) says : "Can any one tell me the origin of a cake called a cop-a-loaf or cop loaf? It was a piece of paste made in the shape of a box or casket, ornamented at the top with the head of a cock or dragon, with currants for eyes. It was always placed, in my young days, at the bedside on Christmas morning, and, it is scarcely necessary to say, eaten before breakfast. Inside was an apple." Brand says : "In Yorkshire

Yorkshire (Cleveland) the children eat, at the present season, a kind of gingerbread, baked in large and thick cakes, or flat loaves, called *Pepper Cakes*. They are also usual at the birth of a child. One of these cakes is provided, and a cheese ; the latter is on a large platter or dish, and the pepper cake upon it. The cutting of the Christmas cheese is done by the master of the house on Christmas Eve, and is a ceremony not to be lightly omitted. All comers to the house are invited to partake of the pepper cake and Christmas cheese."

Any notice of Christmas cheer would be incomplete without mention being made of *Snap-dragon*. It is an old sport, and is alluded to by Shakespeare in *Henry IV.*, part ii. Act ii. sc. 4, where Falstaff says—

> And drinks off candles' ends for flap-dragons.

And in *Love's Labour's Lost*, Act v. sc. 1—

> Thou art easier swallowed than a flap-dragon.

It is a kind of game, in which brandy is poured over a large dish full of raisins, and then set alight. The object is to snatch the raisins out of the flame and devour them without burning oneself. This can be managed by sharply seizing them, and shutting the mouth at once. It is suggested that the name is derived from the German *schnapps*, spirit, and *drache*, dragon.

CHAPTER XXIII

The First Carol—Anglo-Norman Carol—Fifteenth-Century Carol—" The Twelve Good Joys of Mary "—Other Carols—" A Virgin most Pure "—" Noel "— Festive Carol of Fifteenth Century—" A Christenmesse Carroll."

BISHOP Jeremy Taylor very appropriately said that the first Christmas carol was sung by the angels at the Nativity of our Saviour—"GLORY TO GOD IN THE HIGHEST, AND ON EARTH PEACE, GOODWILL TOWARD MEN." No man knows when the custom began of singing carols, or hymns on Christmas day in honour of the Nativity; but there can be no doubt that it was of very ancient date in the English Church, and that it has been an unbroken custom to this day, when the practice is decidedly on the increase, as may be judged from the many collections of ancient carols, and of modern ones as well. It would be impossible for me to give anything like a representative collection of Christmas carols, because of space, but I venture to reproduce a few old ones, and first, perhaps the oldest we have, an Anglo-Norman carol, which is in the British Museum, and with it I give Douce's very free translation. It will be seen by this that all carols were not of a religious kind, but many were songs appropriate to the festive season :—

Seignors ore entendez a nus,
De loinz sumes venuz a wous,
   Pur quere Noel ;
Car lun nus dit que en cest hostel
Soleit tenir sa feste anuel
   Ahi cest iur.
      Deu doint a tuz icels joie
       d'amurs
      Qi a DANZ NOEL ferunt
      honors.

Seignors io vus di por veir
KE DANZ NOEL ne uelt aveir
   Si joie non :
E replein sa maison
De payn, de char, e de peison,
   Por faire honor.
      Deu doint, etc.

Seignors il est crie en lost
Qe cil qui despent bien e tost,
   E largement ;

E

E fet les granz honors sovent
Deu li duble quanque il despent
   Por faire honor.
      Deu doint, etc.

Seignors escriez les malveis,
Car vus nel les troverez jameis
   De bone part ;
Botun, batun, ferun groinard,
Car tot dis a le quer cunard
   Por faire honor.
      Deu doint, etc.

NOEL beyt bein li vin Engleis

E li Gascoin e li Franceys
   E l'Angeuin ;
NOEL fait beivre son veisin,
Si quil se dort, le chief en clin,
   Sovent le ior.
      Deu doint, etc.

Seignors io vus di par NOEL,
E par li sires de cest hostel,
   Car benez ben :
E io primes beurai le men,
E pois apres chescon le soen,
   Par mon conseil.
Si io vus di trestoz Wesseyl
Dehaiz eil.qui ne dirra Drincheyl.

TRANSLATION.

Now, lordings, listen to our ditty,
   Strangers coming from afar ;
Let poor minstrels move your pity,
   Give us welcome, soothe our care :
In this mansion, as they tell us,
   Christmas wassell keeps to-day ;
And, as the king of all good fellows,
   Reigns with uncontrouled sway.

Lordings, in these realms of plea-
     sure,
   Father Christmas yearly dwells ;
Deals out joy with liberal measure,
   Gloomy sorrow soon dispels :
Numerous guests, and viands dainty,
   Fill the hall and grace the board ;
Mirth and beauty, peace and plenty,
   Solid pleasures here afford.

Lordings, 'tis said the liberal mind,
   That on the needy much bestows,
From Heav'n a sure reward shall find ;
   From Heav'n, whence ev'ry bless-
     ing flows.
Who largely gives with willing hand,
   Or quickly gives with willing heart,
His fame shall spread throughout
     the land,
   His mem'ry thence shall ne'er de-
     part.

Lordings, grant not your protection
   To a base unworthy crew,
But cherish, with a kind affection,
   Men that are loyal, good, and true.
Chase from your hospitable dwelling
   Swinish souls that ever crave ;
Virtue they can ne'er excel in,
   Gluttons never can be brave.

Lordings, Christmas loves good drink-
     ing,
   Wines of Gascoigne, France, Anjou,
English ale that drives out thinking,
   Prince of liquors, old or new.
Every neighbour shares the bowl,
   Drinks of the spicy liquor deep,
Drinks his fill without controul,
   Till he drowns his care in sleep.

And now—by Christmas, jolly soul !
   By this mansion's generous sieur !
By the wine, and by the bowl,
   And all the joys they both
     inspire !
Here I'll drink a health to all :
   The glorious task shall first be
     mine :
And ever may foul luck befall
   Him that to pledge me shall de-
     cline.
               THE

THE CHORUS.

Hail, Father Christmas! hail to Thee!
Honour'd ever shalt thou be!
All the sweets that love bestows,
Endless pleasures, wait on those
Who, like vassals brave and true,
Give to Christmas homage due.

Wynkyn de Worde first printed Christmas carols in 1521, but there were many MS. carols in existence before then. Here is a very pretty one from Mr. Wright's fifteenth-century MS. :—

To blys God bryng us al and sum.
Christe, redemptor omnium.

In Bedlem, that fayer cyte,
Was born a chyld that was so fre,
Lord and prince of hey degre,
Jam lucis orto sidere.

As the sune schynyth in the glas,
So Jhesu of hys moder borne was;
Hym to serve God gyffe us grace,
O Lux beata Trinitas.

Jhesu, for the lowe of the,
Chylder wer slayn grett plente
In Bedlem, that fayer cyte,
A solis ortus cardine.

Now is he oure Lord Jhesus;
Thus hath he veryly vysyt us;
Now to mak mery among us
Exultet cœlum laudibus.

The next carol I give has always been a popular favourite, and can be traced back to the fourteenth century, when it was called "Joyes Fyve." In Mr. Wright's fifteenth-century MS. it is "Off the Five Joyes of Our Lady." It afterwards became the "Seven Joys of Mary," and has expanded to

THE TWELVE GOOD JOYS OF MARY.

The first good joy our Mary had,
It was the joy of One,
To see her own Son Jesus
To suck at her breast-bone.
To suck at her breast-bone, good man,
And blessed may he be,
Both Father, Son and Holy Ghost,
To all eternity.

The next good joy our Mary had,
It was the joy of Two,
To see her own Son Jesus
To make the lame to go.
To make the lame, etc.

The next good joy our Mary had,
It was the joy of Three,
To see her own Son Jesus
To make the blind to see.
To make the blind to see, etc.

The

182

The next good joy our Mary had,
It was the joy of Four,
To see her own Son Jesus
To read the Bible o'er.
To read, etc.

The next good joy our Mary had,
It was the joy of Five,
To see her own Son Jesus
To raise the dead alive.
To raise, etc.

The next good joy our Mary had,
It was the joy of Six,
To see her own Son Jesus
To wear the crucifix.
To wear, etc.

The next good joy our Mary had,
It was the joy of Seven,
To see her own Son Jesus
To wear the Crown of Heaven.
To wear, etc.

The next good joy our Mary had,
It was the joy of Eight,

To see our blessed Saviour
Turn darkness into light.
Turn darkness, etc.

The next good joy our Mary had,
It was the joy of Nine,
To see our blessed Saviour
Turn water into wine.
Turn water, etc.

The next good joy our Mary had,
It was the joy of Ten,
To see our blessed Saviour
Write without a pen.
Write without, etc.

The next good joy our Mary had,
It was the joy of Eleven,
To see our blessed Saviour
Shew the gates of Heaven.
Shew the gates, etc.

The next good joy our Mary had,
It was the joy of Twelve,
To see our blessed Saviour
Shut close the gates of Hell.
Shut close, etc.

"On Christmas Day in the Morning" and "God rest You, Merry Gentlemen," are both very old and popular, the latter extremely so; in fact, it is the carol most known. The next example was first printed by the Rev. Arthur Bedford, who wrote many books and published sermons between 1705 and 1743, but his version began somewhat differently :—

A Virgin unspotted, the Prophets did tell,
Should bring forth a Saviour, as now it befell.

A VIRGIN MOST PURE.

A Virgin most pure, as the Prophets did tell,
Hath brought forth a Baby, as it hath befell,
To be our Redeemer from death, hell and Sin,
Which Adam's transgression hath wrapped us in.
Rejoice and be merry, set sorrow aside,
Christ Jesus, our Saviour, was born on this tide.

In

183

In Bethlehem, a city in Jewry it was—
Where Joseph and Mary together did pass,
And there to be taxed, with many ane mo,
For Cæsar commanded the same should be so.
    Rejoice, etc.

But when they had entered the city so fair,
A number of people so mighty was there,
That Joseph and Mary, whose substance was small,
Could get in the city no lodging at all.
    Rejoice, etc.

Then they were constrained in a stable to lie,
Where oxen and asses they used to tie;
Their lodging so simple, they held it no scorn,
But against the next morning our Saviour was born.
    Rejoice, etc.

Then God sent an Angel from heaven so high,
To certain poor shepherds in fields where they lie,
And bid them no longer in sorrow to stay,
Because that our Saviour was born on this day.
    Rejoice, etc.

Then presently after, the shepherds did spy
A number of Angels appear in the sky,
Who joyfully talked, and sweetly did sing,
"To God be all Glory, our Heavenly King."
    Rejoice, etc.

Three certain Wise Princes they thought it most meet
To lay their rich offerings at our Saviour's feet;
So then they consented, and to Bethlehem did go,
And when they came thither they found it was so.
    Rejoice, etc.

But all Christmas carols were not religious—many of them were of the most festive description; but here is one, temp. Henry VIII., which is a mixture of both :—

Noel, Noel, Noel, Noel,
Who is there, that singeth so, Noel,
    Noel, Noel?

I am here, Sir Christhismass,
Welcome, my lord Christhismass,
Welcome to all, both more and less.
    Come near, Noel.

Dieu vous garde, beau Sire, tidings I
    you bring,
A maid hath born a Child full young,
The which causeth for to sing,
    Noel.

        Christ

184

Christ is now born of a pure maid,
In an ox stall He is laid,
Wherefore sing we all at a braid,[1]
    Noel.

Buvez bien par toute la compagnie,
Make good cheer, and be right
  merry,
And sing with us, now, joyfully,
    Noel.

Of the purely festive carols here is an example of the fifteenth century, from Mr. Wright's MS. :—

At the begynnyng of the mete
Of a borejs hed ʒe schal hete ;
And in the mustard ʒe xal wete ;
    And ʒe xal syngyn, or ʒe gon.

Wolcom be ʒe that ben here,
And ʒe xal have ryth gud chere,
And also a ryth gud face ;
    And ʒe xal syngyn, or ʒe gon.

Welcum be ʒe everychon,
For ʒe xal syngyn ryth anon ;
Hey ʒow fast that ʒe had don,
    And ʒe xal syngyn, or ʒe gon.

The last I give is of the sixteenth century, and is in the British Museum (MS. Cott. Vesp. A. xxv.) :—

A Christenmesse Carroll

A bonne, God wote !
  Stickes in my throate,
Without I have a draught,
  Of cornie aile,
  Nappy and staile,
My lyffe lyes in great wanste.
  Some ayle or beare,
  Gentell butlere,
Some lycoure thou hus showe,
  Such as you mashe,
  Our throtes to washe
The best were that you brew.

  Saint, master and knight,
  That Saint Mault hight,
Were prest between two stones ;
  That swet humour
  Of his lycoure
Would make us sing at once.

  Mr. Wortley,
  I dar well say,
I tell you as I thinke,
  Would not, I say,
  Byd hus this day,
But that we shuld have drink.

  His men so tall
  Walkes up his hall,
With many a comly dishe ;
  Of his good meat
  I cannot eate,
Without a drink i-wysse.
  Now gyve hus drink,
  And let cat wynke,
I tell you all at once,
  Yt stickes so sore,
  I may sing no more,
Tyll I have dronken once.

[1] Suddenly.

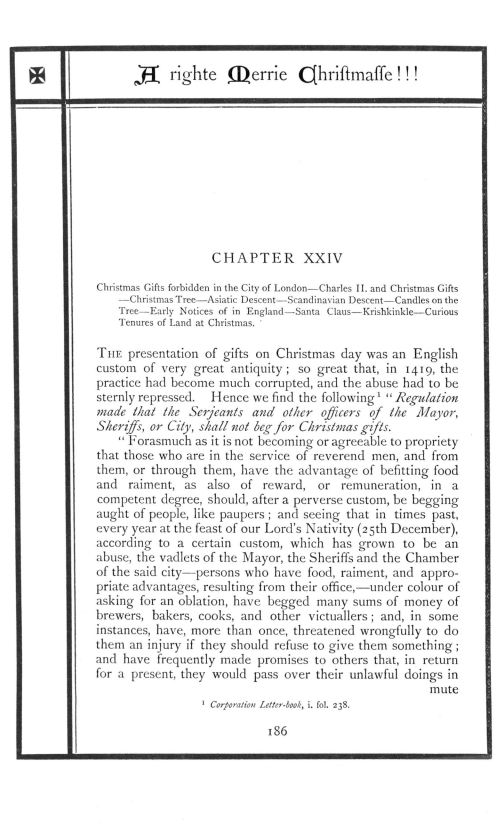

CHAPTER XXIV

Christmas Gifts forbidden in the City of London—Charles II. and Christmas Gifts —Christmas Tree—Asiatic Descent—-Scandinavian Descent—Candles on the Tree—Early Notices of in England—Santa Claus—Krishkinkle—Curious Tenures of Land at Christmas.

THE presentation of gifts on Christmas day was an English custom of very great antiquity; so great that, in 1419, the practice had become much corrupted, and the abuse had to be sternly repressed. Hence we find the following[1] "*Regulation made that the Serjeants and other officers of the Mayor, Sheriffs, or City, shall not beg for Christmas gifts.*

"Forasmuch as it is not becoming or agreeable to propriety that those who are in the service of reverend men, and from them, or through them, have the advantage of befitting food and raiment, as also of reward, or remuneration, in a competent degree, should, after a perverse custom, be begging aught of people, like paupers; and seeing that in times past, every year at the feast of our Lord's Nativity (25th December), according to a certain custom, which has grown to be an abuse, the vadlets of the Mayor, the Sheriffs and the Chamber of the said city—persons who have food, raiment, and appropriate advantages, resulting from their office,—under colour of asking for an oblation, have begged many sums of money of brewers, bakers, cooks, and other victuallers; and, in some instances, have, more than once, threatened wrongfully to do them an injury if they should refuse to give them something; and have frequently made promises to others that, in return for a present, they would pass over their unlawful doings in

mute

[1] *Corporation Letter-book*, i. fol. 238.

mute silence; to the great dishonour of their masters, and to the common loss of all the city: therefore, on Wednesday, the last day of April, in the 7th year of King Henry the Fifth, by William Sevenok, the Mayor, and the Aldermen of London, it was ordered and established that no vadlet, or other sergeant of the Mayor, Sheriffs, or City, should in future beg or require of any person, of any rank, degree, or condition whatsoever, any moneys, under colour of an oblation, or in any other way, on pain of losing his office."

Royalty was not above receiving presents on this day, and as, of course, such presents could not be of small value, it must have been no small tax on the nobility. Pepys (23rd February 1663) remarks: "This day I was told that my Lady Castlemaine hath all the King's Christmas presents, made him by the Peers, given to her, which is a most abominable thing." He records his own Christmas gifts (25th December 1667): "Being a fine, light, moonshine morning, home round the city, and stopped and dropped money at five or six places, which I was the willinger to do, it being Christmas day."

But the prettiest method of distributing Christmas gifts was reserved for comparatively modern times, in the Christmas tree. Anent this wonderful tree there are many speculations, one or two so curious that they deserve mention. It is said of a certain living Professor that he deduces everything from an Indian or Aryan descent; and there is a long and very learned article by Sir George Birdwood, C.S.I., in the *Asiatic Quarterly Review* (vol. i. pp. 19, 20), who endeavours to trace it to an eastern origin. He says: "Only during the past thirty or forty years has the custom become prevalent in England of employing the Christmas tree as an appropriate decoration, and a most delightful vehicle for showering down gifts upon the young, in connection with domestic and public popular celebrations of the joyous ecclesiastical Festival of the Nativity. It is said to have been introduced among us from Germany, where it is regarded as indigenous, and it is, probably, a survival of some observance connected with the pagan Saturnalia of the winter solstice, to supersede which, the Church, about the fifth century of our era, instituted Christmas day.

"It has, indeed, been explained as being derived from the ancient

187

ancient Egyptian practice of decking houses at the time of the winter solstice with branches of the date palm, the symbol of life triumphant over death, and therefore of perennial life in the renewal of each bounteous year; and the supporters of this suggestion point to the fact that pyramids of green paper, covered all over with wreaths and festoons of flowers, and strings of sweetmeats, and other presents for children, are often substituted in Germany for the Christmas Tree.

"But similar pyramids, together with similar trees, the latter, usually, altogether artificial, and often constructed of the costliest materials, even of gems and gold, are carried about at marriage ceremonies in India, and at many festivals, such as the Hoolee, or annual festival of the vernal equinox. These pyramids represent Mount Meru and the earth; and the trees, the Kalpadruma, or 'Tree of Ages,' and the fragrant Parajita, the tree of every perfect gift, which grew on the slopes of Mount Meru; and, in their enlarged sense, they symbolise the splendour of the outstretched heavens, as of a tree, laden with golden fruit, deep-rooted in the earth. Both pyramids and trees are also phallic emblems of life, individual, terrestrial, and celestial. Therefore, if a relationship exists between the Egyptian practice of decking houses at the winter solstice with branches of the date palm, and the German and English custom of using gift-bearing and brilliantly illuminated evergreen trees, which are, nearly always, firs, as a Christmas decoration, it is most probably due to collateral rather than to direct descent; and this is indicated by the Egyptians having regarded the date palm, not only as an emblem of immortality, but, also, of the starlit firmament."

Others attempt to trace the Christmas tree to the Scandinavian legend of the mystic tree Yggdrasil, which sprang from the centre of Mid-gard, and the summit of As-gard, with branches spreading out over the whole earth, and reaching above the highest heavens, whilst its three great roots go down into the lowest hell.

A writer in the *Cornhill Magazine*, December 1886, thus accounts for the candles on the tree—

"But how came the lights on the Christmas tree?

"In the ninth month of the Jewish year, corresponding nearly to our December, and on the twenty-fifth day, the Jews celebrated

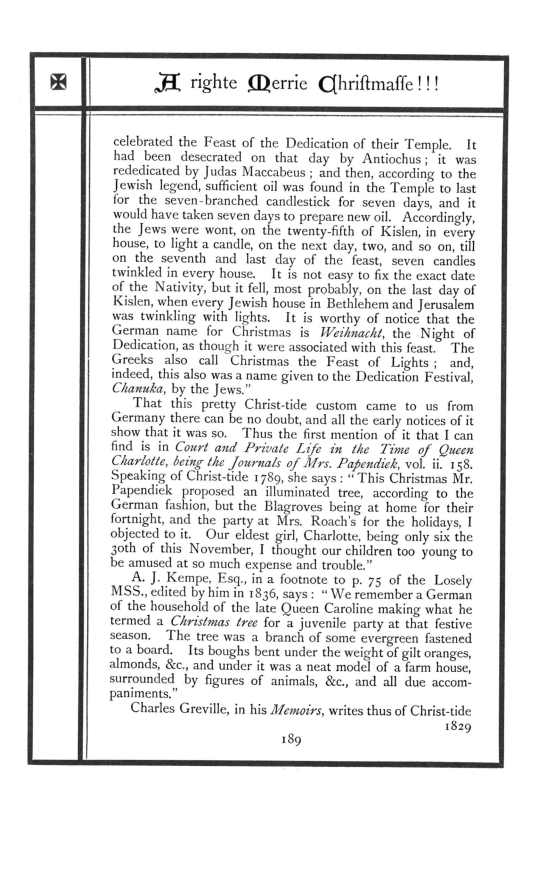
celebrated the Feast of the Dedication of their Temple. It had been desecrated on that day by Antiochus ; it was rededicated by Judas Maccabeus ; and then, according to the Jewish legend, sufficient oil was found in the Temple to last for the seven-branched candlestick for seven days, and it would have taken seven days to prepare new oil. Accordingly, the Jews were wont, on the twenty-fifth of Kislen, in every house, to light a candle, on the next day, two, and so on, till on the seventh and last day of the feast, seven candles twinkled in every house. It is not easy to fix the exact date of the Nativity, but it fell, most probably, on the last day of Kislen, when every Jewish house in Bethlehem and Jerusalem was twinkling with lights. It is worthy of notice that the German name for Christmas is *Weihnacht*, the Night of Dedication, as though it were associated with this feast. The Greeks also call Christmas the Feast of Lights ; and, indeed, this also was a name given to the Dedication Festival, *Chanuka*, by the Jews."

That this pretty Christ-tide custom came to us from Germany there can be no doubt, and all the early notices of it show that it was so. Thus the first mention of it that I can find is in *Court and Private Life in the Time of Queen Charlotte, being the Journals of Mrs. Papendiek*, vol. ii. 158. Speaking of Christ-tide 1789, she says : " This Christmas Mr. Papendiek proposed an illuminated tree, according to the German fashion, but the Blagroves being at home for their fortnight, and the party at Mrs. Roach's for the holidays, I objected to it. Our eldest girl, Charlotte, being only six the 30th of this November, I thought our children too young to be amused at so much expense and trouble."

A. J. Kempe, Esq., in a footnote to p. 75 of the Losely MSS., edited by him in 1836, says : " We remember a German of the household of the late Queen Caroline making what he termed a *Christmas tree* for a juvenile party at that festive season. The tree was a branch of some evergreen fastened to a board. Its boughs bent under the weight of gilt oranges, almonds, &c., and under it was a neat model of a farm house, surrounded by figures of animals, &c., and all due accompaniments."

Charles Greville, in his *Memoirs*, writes thus of Christ-tide 1829

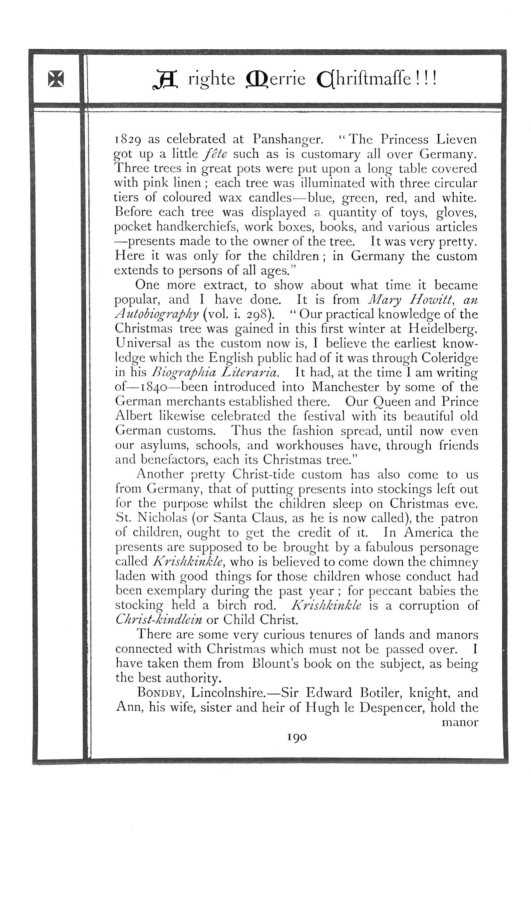

1829 as celebrated at Panshanger. "The Princess Lieven got up a little *fête* such as is customary all over Germany. Three trees in great pots were put upon a long table covered with pink linen; each tree was illuminated with three circular tiers of coloured wax candles—blue, green, red, and white. Before each tree was displayed a quantity of toys, gloves, pocket handkerchiefs, work boxes, books, and various articles —presents made to the owner of the tree. It was very pretty. Here it was only for the children; in Germany the custom extends to persons of all ages."

One more extract, to show about what time it became popular, and I have done. It is from *Mary Howitt, an Autobiography* (vol. i. 298). "Our practical knowledge of the Christmas tree was gained in this first winter at Heidelberg. Universal as the custom now is, I believe the earliest know-ledge which the English public had of it was through Coleridge in his *Biographia Literaria*. It had, at the time I am writing of—1840—been introduced into Manchester by some of the German merchants established there. Our Queen and Prince Albert likewise celebrated the festival with its beautiful old German customs. Thus the fashion spread, until now even our asylums, schools, and workhouses have, through friends and benefactors, each its Christmas tree."

Another pretty Christ-tide custom has also come to us from Germany, that of putting presents into stockings left out for the purpose whilst the children sleep on Christmas eve. St. Nicholas (or Santa Claus, as he is now called), the patron of children, ought to get the credit of it. In America the presents are supposed to be brought by a fabulous personage called *Krishkinkle*, who is believed to come down the chimney laden with good things for those children whose conduct had been exemplary during the past year; for peccant babies the stocking held a birch rod. *Krishkinkle* is a corruption of *Christ-kindlein* or Child Christ.

There are some very curious tenures of lands and manors connected with Christmas which must not be passed over. I have taken them from Blount's book on the subject, as being the best authority.

Bondby, Lincolnshire.—Sir Edward Botiler, knight, and Ann, his wife, sister and heir of Hugh le Despencer, hold the

manor

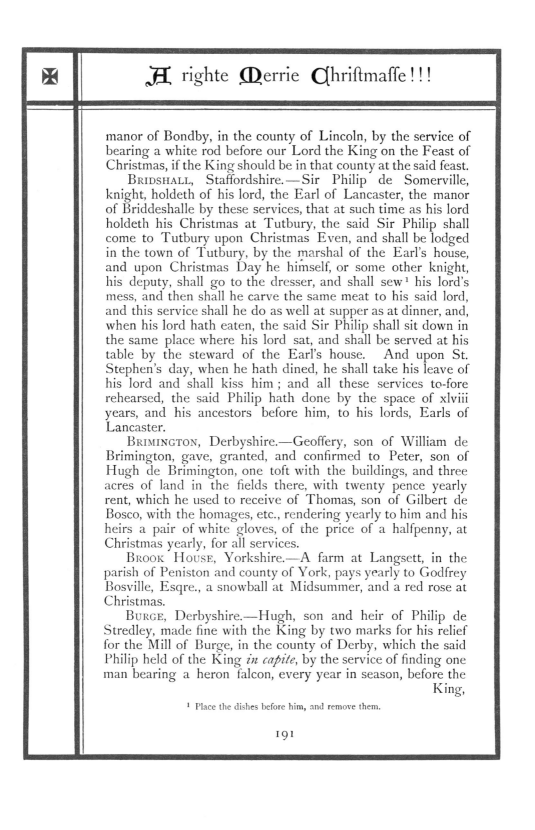

manor of Bondby, in the county of Lincoln, by the service of bearing a white rod before our Lord the King on the Feast of Christmas, if the King should be in that county at the said feast.

BRIDSHALL, Staffordshire.—Sir Philip de Somerville, knight, holdeth of his lord, the Earl of Lancaster, the manor of Briddeshalle by these services, that at such time as his lord holdeth his Christmas at Tutbury, the said Sir Philip shall come to Tutbury upon Christmas Even, and shall be lodged in the town of Tutbury, by the marshal of the Earl's house, and upon Christmas Day he himself, or some other knight, his deputy, shall go to the dresser, and shall sew[1] his lord's mess, and then shall he carve the same meat to his said lord, and this service shall he do as well at supper as at dinner, and, when his lord hath eaten, the said Sir Philip shall sit down in the same place where his lord sat, and shall be served at his table by the steward of the Earl's house. And upon St. Stephen's day, when he hath dined, he shall take his leave of his lord and shall kiss him ; and all these services to-fore rehearsed, the said Philip hath done by the space of xlviii years, and his ancestors before him, to his lords, Earls of Lancaster.

BRIMINGTON, Derbyshire.—Geoffery, son of William de Brimington, gave, granted, and confirmed to Peter, son of Hugh de Brimington, one toft with the buildings, and three acres of land in the fields there, with twenty pence yearly rent, which he used to receive of Thomas, son of Gilbert de Bosco, with the homages, etc., rendering yearly to him and his heirs a pair of white gloves, of the price of a halfpenny, at Christmas yearly, for all services.

BROOK HOUSE, Yorkshire.—A farm at Langsett, in the parish of Peniston and county of York, pays yearly to Godfrey Bosville, Esqre., a snowball at Midsummer, and a red rose at Christmas.

BURGE, Derbyshire.—Hugh, son and heir of Philip de Stredley, made fine with the King by two marks for his relief for the Mill of Burge, in the county of Derby, which the said Philip held of the King *in capite*, by the service of finding one man bearing a heron falcon, every year in season, before the
King,

---

[1] Place the dishes before him, and remove them.

King, when he should be summoned, and to take for performing the said service, at the cost of the King, two robes at
Whitsuntide and Christmas.

GREENS-NORTON, Northamptonshire.—This, so named of
the Greens (persons famed in the sixteenth century for their
wealth), called before Norton-Dauncy, was held of the King
in capite by the service of lifting up their right hands towards
the King yearly, on Christmas day, wheresoever the King
should then be in England.

HAWARDEN AND BOSELE, Cheshire.—The manors of
Hawarden and Bosele, with the appurtenances in the county
of Cheshire, are held of the King *in capite* by Robert de
Monhault, Earl of Arundel, by being steward of the county of
Cheshire, *viz.* by the service of setting down the first dish
before the Earl of Chester at Chester on Christmas day.

HEDSOR, Bucks.—An estate in this parish, called Lambert
Farm, was formerly held under the manor by the service of
bringing in the first dish at the lord's table on St. Stephen's
day, and presenting him with two hens, a cock, a gallon of ale,
and two manchets of white bread; after dinner the lord
delivered to the tenant a sparrow hawk and a couple of
spaniels, to be kept at his costs and charges for the lord's use.

HEMINGSTON, Suffolk.—Rowland le Sarcere held one
hundred and ten acres of land in Hemingston by serjeanty;
for which, on Christmas day every year, before our sovereign
lord the King of England, he should perform altogether, and at
once, a leap, puff up his cheeks, therewith making a sound,
and let a crack.

LEVINGTON, Yorkshire.—Adam de Bras, lord of Skelton,
gave in marriage with his daughter Isabel, to Henry de
Percy, eldest son and heir of Joceline de Lovain (ancestor
to the present Duke of Northumberland), the manor of
Levington, for which he and his heirs were to repair to Skelton
Castle every Christmas day, and lead the lady of that castle
from her chamber to the chapel to mass, and thence to her
chamber again, and after dining with her, to depart.

REDWORTH, Co. Durham.—In the fourth year of Bishop
Skirlawe, 1391, John de Redworth died, seised in his
demesne, &c. of two messuages and twenty-six acres of land
and meadow, with the appurtenances, in Redworth, held of
the

the said Lord Bishop *in capite* by homage and fealty, and the service of four shillings and ten pence a year, to be paid at the Exchequer at Durham, and the rent of one hen and two parts of a hen to be paid at the same Exchequer yearly at Christmas.

STAMFORD, Lincolnshire.—William, Earl Warren, lord of this town in the time of King John, standing upon the castle walls, saw two bulls fighting for a cow in the Castle Meadow, till all the butchers' dogs pursued one of the bulls (maddened with noise and multitude) clean through the town. This sight so pleased the Earl that he gave the Castle Meadow, where the bulls' duel had begun, for a common to the butchers of the town, after the first grass was mown, on condition that they should find a mad bull the day six weeks before Christmas day, for the continuance of the sport for ever.

THURGARTON AND HORSEPOLL, Notts.—The tenants of these manors held their lands by these customs and services. Every native and villein (which were such as we call husbandmen) paid each a cock and a hen, besides a small rent in money, for a toft and one bovate of land, held of the Priory of Thurgarton. These cocks and hens were paid the second day in Christmas, and that day every one, both cottagers and natives, dined in the hall; and those who did not had a white loaf and a flagon of ale, with one mess from the kitchen. And all the reapers in harvest, which were called hallewimen, were to eat in the hall one day in Christmas, or afterwards, at the discretion of the cellarer.

There is a curious custom still carried out at Queen's College, Oxford. On the feast of the Circumcision the bursar gives to every member a needle and thread, adding the injunction, "Take this and be thrifty." It is said, I know not with what truth, that it is to commemorate the name of the founder, Robert Egglesfield—by the visible pun, *aiguille* (needle) and *fil* (thread).

CHAPTER XXV

Christ-tide Literature—Christmas Cards—Their Origin—Lamplighter's Verses—
Watchman's Verses—Christmas Pieces.

THE literature specially designed nowadays for Christmas reading is certainly not of a high order, whether we take books—which are issued at this time by the hundred—or the special numbers of magazines and newspapers, all of which have rubbishing stories with some tag in them relating to Christ-tide. Tales of ghosts, etc., were at one time very fashionable, and even Dickens pandered to this miserable style of writing, not enhancing his reputation thereby.

Akin in merit to this literature are the mottoes we find in the *bon bon* crackers, and the verses on Christmas cards, which are on a par with those which adorned the defunct valentine. When first Christmas cards came into vogue they were expensive and comparatively good; now they are simply rubbish, and generally have no allusion either in the design, or doggrel to Christ-tide, to which they owe their existence. Their origin was thoroughly threshed out in *Notes and Queries*, and I give the correspondence thereon (6th series, v. 155).

"Christmas cards were first published and issued from Summerly's *Home Treasury* Office, 12 Old Bond Street, in the year 1846. The design was drawn by J. C. Horsley, R.A., at the suggestion of Sir Henry Cole, K.C.B., and carried out by De la Rue and Co."

(*Ib.* 376) "Mr. Platt is somewhat in error in stating that the first Christmas card was carried out by De la Rue and Co. This firm republished it last year (1881) in chromo-lithography, but in 1846 it was produced in outline by lithography, and coloured

coloured by hand by a colourer of that time named Mason, when it could not have been sold for less than a shilling. Last year. chromo-lithography enabled it to be produced for two pence. The original publisher was Mr. Joseph Cundall. It may be well to place the design on record. A trellis of rustic work in the Germanesque style divided the card into a centre and two side panels. The sides were filled by representations of the feeding of the hungry and the clothing of the naked ; in the central compartment a family party was shown at table—an old man and woman, a maiden and her young man, and several children,—and they were pictured drinking healths in wine. On this ground certain total abstainers have called in question the morality of Mr. Horsley's design."

The Publishers' Circular, 31st December 1883 (p. 1432), says : " Several years ago, in the Christmas number of *The Publishers' Circular,* we described the original Christmas card, designed by Mr. J. C. Horsley, R.A., at the suggestion of Sir Henry Cole, and no contradiction was then offered to our theory that this must have been the real and original card. On Thursday, however, Mr. John Leighton, writing under his *nom de plume,* 'Luke Limner,' comes forward to contest the claim of priority of design, and says : 'Occasional cards of a purely private character have been done years ago, but the Christmas card pure and simple is the growth of our town and our time. It began in 1862, the first attempts being the size of the ordinary gentleman's address card, on which were simply put "A Merry Christmas" and "A Happy New Year"; after that there came to be added robins and holly branches, embossed figures and landscapes. Having made the original designs for these, I have the originals before me now ; they were produced by Goodall and Son. Seeing a growing want, and the great sale obtained abroad, this house produced (1868) a "Little Red Riding Hood," a "Hermit and his Cell," and many other subjects in which snow and the robin played a part.' We fail to see how a card issued in 1862 can ante-date the production of 1846, a copy of which is in our possession ; and although there is no copyright in an idea, the title to the honour of originating the pretty trifle now so familiar to us seems to rest with Sir Henry Cole."

The Times of 2nd January 1884 has the following letter :—
"Sɪʀ—

"SIR—The writer of the article on Christmas Cards in *The Times* of December 25th is quite right in his assertion. The first Christmas card ever published was issued by me in the usual way, in the year 1846, at the office of *Felix Summerly's Home Treasury*, at 12 Old Bond Street. Mr. Henry Cole (afterwards Sir Henry) originated the idea. The drawing was made by J. C. Horsley, R.A. ; it was printed in lithography by Mr. Jobbins of Warwick Court, Holborn, and coloured by hand. Many copies were sold, but possibly not more than 1000. It was of the usual size of a lady's card. Those my friend Luke Limner speaks of were not brought out, as he says, till many years after.—JOSEPH CUNDALL."

As works of art—compared with the majority of Christmas cards, which are mostly "made in Germany"—the card almanacs presented by tradesmen to their customers are generally of a very superior character.

In the old days, when there were oil lamps in the streets, the lamplighter, like the bellman and the watchman, used annually at Christmas to leave some verses at every house to remind its occupier that Boxing day drew nigh. One example will suffice, and its date is 1758 :—

THE LAMPLIGHTER'S POEM :

Humbly Presented to all His worthy Masters and Mistresses.

Compos'd by a Lamplighter.

Revolving Time another Glass has run,
Since I, last year, this Annual Task begun,
And Christmas now beginning to appear
(Which never comes, you know, but once a year),
I have presum'd to bring my Mite once more,
Which, tho' it be but small, is all my Store ;
And I don't doubt you'll take it in good Part,
As 'tis the Tribute of a grateful Heart.
  Brave Prussia's king, that true Protestant Prince,
For Valour Fam'd, endow'd with Martial Sense ;
Against three mighty Potentates did stand,
Who would have plundered him of all his Land :
But God, who knew his Cause was Just and Right,
Gave him such Courage and Success in Fight :
Born to oppose the Pope's malignant clan,
He'll do whatever Prince or Hero can ;

Retrieve

Retrieve that martial Fame by Britons lost,
And prove that Faith which graceless Christians boast.
O! make his Cause, ye Powers above! your Care;
Let Guilt shrink back, and Innocence appear.
  But, now, with State Affairs I must have done,
And to the Business of my Lamps must run;
When Sun and Moon from you do hide their Head,
Your busy Streets with artful Lights are spread,
And gives you Light with great indulgent Care,
Makes the dark Night like the bright Day appear;
Then we poor useful Mortals nimbly run
To light your Lamps before the Day is gone:
With strictest Care, we to each Lamp give Fire,
The longest Night to burn: you do require
Of us to make each Lamp to burn that time,
But, oft, we do fall short of that Design:
Sometimes a Lamp goes out at Master's Door,
This happens once which ne'er did so before:
The Lamp-man's blamed, and ask'd the reason why
That should go out, and others burning by?
Kind, worthy Sirs, if I may be so bold,
A truer Tale to you was never told;
We trim, we give each Lamp their Oil alike,
Yet some goes out, while others keep alight:
Why they do so, to you we can't explain,
It ne'er did sink into our shallow Brain:
Nor have we heard that any one could tell,
That secret Place where Life of Fire does dwell,
Such various Motions in it we do find,
And a hard Task with it to please Mankind.
  Now, our kind Master, who Contractor is,
If a Complaint he hears of Lamps amiss,
With strictest Care the Streets looks round about,
And views the Lamps, takes Notice which are out;
Then, in great Fury, he to us replies,
Such Lamps were out, why have I all this Noise?
Go fetch those Burners all down here to me,
That where the Fault is I may plainly see:
Then straight he views them, with Remains of Oil,
Crys, ah! I thought you did these Lamps beguile;
But now the thing I do more plainly see,
The Burning Oil is a great Mystery:
Then come, my Boys, to work, make no delay,
Keep from Complaints, if possible you may;
Clean well each Glass, I'll spare for no Expence
Where I contract, to please th' Inhabitants.

Since

Since Time still flies, and Life is but a Vapour,
'Tis now high time that I conclude my Paper,
And, if my Verses have the Luck to Please,
My Mind will be exceedingly at ease;
But, if this shouldn't Please, I know what will,
And that's with Diligence to serve you still.

FINIS.

Hone, in his *Every-Day Book* (vol. i. p. 1627), gives, date 1823 :—

A COPY OF CHRISTMAS VERSES,

presented to the

INHABITANTS OF BUNGAY

By their Humble Servants, the late Watchmen,

JOHN PYE and JOHN TYE.

Your pardon, Gentles, while we thus implore,
In strains not less *awakening* than of yore,
Those smiles we deem our best reward to catch,
And, for the which, we've long been on the *Watch;*
Well pleas'd if we that recompence obtain,
Which we have ta'en so many *steps* to gain.
Think of the perils in our *calling past,*
The chilling coldness of the midnight blast,
The beating rain, the swiftly-driving snow,
The various ills that we must undergo,
Who roam, the glow-worms of the human race,
The living Jack-a-Lanthorns of the place.
  'Tis said by some, perchance to mock our toil,
That we are prone to "*waste the midnight oil!*"
And that a task thus idle to pursue
Would be an idle *waste of money,* too!
How hard that we the *dark* designs should rue
Of those who'd fain make *light* of all we do!
But such the fate which oft doth merit greet,
And which now drives us fairly off our beat!
Thus it appears from this, our dismal plight,
That *some* love *darkness* rather than the *light.*
  Henceforth, let riot and disorder reign,
With all the ills that follow in their train;
Let TOMS and JERRYS unmolested brawl
(No *Charlies* have they now to *floor* withal).
And "rogues and vagabonds" infest the Town,
Far cheaper 'tis to *save* than *crack a crown.*
  To brighter scenes we now direct our view—

And,

And, first, fair Ladies, let us turn to you.
May each NEW YEAR new joys, new pleasures bring,
And Life for you be one delightful spring!
No summer's sun annoy with fev'rish rays,
No winter chill the evening of your days!
　To you, kind Sirs, we next our tribute pay:
May smiles and sunshine greet you on your way!
If married, calm and peaceful be your lives;
If single, may you, forthwith, get you wives!
　Thus, whether Male or Female, Old or Young
Or Wed, or Single, be this burden sung:
Long may you live to hear, and we to call,
"A Happy Christmas and New Year to all."

The present generation has never seen, and probably never heard of, "Christmas pieces," or specimens of hand-writing, which went out of vogue fifty years ago. It was very useful, as the boy took great pride in its writing, and parents could judge of their children's proficiency in penman-ship. Sometimes these sheets were surrounded with elaborate flourishings of birds, pens, scrolls, etc., such as the writing-master of the last century delighted in; others were headed with copper-plate engravings, sometimes coloured. Here are a few of the subjects: Ruth and Boaz, Measuring the Temple (Ezekiel), Philip Baptising the Eunuch, The Good Samaritan, Joshua's Command, John the Baptist Preaching in the Wilderness, The Seven Wonders of the World, King William III., St. Paul's Shipwreck, etc., etc.

A publisher, writing to *Notes and Queries* in 1871 (4 series, vi. 462) about these "Christmas Pieces," says: "As a youngster, some thirty years ago, in my father's establish-ment, the sale of "school pieces," or "Christmas pieces," as they were called, was very large. My father published some thirty different subjects (a new one every year, one of the old ones being let go out of print). There were also three other publishers of them. The order to print used to average about 500 of each kind, but double of the Life of our Saviour. Most of the subjects were those of the Old Testament. I only recollect four subjects not sacred. Printing at home, we generally commenced the printing in August from the copper-plates, as they had to be coloured by hand. They sold, retail, at sixpence each, and we used to supply them to the

the trade at thirty shillings per gross, and to schools at three
shillings and sixpence per dozen, or two dozen for six shillings
and sixpence.   Charity boys were large purchasers of these
pieces, and at Christmas time used to take them round their
parish to show, and, at the same time, solicit a trifle.   The
sale never began before October in the country, and December in London ; and early in January the stock left used to be
put by until the following season.   It is over fifteen years
since any were printed by my firm, and the last new one I
find was done in lithography."

CHAPTER XXVI

Carol for St. Stephen's Day—Boxing Day—Origin of Custom—Early Examples
—The Box—Bleeding Horses—Festivity on this Day—Charity at
Bampton—Hunting the Wren in Ireland—Song of the Wren Boys.

On the day succeeding Christmas day the Church com-
memorates the death of the proto-martyr Stephen, and in
honour of this festival the following carol is sung :—

In friendly Love and Unity,
   For good *St. Stephen's* Sake,
Let us all, this blessed Day,
   To Heaven our Prayers make :
That we with him the Cross of Christ
   May freely undertake.
      And Jesus *will send you his*
      Blessing.

Those accursed Infidels
   That stoned him to Death,
Could not by their cruelties
   Withhold him from his Faith,
In such a godly Martyrdom
   Seek we all the Path.
      And Jesus, etc.

And whilst we sit here banqueting,
   Of dainties having Store,
Let us not forgetful be
   To cherish up the Poor ;
And give what is convenient
   To those that ask at Door.
      And Jesus, etc.

For God hath made you Stewards
   here,
   Upon the Earth to dwell ;
He that gathereth for himself,
   And will not use it well,
Lives far worse than *Dives* did,
   That burneth now in Hell.
      And Jesus, etc.

And, now, in Love and Charity,
   See you your Table spread,
That I may taste of your good Cheer,
   Your *Christmas* Ale and Bread :
Then I may say that I full well
   For this, my Carol, sped.
      And Jesus, etc.

For Bounty is a blessed Gift,
   The Lord above it sends,
And he that gives it from His Hands,
   Deserveth many Friends :
I see it on my Master's Board,
   And so my Carol ends.
      Lord Jesus, etc.

But St. Stephen's day is much better known in England
as "Boxing Day," from the kindly custom of recognising
                        little

201

little services rendered during the year by giving a Christmas box—a custom which, of course, is liable to abuse, and especially when, as in many instances, it is regarded as a right, in which case it loses its pleasant significance. No one knows how old this custom is, nor its origin. Hutchinson, in his *History of Northumberland* (vol. ii. p. 20), says: "The Paganalia of the Romans, instituted by Servius Tullius, were celebrated in the beginning of the year; an altar was erected in each village, where all persons gave money." There is a somewhat whimsical account of its origin in the first attempt at *Notes and Queries*, *The Athenian Oracle*, by John Dunton (1703, vol. i. 360).

"Q. *From whence comes the custom of gathering of* Christmas Box Money? *And how long since?*

"A. It is as Ancient as the word *Mass*, which the Romish Priests invented from the *Latin* word *Mitto*, to send, by putting People in Mind to send Gifts, Offerings, Oblations, to have Masses said for everything almost, that a Ship goes not out to the *Indies*, but the Priest have a Box in that Ship, under the Protection of some Saint. And for Masses, as they Cant, to be said for them to that Saint, etc., the Poor People must put something into the Priest's Box, which is not to be Opened till the Ship Return. Thus the Mass at that time was called *Christ's Mass*, and the Box, *Christ's Mass Box*, or Money gathered against that time, that Masses might be made by the Priests to the Saints, to forgive the People the Debaucheries of that time; and from this, Servants had the Liberty to get Box-money, because they might be able to pay the Priest for his Masses, because *No Penny, No Paternoster*."

At all events, the Christmas box was a well-known institution in the early seventeenth century. We have already seen Pepys "dropping money" here and there at Christ-tide, and on 28th December 1668 he notes: "Called up by drums and trumpets; these things and boxes having cost me much money this Christmas already, and will do more." Yet the custom must have been much older, for in the accounts of Dame Agnes Merett, Cellaress of Syon Monastery, at Isleworth, in 29 Henry VIII., 1537-38 (*Record Office Roll*, T.G. 18,232), the following are entered among

among the *Foreigne Paymentes*: "Reward to the servauntes at Crystemas, with their aprons xxs. Reward to the Clerk of the Kechyn, xiijs. iiijd. Reward to the Baily of the Husbandry, vis. viijd. Reward to the Keeper of the Covent Garden, vis. viijd."

As time went on we find increasing notices of Christmas boxes. In Beaumont and Fletcher's *Wit without Money* (Act ii. sc. 2) "A Widow is a Christmas box that sweeps all."

Swift, in his *Journal to Stella*, mentions them several times. 26th December 1710: "By the Lord Harry, I shall be undone here with Christmas boxes. The rogues at the Coffee-house have raised their tax, every one giving a crown, and I gave mine for shame, besides a great many half-crowns to great men's porters," etc.

24th December 1711: "I gave Patrick half a crown for his Christmas box, on condition he would be good; and he came home drunk at midnight."

2nd January 1712: "I see nothing here like Christmas, excepting brawn and mince pies in places where I dine, and giving away my half crowns like farthings to great men's porters and butlers."

Gay, in his *Trivia*, thus mentions it :—

> Some boys are rich by birth beyond all wants,
> Belov'd by uncles, and kind, good, old aunts ;
> When Time comes round, a *Christmas Box* they bear,
> And one day makes them rich for all the year.

But the Christmas *box* was an entity, and tangible; it was a saving's box made of earthenware, which must be broken before the cash could be extracted, as can be proved by several quotations, and the gift took its name from the receptacle for it.

In Mason's *Handful of Essaies* 1621 : "Like a swine, he never doth good till his death; as an apprentice's box of earth, apt he is to take all, but to restore none till hee be broken."

In the frontispiece to Blaxton's *English Usurer*, 1634, the same simile is used :—

> Both with the Christmas Boxe may well comply,
> It nothing yields till broke ; they till they die.

And

And again, in Browne's *Map of the Microcosme*, 1642, speaking of a covetous man, he says, he "doth exceed in receiving, but is very deficient in giving; like the Christmas earthen Boxes of apprentices, apt to take in money, but he restores none till hee be broken, like a potter's vessell, into many shares."

Aubrey, in his *Wiltshire Collections, circ.* 1670 (p. 45), thus describes a *trouvaille* of Roman coins. "Among the rest was an earthen pott of the colour of a Crucible, and of the shape of a prentice's Christmas Box, with a slit in it, containing about a quart, which was near full of money. This pot I gave to the Repository of the Royal Society at Gresham College."

And, to wind up these Christmas box notices, I may quote a verse from Henry Carey's "Sally in our Alley" (1715?)

> When Christmas comes about again,
> Oh! then I shall have money;
> I'll hoard it up, and box and all,
> I'll give it to my honey.

There used to be a very curious custom on St. Stephen's day, which Douce says was introduced into this country by the Danes—that of bleeding horses. That it was usual is, I think, proved by very different authorities. Tusser says:—

> Yer Christmas be passed, let horsse be let blood,
> For manie a purpose it dooth him much good;
> The day of S. Steeven old fathers did use;
> If that do mislike thee, some other day chuse.

And Barnebe Googe, in his translation of Naogeorgus, remarks:—

> Then followeth Saint Stephen's day, whereon doth every man
> His horses iaunt and course abrode, as swiftly as he can;
> Untill they doe extreemely sweate, and than they let them blood,
> For this being done upon this day, they say doth do them good,
> And keepes them from all maladies and secknesse through the yeare,
> As if that Steuen any time tooke charge of horses heare.

Aubrey, also, in his *Remains of Gentilisme*, says: "On St. Stephen's day the farrier came constantly, and blouded all our cart horses."

It was occasionally the day of great festivity, even though it it came so very closely after Christmas day; and Mr. J. G. Nichols, in *Notes and Queries* (2 ser. viii. 484), quotes a letter, dated 2nd January 1614, in confirmation. It is from an alderman of Leicester to his brother in Wood Street, Cheapside. "Yow wryte how yow reacayved my lettar on St. Steven's day, and that, I thanke yow, yow esteemed yt as welcoom as the 18 trumpytors; w^t in so doing, I must and will esteme yowres, God willing, more wellcoom then trumpets and all the musicke we have had since Christmas, and yet we have had prety store bothe of owre owne and othar, evar since Christmas. And the same day we were busy w^t hollding up hands and spoones to yow, out of porredge and pyes, in the remembraunce of yowre greate lyberality of frute and spice, which God send yow long lyffe to contynew, for of that day we have not myssed anny St. Steven this 47 yeare to have as many gas (*guests*) as my howse will holld, I thank God for yt."

In Southey's *Common Place Book* it is noted that the three Vicars of Bampton, Oxon., give beef and beer on the morning of St. Stephen's day to those who choose to partake of it. This is called St. Stephen's breakfast. The same book also mentions a singular custom in Wales, that on this day everybody is privileged to whip another person's legs with holly, which is often reciprocated till the blood streams down; and this is corroborated in Mason's *Tales and Traditions of Tenby*, where it is mentioned as being practised in that town.

We have heard of hunting the wren in the Isle of Man; the same custom obtains in the south of Ireland, only it takes place on St. Stephen's day. There is a tradition which is supposed to account for this animosity against this pretty and harmless little bird. In one of the many Irish rebellions a night march was made by a body of rebels on a party of royalists, and when, about dawn of day, they neared the sleeping out-posts, a slumbering drummer was aroused by a tapping on his drum; and, giving the alarm, the rebels were repulsed. The tapping was caused by a wren pecking at the crumbs left on the drum-head after the drummer's last meal. Henceforward a grudge was nursed against the wren, which has existed until now.

The

The "wren boys" go round, calling at houses, either having a dead wren in a box, or hung on a holly bush, and they sing a song :—

> The Wran, the Wran, the king of all birds,
> On St. Stephen's day she's cotched in the furze ;
> Although she's but wee, her family's great,
> So come down, Lan'leddy, and gie us a trate.
>> Then up wi' the kettle, an' down wi' the pan,
>> An' let us ha' money to bury the Wran.

Croker, in his *Researches in the South of Ireland* (p. 233), gives us more of this song :—

> The Wren, the Wren, the King of all birds,
> St. Stephen's day was caught in the furze ;
> Although he is little, his family's great,
> I pray you, good landlady, give us a treat.
>
> My box would speak if it had but a tongue,
> And two or three shillings would do it no wrong ;
> Sing holly, sing ivy—sing ivy, sing holly,
> A drop just to drink, it would drown melancholy.
>
> And, if you draw it of the best,
> I hope in Heaven your soul may rest ;
> But, if you draw it of the small,
> It won't agree with the Wren boys at all, etc. etc.

"A small piece of money is usually bestowed on them, and the evening concludes in merrymaking with the money thus collected."

CHAPTER XXVII

St. John's Day—Legend of the Saint—Carols for the Day—Holy Innocents—
Whipping Children—Boy Bishops—Ceremonies connected therewith—The
King of Cockney's Unlucky Day—Anecdote thereon—Carol for the Day.

THE 27th December is set apart by the Church to commemorate St. John the Evangelist. Googe, in his translation of Naogeorgus, says :—

Next *John* the sonne of *Zebedee* hath his appoynted day,
Who once by cruell tyraunts will, constrayned was, they say,
Strong poyson up to drinke, therefore the Papistes doe beleeve
That whoso puts their trust in him, no poyson them can greeue.
The wine beside that hallowed is, in worship of his name,
The priestes doe giue the people that bring money for the same.
And, after, with the selfe same wine are little manchets made,
Agaynst the boystrous winter stormes, and sundrie such like trade.
The men upon this solemne day do take this holy wine,
To make them strong, so do the maydes, to make them faire and fine.

In explanation of this I may quote from Mrs. Jameson's *Sacred and Legendary Art* (ed. 1857, p. 159): "He (St. John) bears in his hand the sacramental cup, from which a serpent is seen to issue. St. Isidore relates that at Rome an attempt was made to poison St. John in the cup of the sacrament; he drank of the same, and administered it to the communicants without injury, the poison having, by a miracle, issued from the cup in the form of a serpent, while the hired assassin fell down dead at his feet. According to another version of this story the poisoned cup was administered by order of the Emperor Domitian. According to a third version, Aristodemus, the high priest of Diana at Ephesus, defied him to drink of the poisoned chalice, as a test of the truth

truth of his mission. St. John drank unharmed—the priest fell dead."

Wright gives two very pretty carols for St. John's day.

To almyghty God pray for pees.

Amice Christi Johannes.

O glorius Johan Evangelyste,
Best belovyd with Jhesu Cryst,
In Cena Domini upon hys bryst
    Ejus vidisti archana.

Chosen thou art to Cryst Jhesu,
Thy mynd was never cast frome
    vertu;
Thi doctryne of God thou dydest
    renu,
    Per ejus vestigia.

Cryst on the rod, in hys swet pas-
    syon,
Toke the hys moder as to hyr sone;
For owr synnes gett grace and par-
    don,
    Per tua sancta merita.

O most nobble of evangelystes all,
Grace to owr maker for us thou call,
And off swetenesse celestyall,
    Prebe nobis pocula.

And aftur the cowrs of mortalite,
In heven with aungels for to be,
Sayyng Ozanna to the Trinitye.
    Per seculorum secula.

Pray for us, thou prynce of pes.

Amici Christi, Johannes.

To the now, Crystys der derlyng,
That was a mayd bothe old and ȝyng,
Myn hert is sett for to syng
    Amici Christi, Johannes.

For he was so clene a maye,
On Crystys brest aslepe he laye,
The prevyteys of hevyn ther he saye.
    Amici Christi, Johannes.

Qwhen Cryst beforne Pilate was
    browte,
Hys clene mayd forsoke hym nowte,
To deye with hym was all hys
    thowte,
    Amici Christi, Johannes.

Crystys moder was hym betake,
Won mayd to be anodyris make,
To help that we be nott forsake,
    Amici Christi, Johannes.

On 28th December the Holy Innocents, or the children slain by order of Herod, are borne in mind. Naogeorgus says of this day :—

Then

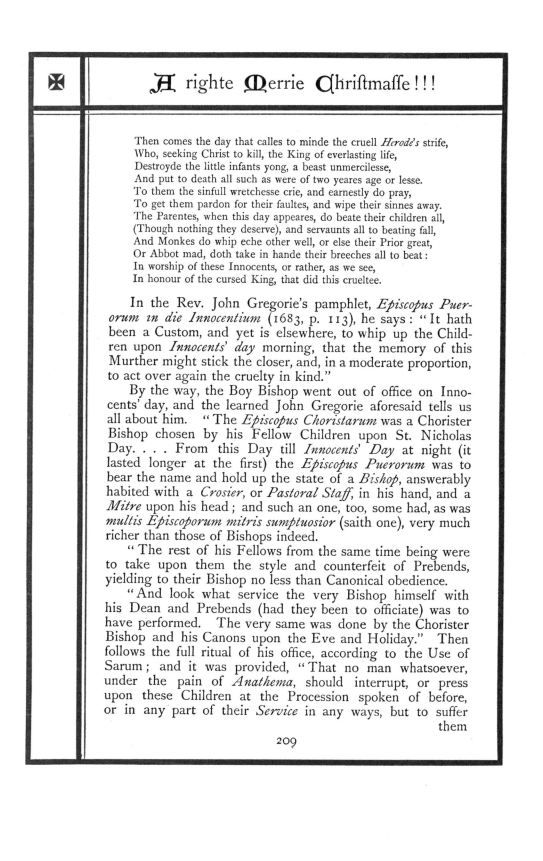

Then comes the day that calles to minde the cruell *Herode's* strife,
Who, seeking Christ to kill, the King of everlasting life,
Destroyde the little infants yong, a beast unmercilesse,
And put to death all such as were of two yeares age or lesse.
To them the sinfull wretchesse crie, and earnestly do pray,
To get them pardon for their faultes, and wipe their sinnes away.
The Parentes, when this day appeares, do beate their children all,
(Though nothing they deserve), and servaunts all to beating fall,
And Monkes do whip eche other well, or else their Prior great,
Or Abbot mad, doth take in hande their breeches all to beat:
In worship of these Innocents, or rather, as we see,
In honour of the cursed King, that did this crueltee.

In the Rev. John Gregorie's pamphlet, *Episcopus Puerorum in die Innocentium* (1683, p. 113), he says: "It hath been a Custom, and yet is elsewhere, to whip up the Children upon *Innocents' day* morning, that the memory of this Murther might stick the closer, and, in a moderate proportion, to act over again the cruelty in kind."

By the way, the Boy Bishop went out of office on Innocents' day, and the learned John Gregorie aforesaid tells us all about him. "The *Episcopus Choristarum* was a Chorister Bishop chosen by his Fellow Children upon St. Nicholas Day. . . . From this Day till *Innocents' Day* at night (it lasted longer at the first) the *Episcopus Puerorum* was to bear the name and hold up the state of a *Bishop*, answerably habited with a *Crosier*, or *Pastoral Staff*, in his hand, and a *Mitre* upon his head; and such an one, too, some had, as was *multis Episcoporum mitris sumptuosior* (saith one), very much richer than those of Bishops indeed.

"The rest of his Fellows from the same time being were to take upon them the style and counterfeit of Prebends, yielding to their Bishop no less than Canonical obedience.

"And look what service the very Bishop himself with his Dean and Prebends (had they been to officiate) was to have performed. The very same was done by the Chorister Bishop and his Canons upon the Eve and Holiday." Then follows the full ritual of his office, according to the Use of Sarum; and it was provided, "That no man whatsoever, under the pain of *Anathema*, should interrupt, or press upon these Children at the Procession spoken of before, or in any part of their *Service* in any ways, but to suffer them

them quietly to perform and execute what it concerned them to do.

"And the part was acted yet more earnestly, for *Molanus* saith that this Bishop, in some places, did receive Rents, Capons, etc., during his year; And it seemeth by the statute of *Sarum*, that he held a kind of Visitation, and had a full correspondency of all other State and Prerogative. . . . In case the Chorister Bishop died within the Month, his Exequies were solemnized with an answerable glorious pomp and sadness. He was buried (as all other Bishops) in all his Ornaments, as by the Monument in stone spoken of before,[1] it plainly appeareth."

Hone, in his *Every-Day Book* (vol. i. pp. 1559-60), gives a facsimile of this monument from Gregorie's book, and says : "The ceremony of the boy bishop is supposed to have existed, not only in collegiate churches, but in almost every parish in England. He and his companions walked the streets in public procession. A statute of the Collegiate Church of St. Mary Overy, in 1337, restrained one of them to the limits of his own parish. On December 7, 1229, the day after St. Nicholas' Day, a boy bishop in the chapel at Heton, near Newcastle-on-Tyne, said vespers before Edward I. on his way to Scotland, who made a considerable present to him, and the other boys who sang with him. In the reign of King Edward III. a boy bishop received a present of nineteen shillings and sixpence for singing before the king in his private chamber on Innocents' day. Dean Colet, in the statutes of St. Paul's School, which he founded in 1512, expressly ordains that his scholars should, every Childermas Day,[2] 'come to Paulis Churche, and hear the Chylde Bishop's Sermon ; and, after, be at hygh masse, and each of them offer a penny to the Chylde-Bishop; and with them, the maisters and surveyors of the Scole.'"

By a proclamation of Henry VIII., dated 22nd July 1542, the show of the boy bishop was abrogated, but in the reign of Mary it was revived with other Romish ceremonials. A flattering song was sung before that queen by a boy bishop, and

---

[1] A stone monument of a boy bishop found in Salisbury Cathedral.
[2] The Anglo-Saxons called Innocents' day Childe-mass or Childer-mass.

and printed. It was a panegyric on her devotion, and compared her to Judith, Esther, the Queen of Sheba, and the Virgin Mary.

The accounts of St. Mary at Hill, London, in the 10th Henry VI., and for 1549 and 1550, contain charges for boy bishops for those years. At that period his estimation in the Church seems to have been undiminished; for on 13th November 1554 the Bishop of London issued an order to all the clergy of his diocese to have boy bishops and their processions; and in the same year these young sons of the old Church paraded St. Andrew's, Holborn, and St. Nicholas, Olaves, in Bread Street, and other parishes. In 1556 Strype says that "the boy bishops again went abroad, singing in the old fashion, and were received by many ignorant but well-disposed persons into their houses, and had much good cheer."

Speaking of the Christmas festivities at Lincoln's Inn, Dugdale[1] says: "Moreover, that the *King of Cockneys*, on *Childermass* Day, should sit and have due service; and that he and all his officers should use honest manner and good Order, without any wast or destruction making, in Wine, Brawn, Chely, or other Vitaills."

In Chambers's *Book of Days* we find that, "In consequence probably of the feeling of horror attached to such an act of atrocity, Innocents' Day used to be reckoned about the most unlucky throughout the year, and in former times no one who could possibly avoid it began any work, or entered on any undertaking on this anniversary. To marry on Childermas Day was specially inauspicious. It is said of the equally superstitious and unprincipled monarch, Louis XV., that he would never perform any business or enter into any discussion about his affairs on this day, and to make to him then any proposal of the kind was certain to exasperate him to the utmost. We are informed, too, that in England, on the occasion of the coronation of King Edward IV., that solemnity, which had been originally intended to take place on a Sunday, was postponed till the Monday, owing to the former day being, in that year, the festival of Childermas. The idea of

[1] *Orig. Jur.*, p. 246.

of the inauspicious nature of the day was long prevalent, and is even not yet wholly extinct. To the present hour, we understand, the housewives in Cornwall, and probably also in other parts of the country, refrain scrupulously from scouring or scrubbing on Innocents' Day."

At the churches in several parts of the country muffled peals are rung on this day, and with the Irish it is called "La crosta na bliana," or "the cross day of the year," and also, "Diar daoin darg," or "Bloody Thursday," and on that day the Irish housewife will not warp thread, nor permit it to be warped; and the Irish say that anything begun upon that day must have an unlucky ending.

A writer in *Notes and Queries* (4 ser. xii. 185) says: "The following legend regarding the day is current in the county of Clare. Between the parishes of Quin and Tulla, in that county, is a lake called Turlough. In the lake is a little island; and among a heap of loose stones in the middle of the island rises a white thorn bush, which is called 'Scagh an Earla' (the Earl's bush). A suit of clothes made for a child on the 'Cross day' was put on the child; the child died. The clothes were put on a second and on a third child; they also died. The parents of the children at length put out the clothes on the 'Scag an Earla,' and when the waters fell the clothes were found to be full of dead eels."

Here is a good carol for Innocents' day, published in the middle of the sixteenth century:—

A CAROL OF THE INNOCENTS.

Mark this song, for it is true,
For it is true, as clerks tell:
In old time strange things came to pass,
Great wonder and great marvel was
    In Israel.

There was one, Octavian,
Octavian of Rome Emperor,
As books old doth specify,
Of all the wide world truly
    He was lord and governor.

The Jews, that time, lack'd a king,
They lack'd a king to guide them well,
The Emperor of power and might,
Chose one Herod against all right,
    In Israel.

This Herod, then, was King of Jews
Was King of Jews, and he no Jew,
Forsooth he was a Paynim born,
Wherefore on faith it may be sworn
    He reigned King untrue.

By

By prophecy, one Isai,
One Isai, at least, did tell
A child should come, wondrous news,
That should be born true King of
　　Jews
　　In Israel.

This Herod knew one born should be,
One born should be of true lineage,
That should be right heritor;
For he but by the Emperor
　　Was made by usurpage.

Wherefore of thought this King
　　Herod,
This King Herod in great fear fell,
For all the days most in his mirth,
Ever he feared Christ his birth
　　In Israel.

The time came it pleased God,
It pleased God so to come to pass,
For man's soul indeed
His blessed Son was born with speed,
　　As His will was.

Tidings came to King Herod,
To King Herod, and did him tell,
That one born forsooth is he,
Which lord and king of all shall be
　　In Israel.

Herod then raged, as he were wode
　　(mad),
As he were wode of this tyding,
And sent for all his scribes sure,
Yet would he not trust the Scripture,
　　Nor of their counselling.

This, then, was the conclusion,
The conclusion of his counsel,
To send unto his knights anon
To slay the children every one
　　In Israel.

This cruel king this tyranny,
This tyranny did put in ure (practice),
Between a day and years two,
All men-children he did slew,
　　Of Christ for to be sure.

Yet Herod missed his cruel prey,
His cruel prey, as was God's will;
Joseph with Mary then did flee
With Christ to Egypt, gone was she
　　From Israel.

All the while these tyrants,
These tyrants would not convert,
But innocents young
That lay sucking,
　　They thrust to the heart.

This Herod sought the children
　　young,
The children young, with courage
　　fell.
But in doing this vengeance
His own son was slain by chance
　　In Israel.

Alas! I think the mothers were woe,
The mothers were woe, it was great
　　skill,
What motherly pain
To see them slain,
　　In cradles lying still!

But God Himself hath them elect,
Hath them elect in heaven to dwell,
For they were bathed in their blood,
For their Baptism forsooth it stood
　　In Israel.

Alas! again, what hearts had they,
What hearts had they those babes to
　　kill,
With swords when they them caught,
In cradles they lay and laughed,
　　And never thought ill.

213

CHAPTER XXVIII

New Year's Eve—Wassail—New Year's Eve Customs—Hogmany—The Clāvie
—Other Customs—Weather Prophecy

NEW YEAR'S EVE is variously kept — by some in harmless mirth, by others in religious exercises. Many churches in England have late services, which close at midnight with a carol or appropriate hymn, and this custom is especially held by the Wesleyan Methodists in their "Watch Night," when they pray, etc., till about five minutes to twelve, when there is a dead silence, supposed to be spent in introspection, which lasts until the clock strikes, and then they burst forth with a hymn of praise and joy.

The wassail bowl used to hold as high a position as at Christmas eve, and in Lyson's time it was customary in Gloucestershire for a merry party to go from house to house carrying a large bowl, decked with garlands and ribbons, singing the following wassail song :—

> Wassail ! Wassail ! all over the town,
> Our toast it is white, our ale it is brown,
> Our bowl it is made of a maplin tree ;
> We be good fellows all, I drink to thee.
>
> Here's to our horse, and to his right ear,
> God send our maister a happy New Year ;
> A happy New Year as e'er he did see—
> With my wassailing bowl I drink to thee.
>
> Here's to our mare, and to her right eye,
> God send our mistress a good Christmas pye :
> A good Christmas pye as e'er I did see—
> With my wassailing bowl I drink to thee.

Here's

214

Here's to Fill-pail (cow) and to her long tail,
God send our measter us never may fail
Of a cup of good beer, I pray you draw near,
And our jolly wassail it's then you shall hear.

Be here any maids ?   I suppose there be some,
Sure they will not let young men stand on the cold stone
Sing hey, O maids, come trole back the pin,
And the fairest maid in the house let us all in.

Come, butler, come bring us a bowl of the best :
I hope your soul in heaven will rest :
But, if you do bring us a bowl of the small,
Then down fall butler, bowl, and all.

Until recently, a similar custom obtained in Nottingham-shire ; but, in that case, the young women of the village, dressed in their best, carried round a decorated bowl filled with ale, roasted apples, and toast, seasoned with nutmeg and sugar, the regulation wassail compound.   This they offered to the inmates of the house they called at, whilst they sang the following, amongst other verses :—

Good master, at your door,
Our wassail we begin ;
We are all maidens poor,
So we pray you let us in,
And drink our wassail.
All hail, wassail !
Wassail ! wassail !
And drink our wassail.

In Derbyshire, on this night, a cold posset used to be prepared, made of milk, ale, eggs, currants, and spices, and in it is placed the hostess's wedding ring.   Each of the party takes out a ladleful, and in so doing tries to fish out the ring, believing that whoever shall be fortunate enough to get it will be married before the year is out.   It was also custom-ary in some districts to throw open all the doors of the house just before midnight, and, waiting for the advent of the New Year, to greet him as he approaches with cries of "Welcome!"

At Muncaster, in Cumberland, on this night the children used to go from house to house singing a song, in which they

crave

215

crave the bounty "they were wont to have in old King Edward's time"; but what that was is not known.

It was a custom at Merton College, Oxford, according to Pointer (*Oxoniensis Academia*, ed. 1749, p. 24), on the last night in the year, called Scrutiny Night, for the College servants, all in a body, to make their appearance in the Hall, before the Warden and Fellows (after supper), and there to deliver up their keys, so that if they have committed any great crime during the year their keys are taken away, and they consequently lose their places, or they have them delivered to them afresh.

On this night a curious custom obtained at Bradford, in Yorkshire, where a party of men and women, with blackened faces, and fantastically attired, used to enter houses with besoms, and "sweep out the Old Year."

Although Christmas is kept in Scotland, there is more festivity at the New Year, and perhaps one of the most singular customs is that which was told by a gentleman to Dr. Johnson during his tour in the Hebrides. On New Year's eve, in the hall or castle of the Laird, where at festal seasons there may be supposed to be a very numerous company, one man dresses himself in a cow's hide, upon which the others beat with sticks. He runs, with all this noise, round the house, which all the company quit in a counterfeited fright, and the door is then shut. On New Year's eve there is no great pleasure to be had out of doors in the Hebrides. They are sure soon to recover sufficiently from their terror to solicit for readmission, which is not to be obtained but by repeating a verse, with which those who are knowing and provident are provided.

In the Orkney Islands it was formerly the custom for bands of people to assemble and pay a round of visits, singing a song which began—

> This night it is guid New'r E'en's night,
> We're a' here Queen Mary's men:
> And we're come here to crave our right,
> And that's before our Lady!

In the county of Fife this night was called "Singen E'en," probably from the custom of singing carols then. This day

is

is popularly known in Scotland as *Hogmany*, and the following is a fragment of a Yorkshire *Hagmena* song :—

> To-night it is the New Year's night, to-morrow is the day,
> And we are come for our right and for our ray,
> As we used to do in Old King Henry's day :
>   Sing, fellows! sing, Hagman-ha!
>
> If you go to the bacon flick, cut me a good bit ;
> Cut, cut and low, beware of your maw.
> Cut, cut and round, beware of your thumb,
> That me and my merry men may have some :
>   Sing, fellows! sing, Hag-man-ha!
>
> If you go to the black ark (chest), bring me ten marks ;
> Ten marks, ten pound, throw it down upon the ground,
> That me and my merry men may have some :
>   Sing, fellows! sing, Hog-man-ha!

The meaning of this word "Hogmany" is not clear, and has been a source of dispute among Scottish antiquaries ; but two suggestions of its derivation are probable   One is that it comes from *Au qui menez* (To the mistleto go), which mummers formerly cried in France at Christmas; and the other is that it is derived from *Au gueux menez, i.e.* bring the beggars —which would be suitable for charitable purposes at such a time.   In some remote parts of Scotland the poor children robe themselves in a sheet, which is so arranged as to make a large pocket in front, and going about in little bands, they call at houses for their Hogmany, which is given them in the shape of some oat cake, and sometimes cheese, the cakes being prepared some days beforehand, in order to meet the demand.   On arriving at a house they cry " Hogmany," or sing some rough verse, like—

> Hogmanay,
> Trollolay,
> Give us of your white bread, and none of your grey !

In *Notes and Queries* (2 ser. ix. 38) a singular Scotch custom is detailed.   Speaking of the village of Burghead, on the southern shore of the Moray Frith, the writer says : "On the evening of the last day of December (old style) the youth of the village assemble about dusk, and make the

217

the necessary preparations for the celebration of the 'clāvie.' Proceeding to some shop, they demand a strong empty barrel, which is usually gifted at once; but if refused, taken by force. Another for breaking up, and a quantity of tar are likewise procured at the same time. Thus furnished, they repair to a particular spot close to the sea shore, and commence operations.

"A hole, about four inches in diameter, is first made in the bottom of the stronger barrel, into which the end of a stout pole, five feet in length, is firmly fixed; to strengthen their hold, a number of supports are nailed round the outside of the former, and also closely round the latter. The tar is then put into the barrel, and set on fire; and the remaining one being broken up, stave after stave is thrown in, until it is quite full. The 'clāvie,' already burning fiercely, is now shouldered by some strong young man, and borne away at a rapid pace. As soon as the bearer gives signs of exhaustion, another willingly takes his place; and should should any of those who are honoured to carry the blazing load meet with an accident, as sometimes happens, the misfortune excites no pity, even among his near relatives.

"In making the circuit of the village they are said to confine themselves to their old boundaries. Formerly the procession visited all the fishing boats, but this has been discontinued for some time. Having gone over the appointed ground, the 'clāvie' is finally carried to a small artificial eminence near the point of the promontory, and, interesting as being a portion of the ancient fortifications, spared, probably on account of its being used for this purpose, where a circular heap of stones used to be hastily piled up, in the hollow centre of which the 'clāvie' was placed, still burning. On this eminence, which is termed the 'durie,' the present proprietor has recently erected a small round column, with a cavity in the centre, for admitting the free end of the pole, and into this it is now placed. After being allowed to burn on the 'durie' for a few minutes, the 'clāvie' is most unceremoniously hurled from its place, and the smoking embers scattered among the assembled crowd, by whom, in less enlightened times, they were eagerly caught at, and fragments of them carried home, and carefully preserved as charms against witchcraft."

witchcraft." Some discussion took place on the origin of this custom, but nothing satisfactory was eliminated.

Another correspondent to the same periodical (2 ser. ix. 322) says : "A practice, which may be worth noting, came under my observation at the town of Biggar (in the upper ward of Lanarkshire) on 31st December last. It has been customary there, from time immemorial, among the inhabitants to celebrate what is called ' Burning out the Old Year.' For this purpose, during the day of the 31st, a large quantity of fuel is collected, consisting of branches of trees, brushwood, and coals, and placed in a heap at the ' Cross ' ; and about nine o'clock at night the lighting of the fire is commenced, surrounded by a crowd of onlookers, who each thinks it a duty to cast into the flaming mass some additional portion of material, the whole becoming sufficient to maintain the fire till next, or New Year's morning is far advanced. Fires are also kindled on the adjacent hills to add to the importance of the occasion."

In Ireland, according to Croker (*Researches in the South of Ireland*, p. 233), on the last night of the year a cake is thrown against the outside door of each house, by the head of the family, which ceremony is said to keep out hunger during the ensuing year :—

> If New Year's Eve night wind blow South,
> It betokeneth warmth and growth ;
> If West, much milk, and fish in the sea ;
> If North, much cold and storms there will be ;
> If East, the trees will bear much fruit ;
> If North-East, flee it, man and brute.

CHAPTER XXIX

New Year's Day—Carol—New Year's Gifts—" Dipping "—Riding the " Stang "
—Curious Tenures—God Cakes—The " Quaaltagh "—" First-foot " in Scot-
land—Highland Customs—In Ireland—Weather Prophecies—Handsel
Monday.

THERE is a peculiar feeling of satisfaction that comes over
us with the advent of the New Year. The Old Year, with its
joys and sorrows, its gains and disappointments, is irrevocably
dead—dead without hope of resurrection, and there is not one
of us who does not hope that the forthcoming year may be a
happier one than that departed.

The following very pretty "Carol for New Year's Day"
is taken from *Psalmes, Songs, and Sonnets*, composed by
William Byrd, Lond. 1611 :—

O God, that guides the cheerful sun
  By motions strange the year to frame,
Which now, returned whence it begun,
  From Heaven extols Thy glorious Name ;
This New Year's season sanctify
  With double blessings of Thy store,
That graces new may multiply,
  And former follies reign no more.
So shall our hearts with Heaven agree,
And both give laud and praise to Thee.   Amen.

Th' old year, by course, is past and gone,
  Old Adam, Lord, from us expel ;
New creatures make us every one,
  New life becomes the New Year well.
As new-born babes from malice keep,
  New wedding garments, Christ, we crave ;

That

That we Thy face in Heaven may see,
With Angels bright, our souls to save.
So shall our hearts with Heaven agree,
And both give laud and praise to Thee. Amen.

The Church takes no notice of the first of January as the beginning of a New Year, but only as the Feast of the Circumcision of our Lord, and consequently, being included in the twelve days of Christ-tide festivity, it was only regarded as one of them, and no particular stress was placed upon it. There were, and are, local customs peculiar to the day, but, with the exception of some special festivity, general good wishes for health and prosperity, and the giving of presents, there is no extraordinary recognition of the day.

Naogeorgus says of it :—

The next to this is New Yeares day, whereon to every frende,
They costly presents in do bring, and Newe Yeares giftes do sende.
These giftes the husband gives his wife, and father eke the childe,
And maister on his men bestowes the like, with favour milde.
And good beginning of the yeare, they wishe and wishe againe,
According to the auncient guise of heathen people vaine.
These eight dayes no man doth require his dettes of any man,
Their tables do they furnish out with all the meate they can :
With Marchpaynes, Tartes, and Custards great, they drink with staring eyes,
They rowte and revell, feede and feast, as merry all as Pyes :
As if they should at th' entrance of this newe yeare hap to die,
Yet would they have theyr bellyes full, and auncient friendes allie.

The custom of mutual gifts on this day still obtains in England, but is in great force in France. Here it was general among all classes, and many are the notices of presents to Royalty, but nowadays a present at Christmas has very greatly superseded the old custom. We owe the term "pin-money" to the gift of pins at this season. They were expensive articles, and occasionally money was given as a commutation. Gloves were, as they are now, always an acceptable present, but to those who were not overburdened with this world's goods an orange stuck with cloves was deemed sufficient for a New Year's gift.

Among the many superstitious customs which used to obtain in England was a kind of "Sortes Virgilianæ," or divination, as to the coming year. Only the Bible was the medium,

medium, and the operation was termed "dipping." The ceremony usually took place before breakfast, as it was absolutely necessary that the rite should be performed fasting. The Bible was laid upon a table, and opened haphazard, a finger being placed, without premeditation, upon a verse, and the future for the coming year was dependent upon the sense of the verse pitched upon. A correspondent in *Notes and Queries* (2 ser. xii. 303) writes: "About eight years ago I was staying in a little village in Oxfordshire on the first day of the year, and happening to pass by a cottage where an old woman lived whom I knew well, I stepped in, and wished her 'A Happy New Year.' Instead of replying to my salutation, she stared wildly at me, and exclaimed in a horrified tone, 'New Year's Day! and I have never dipped.' Not having the slightest idea of her meaning, I asked for an explanation, and gathered from her that it was customary to *dip* into the Bible before twelve o'clock on New Year's Day, and the first verse that met the eye indicated the good or bad fortune of the inquirer through the ensuing year. My old friend added: 'Last year I dipped, and I opened on Job, and sure enough, I have had nought but trouble ever since.' Her consternation on receiving my good wishes was in consequence of her having let the opportunity of dipping go by for that year, it being past twelve o'clock."

Another singular custom which used to obtain in Cumberland and Westmoreland is noted in a letter in the *Gentleman's Magazine* for 1791, vol. lxi., part ii. p. 1169: "Early in the morning of the first of January the *Fœx Populi* assemble together, carrying *stangs*[1] and baskets. Any inhabitant, stranger, or whoever joins not this ruffian tribe in sacrificing to their favourite Saint day, if unfortunate enough to be met by any of the band, is immediately mounted across the stang (if a woman, she is basketed), and carried, shoulder height, to the nearest public-house, where the payment of sixpence immediately liberates the prisoner. No respect is paid to any person; the cobler on that day thinks himself equal to the parson, who generally gets mounted like the rest of his flock ;

[1] Poles. To ride the stang was a popular punishment for husbands who behaved cruelly to their wives.

flock; whilst one of his porters *boasts and prides himself* in having, but just before, got the *Squire* across the pole. None, though ever so industriously inclined, are permitted to follow their respective avocations on that day."

Blount, in his *Tenures of Land,* etc., gives a very curious tenure by which the Manor of Essington, Staffordshire, was held; the lord of which manor (either by himself, deputy, or steward) oweth, and is obliged yearly to perform, service to the lord of the Manor of Hilton, a village about a mile distant from this manor. The Lord of Essington is to bring a goose every New Year's day, and drive it round the fire, at least three times, whilst Jack of Hilton is blowing the fire. This Jack of Hilton is an image of brass, of about twelve inches high, having a little hole at the mouth, at which, being filled with water, and set to a strong fire, which makes it evaporate like an *æolipole,* it vents itself in a constant blast, so strongly that it is very audible, and blows the fire fiercely.

When the Lord of Essington has done his duty, and the other things are performed, he carries his goose into the kitchen of Hilton Hall, and delivers it to the cook, who, having dressed it, the Lord of Essington, or his deputy, by way of farther service, is to carry it to the table of the lord paramount of Hilton and Essington, and receives a dish from the Lord of Hilton's table for his own mess, and so departs.

He also gives a curious tenure at Hutton Conyers, Yorkshire: "Near this town, which lies a few miles from Ripon, there is a large common, called Hutton Conyers Moor. . . . The occupiers of messuages and cottages within the several towns of Hutton Conyers, Melmerby, Baldersby, Rainton, Dishforth, and Hewick have right of estray for their sheep to certain limited boundaries on the common, and each township has a shepherd.

"The lord's shepherd has a pre-eminence of tending his sheep on any part of the common, and, wherever he herds the lord's sheep, the several other shepherds have to give way to him, and give up their hoofing place, so long as he pleases to depasture the lord's sheep thereon. The lord holds his court the first day in the year, and, to entitle those several townships to such right of estray, the shepherd of each township attends the court, and does fealty by bringing to the court

court a large apple-pie and a twopenny sweet cake, except
the shepherd of Hewick, who compounds by paying sixteenpence for ale (which is drunk as aftermentioned) and a
wooden spoon ; each pie is cut in two, and divided by the
bailiff, one half between the steward, bailiff, and the tenant of
a coney warren, and the other half into six parts, and divided
amongst the six shepherds of the beforementioned six townships. In the pie brought by the shepherd of Rainton, an
inner one is made, filled with prunes. The cakes are divided
in the same manner. The bailiff of the manor provides
furmety and mustard, and delivers to each shepherd a slice of
cheese and a penny roll. The furmety, well mixed with
mustard, is put into an earthen pot, and placed in a hole in
the ground in a garth belonging to the bailiff's house, to
which place the steward of the court, with the bailiff, tenant
of the warren, and six shepherds adjourn, with their respective wooden spoons. The bailiff provides spoons for the
steward, the tenant of the warren, and himself. The steward
first pays respect to the furmety by taking a large spoonful ;
the bailiff has the next honour, the tenant of the warren next,
then the shepherd of Hutton Conyers, and afterwards the
other shepherds by regular turns ; then each person is served
with a glass of ale (paid for by the sixteenpence brought by
the Hewick shepherd), and the health of the Lord of the
Manor is drunk ; then they adjourn back to the bailiff's house,
and the further business of the court is proceeded with."

The question was asked (*Notes and Queries*, 2 ser. ii.
229), but never answered, Whether any reader could give
information respecting the ancient custom in the city of
Coventry of sending God Cakes on the first day of the year ?
"They are used by all classes, and vary in price from a halfpenny to one pound. They are invariably made in a tri-
angular shape, an inch thick, and filled with a kind of mince
meat. I believe the custom is peculiar to that city, and
should be glad to know more about its origin. So general is
the use of them on January 1st, that the cheaper sorts are
hawked about the streets, as hot Cross buns are on Good
Friday in London."

In Nottinghamshire it is considered unlucky to take anything out of a house on New Year's day before something
has

has been brought in ; consequently, as early as possible in the morning, each member of the family brings in some trifle. Near Newark this rhyme is sung :—

> Take out, and take in,
> Bad luck is sure to begin ;
> But take in and take out,
> Good luck will come about.

Train, in his *History of the Isle of Man* (ed. 1845, vol. ii. 115), says that on 1st January an old custom is observed, called the *quaaltagh*. In almost every parish throughout the island a party of young men go from house to house singing the following rhyme :—

> Again we assemble, a merry New Year
> To wish to each one of the family here,
> Whether man, woman, or girl, or boy,
> That long life and happiness all may enjoy ;
> May they of potatoes and herrings have plenty,
> With butter and cheese, and each other dainty ;
> And may their sleep never, by night or day,
> Disturbed be by even the tooth of a flea :
> Until at the Quaaltagh again we appear,
> To wish you, as now, all a happy New Year.

When these lines are repeated at the door, the whole party are invited into the house to partake of the best the family can afford. On these occasions a person of dark complexion always enters first, as a light-haired male or female is deemed unlucky to be the first-foot, or *quaaltagh*, on New Year's morning. The actors of the *quaaltagh* do not assume fantastic habiliments like the Mummers of England, or the Guisards of Scotland ; nor do they, like these rude performers of the Ancient Mysteries, appear ever to have been attended by minstrels playing on different kinds of musical instruments."

The custom of *first-footing* is still in vogue in many parts of Scotland, although a very good authority, *Chambers's Book of Days* (vol. i. p. 28), says it is dying out :—

"Till very few years ago in Scotland the custom of the wassail bowl, at the passing away of the old year, might be said to be still in comparative vigour. On the approach of
twelve

twelve o'clock a *hot pint* was prepared—that is, a kettle or flagon full of warm, spiced, and sweetened ale, with an infusion of spirits. When the clock had struck the knell of the departed year, each member of the family drank of this mixture, 'A good health and a happy New Year, and many of them!' to all the rest, with a general hand-shaking, and perhaps a dance round the table, with the addition of a song to the tune of *Hey tuttie taitie*—

> " Weel may we a' be,
> Ill may we never see,
> Here's to the King
> And the gude companie! etc.

"The elders of the family would then most probably sally out, with the hot kettle, and bearing also a competent provision of buns and short cakes, or bread and cheese, with the design of visiting their neighbours, and interchanging with them the same cordial greetings. If they met by the way another party similarly bent whom they knew, they would stop, and give and take sips from their respective kettles. Reaching the friends' house, they would enter with vociferous good wishes, and soon send the kettle a-circulating. If they were the first to enter the house since twelve o'clock, they were deemed the *first-foot;* and, as such, it was most important, for luck to the family in the coming year, that they should make their entry, not empty-handed, but with their hands full of cakes, and bread and cheese; of which, on the other hand, civility demanded that each individual in the house should partake.

"To such an extent did this custom prevail in Edinburgh, in the recollection of persons still living, that, according to their account, the principal streets were more thronged between twelve and one in the morning than they usually were at mid-day. Much innocent mirth prevailed, and mutual good feelings were largely promoted. An unlucky circumstance, which took place on the 1st January of 1812, proved the means of nearly extinguishing the custom. A small party of reckless boys formed the design of turning the innocent festivities of *first-footing* to account, for the purposes of plunder. They kept their counsel well. No sooner had

226

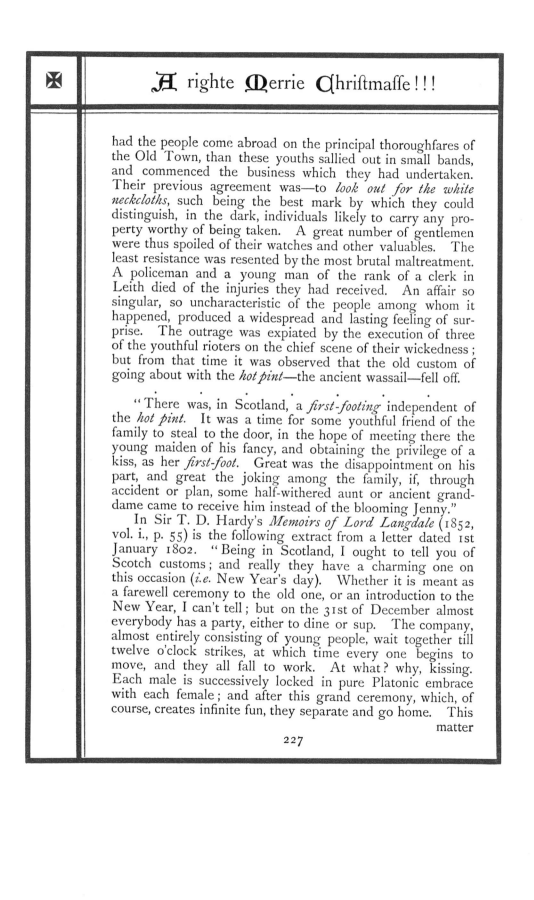

had the people come abroad on the principal thoroughfares of the Old Town, than these youths sallied out in small bands, and commenced the business which they had undertaken. Their previous agreement was—to *look out for the white neckcloths*, such being the best mark by which they could distinguish, in the dark, individuals likely to carry any property worthy of being taken. A great number of gentlemen were thus spoiled of their watches and other valuables. The least resistance was resented by the most brutal maltreatment. A policeman and a young man of the rank of a clerk in Leith died of the injuries they had received. An affair so singular, so uncharacteristic of the people among whom it happened, produced a widespread and lasting feeling of surprise. The outrage was expiated by the execution of three of the youthful rioters on the chief scene of their wickedness; but from that time it was observed that the old custom of going about with the *hot pint*—the ancient wassail—fell off.

.   .   .   .

"There was, in Scotland, a *first-footing* independent of the *hot pint*. It was a time for some youthful friend of the family to steal to the door, in the hope of meeting there the young maiden of his fancy, and obtaining the privilege of a kiss, as her *first-foot*. Great was the disappointment on his part, and great the joking among the family, if, through accident or plan, some half-withered aunt or ancient granddame came to receive him instead of the blooming Jenny."

In Sir T. D. Hardy's *Memoirs of Lord Langdale* (1852, vol. i., p. 55) is the following extract from a letter dated 1st January 1802. "Being in Scotland, I ought to tell you of Scotch customs; and really they have a charming one on this occasion (*i.e.* New Year's day). Whether it is meant as a farewell ceremony to the old one, or an introduction to the New Year, I can't tell; but on the 31st of December almost everybody has a party, either to dine or sup. The company, almost entirely consisting of young people, wait together till twelve o'clock strikes, at which time every one begins to move, and they all fall to work. At what? why, kissing. Each male is successively locked in pure Platonic embrace with each female; and after this grand ceremony, which, of course, creates infinite fun, they separate and go home. This matter

matter is not at all confined to these, but wherever man meets woman it is the peculiar privilege of this hour. The common people think it necessary to drink what they call *hot pint*, which consists of strong beer, whisky, eggs, etc., a most horrid composition, as bad or worse than that infamous mixture called *fig-one*,[1] which the English people drink on Good Friday."

Pennant tells us, in his *Tour in Scotland*, that on New Year's day the Highlanders burned juniper before their cattle; and Stewart, in *Popular Superstitions of the Highlanders of Scotland*, says, as soon as the last night of the year sets in, it is the signal with the Strathdown Highlander for the suspension of his usual employment, and he directs his attention to more agreeable callings. The men form into bands, with tethers and axes, and, shaping their course to the juniper bushes, they return home with mighty loads, which are arranged round the fire to dry until morning. A certain discreet person is despatched to the *dead and living ford*, to draw a pitcher of water in profound silence, without the vessel touching the ground, lest its virtue should be destroyed, and on his return all retire to rest.

Early on New Year's morning, the *usque-cashrichd*, or water from the *dead and living ford*, is drunk, as a potent charm until next New Year's day, against the spells of witchcraft, the malignity of evil eyes, and the activity of all infernal agency. The qualified Highlander then takes a large brush, with which he profusely asperses the occupants of all beds, from whom it is not unusual for him to receive ungrateful remonstrances against ablution. This ended, and the doors and windows being thoroughly closed, and all crevices stopped, he kindles piles of the collected juniper in the different apartments, till the vapour collected from the burning branches condenses into opaque clouds, and coughing, sneezing, wheezing, gasping, and other demonstrations of suffocation ensue. The operator, aware that the more intense the *smuchdan*, the more propitious the solemnity,
disregards

---

[1] Or *Fig-sue*, which is a mixture of ale, sliced figs, bread, and nutmeg, all boiled together, and eaten hot. This mess is made in North Lancashire, and partaken of on Good Friday, probably by way of mortifying the flesh.

disregards these indications, and continues, with streaming eyes and averted head, to increase the fumigation, until, in his own defence, he admits the air to recover the exhausted household and himself. He then treats the horses, cattle, and other bestial stock in the town with the same smothering, to keep them from harm throughout the year.

When the gudewife gets up, and having ceased from coughing, has gained sufficient strength to reach the bottle *dhu*, she administers its comfort to the relief of the sufferers; laughter takes the place of complaint, all the family get up, wash their faces, and receive the visits of their neighbours, who arrive full of congratulations peculiar to the day. *Mu nase choil orst*, "My Candlemas bond upon you," is the customary salutation, and means, in plain words, "You owe me a New Year's gift." A point of great emulation is, who shall salute the other first, because the one who does so is entitled to a gift from the person saluted. Breakfast, consisting of all procurable luxuries, is then served, the neighbours not engaged are invited to partake, and the day ends in festivity.

Of New Year's customs in Ireland a correspondent in *Notes and Queries* (5 ser. iii. 7), writes: "On New Year's day I observed boys running about the suburbs at the County Down side of Belfast, carrying little twisted wisps of straw, which they offer to persons whom they meet, or throw into houses as New Year Offerings, and expect in return to get any small present, such as a little money, or a piece of bread.

"About Glenarm, on the coast of County Antrim, the 'wisp' is not used; but on this day the boys go about from house to house, and are regaled with 'bannocks' of oaten bread, buttered; these bannocks are baked specially for the occasion, and are commonly small, thick, and round, and with a hole through the centre. Any person who enters a house at Glenarm on this day must either eat or drink before leaving it."

It is only natural that auguries for the weather of the year should be drawn from that on which New Year's day falls, and not only so, but, as at Christmas, the weather for the ensuing year was materially influenced, according to the day in

229

in the week on which this commencement of another year happened to fall. It is, however, satisfactory to have persons able to tell us all about it, and thus saith Digges, in his *Prognosticacion Everlasting, of ryghte goode Effect*, Lond., 1596, 4to.

"It is affirmed by some, when New Yeare's day falleth on the Sunday, then a pleasant winter doth ensue: a naturall summer: fruite sufficient: harvest indifferent, yet some winde and raine: many marriages: plentie of wine and honey; death of young men and cattell: robberies in most places: newes of prelates, of kinges; and cruell warres in the end.

"On Monday, a winter somewhat uncomfortable; summer temperate: no plentie of fruite: many fansies and fables opened: agues shall reigne: kings and many others shall dye: marriages shall be in most places: and a common fall of gentlemen.

"On Tuesday, a stormie winter: a wet summer: a divers harvest: corne and fruite indifferent, yet hearbes in gardens shall not flourish: great sicknesse of men, women, and yong children. Beasts shall hunger, starve, and dye of the botch; many shippes, gallies, and hulkes shall be lost; and the bloodie flixes shall kill many men; all things deare, save corne.

"On Wednesday, lo, a warme winter; in the end, snowe and frost: a cloudie summer, plentie of fruite, corne, hay, wine, and honey: great paine to women with childe, and death to infants: good for sheepe: news of kinges: great warres: battell, and slaughter towards the middell.

"On Thursday, winter and summer windie; a rainie harveste: therefore wee shall have overflowings: much fruite: plentie of honey: yet flesh shall be deare: cattell in general shall dye: great trouble; warres, etc.: with a licencious life of the feminine sexe.

"On Friday, winter stormie: summer scant and pleasant: harvest indifferent: little store of fruite, of wine and honey: corne deare: many bleare eyes: youth shall dye: earthquakes are perceived in many places: plentie of thunders, lightnings and tempestes: with a sudden death of cattell.

"On Saturday, a mean winter: summer very hot: a late harvest: good cheape garden hearbs: much burning: plentie of of hempe, flax and honey. Old folke shall dye in most places : fevers and tercians shall grieve many people : great muttering of warres : murthers shall be suddenly committed in many places for light matters."

In Scotland the first Monday is kept as a great holiday among servants and children, to whom *Handsel Monday*, as it is called, is analogous to *Boxing Day* in England, when all expect some little present in token of affection, or in recognition of services rendered during the past year. In the rural districts *Auld Handsel Monday*—that is, the first Monday after the twelfth of the month—is kept in preference. It is also a day for hiring servants for another year, and at farmhouses, after a good substantial breakfast, the remainder of the day is spent as a holiday.

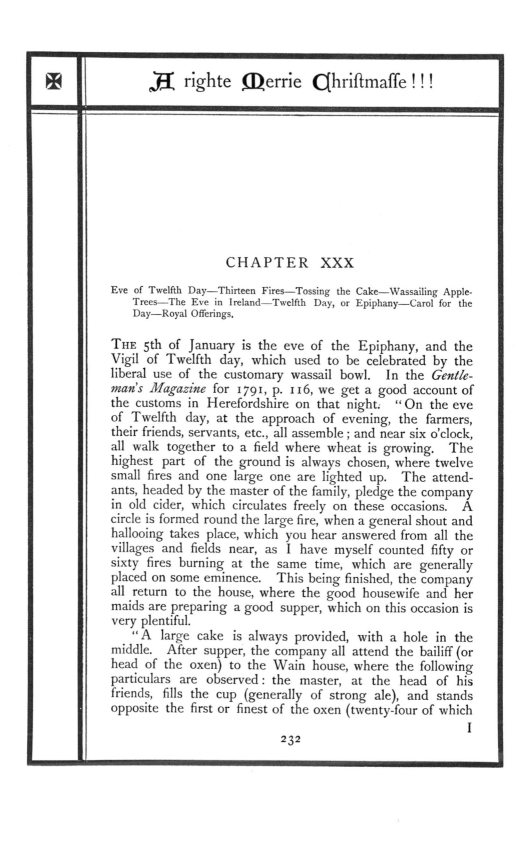

CHAPTER XXX

Eve of Twelfth Day—Thirteen Fires—Tossing the Cake—Wassailing Apple-Trees—The Eve in Ireland—Twelfth Day, or Epiphany—Carol for the Day—Royal Offerings.

THE 5th of January is the eve of the Epiphany, and the Vigil of Twelfth day, which used to be celebrated by the liberal use of the customary wassail bowl. In the *Gentleman's Magazine* for 1791, p. 116, we get a good account of the customs in Herefordshire on that night. "On the eve of Twelfth day, at the approach of evening, the farmers, their friends, servants, etc., all assemble ; and near six o'clock, all walk together to a field where wheat is growing. The highest part of the ground is always chosen, where twelve small fires and one large one are lighted up. The attendants, headed by the master of the family, pledge the company in old cider, which circulates freely on these occasions. A circle is formed round the large fire, when a general shout and hallooing takes place, which you hear answered from all the villages and fields near, as I have myself counted fifty or sixty fires burning at the same time, which are generally placed on some eminence. This being finished, the company all return to the house, where the good housewife and her maids are preparing a good supper, which on this occasion is very plentiful.

"A large cake is always provided, with a hole in the middle. After supper, the company all attend the bailiff (or head of the oxen) to the Wain house, where the following particulars are observed: the master, at the head of his friends, fills the cup (generally of strong ale), and stands opposite the first or finest of the oxen (twenty-four of which

I

I have often seen tied up in their stalls together); he then pledges him in a curious toast; the company then follow his example with all the other oxen, addressing each by their name. This being over, the large cake is produced, and is with much ceremony put on the horn of the first ox, through the hole in the cake; he is then tickled to make him toss his head: if he throws the cake behind, it is the mistress's per-quisite; if before (in what is termed the *boosy*), the bailiff claims the prize. This ended, the company all return to the house, the doors of which are in the meantime locked, and not opened till some joyous songs are sung. On entering, a scene of mirth and jollity commences, and reigns through the house till a late hour the next morning. Cards are introduced, and the merry tale goes round. I have often enjoyed the hospitality, friendship, and harmony I have been witness to on these occasions."

On p. 403 of the same volume another correspondent writes as to the custom on Twelfth day eve in Devonshire. "On the Eve of the Epiphany the farmer, attended by his workmen, with a large pitcher of cyder, goes to the orchard, and there, encircling one of the best-bearing trees, they drink the following toast three several times :—

> "Here's to thee, old apple tree,
> Whence thou may'st bud, and whence thou may'st blow!
> And whence thou may'st bear apples enow!
> Hats full!—Caps full!
> Bushel,—bushel,—sacks full!
> And my pockets full, too! Huzza!

"This done, they return to the house, the doors of which they are sure to find bolted by the females, who, be the weather what it may, are inexorable to all entreaties to open them, till some one has guessed at what is on the spit, which is generally some nice little thing difficult to be hit on, and is the reward of him who first names it. The doors are then thrown open, and the lucky clodpole receives the tit-bit as his recompense. Some are so superstitious as to believe that, if they neglect this custom, the trees will bear no apples that year."

Referring to these customs, Cuthbert Bede remarks (*Notes and*

and Queries, 2 ser. viii. 448): "A farmer's wife told me that where she had lived in Herefordshire, twenty years ago, they were wont, on Twelfth Night Eve, to light in a wheat field twelve small fires, and one large one. . . . She told me that they were designed to represent the blessed Saviour and his twelve Apostles. The fire representing Judas Iscariot, after being allowed to burn for a brief time, was kicked about, and put out. . . . The same person also told me that the ceremony of placing the twelfth cake on the horn of the ox was observed in all the particulars. . . . It was twenty years since she had left the farm, and she had forgotten all the words of the toast used on that occasion : she could only remember one verse out of three or four :—

> " Fill your cups, my merry men all !
> For here's the best ox in the stall ;
> Oh ! he's the best ox, of that there's no mistake,
> And so let us crown him with the Twelfth Cake."

The Derby and Chesterfield Reporter of 7th January 1830 gives the following notice of the Herefordshire customs : " On the eve of Old Christmas day there are thirteen fires lighted in the cornfields of many of the farms, twelve of them in a circle, and one round a pole, much longer and higher than the rest, in the centre. These fires are dignified by the names of the Virgin Mary and the Twelve Apostles, the lady being in the middle ; and while they are burning, the labourers retire into some shed or out-house, where they can behold the brightness of the Apostolic flame. Into this shed they lead a cow, on whose horn a large plum cake has been stuck, and having assembled round the animal, the oldest labourer takes a pail of cider, and addresses the following lines to the cow with great solemnity ; after which the verse is chaunted in chorus by all present :—

> " Here's to thy pretty face and thy white horn,
> God send thy master a good crop of corn,
> Both wheat, rye, and barley, and all sorts of grain,
> And, next year, if we live, we'll drink to thee again.

" He then dashes the cider in the cow's face, when, by a violent toss of her head, she throws the plum cake on the ground ;

ground; and if it falls forward, it is an omen that the next harvest will be good; if backward, that it will be unfavourable. This is the ceremony at the commencement of the rural feast, which is generally prolonged to the following morning."

In Ireland,[1] "on Twelve Eve in Christmas, they use to set up, as high as they can, a sieve of oats, and in it a dozen of candles set round, and in the centre one larger, all lighted. This is in memory of our Saviour and His Apostles—lights of the world."

The 6th of January, or twelfth day after Christmas, is a festival of the Church, called *the Epiphany* (from a Greek word signifying "appearance"), or Manifestation of Christ to the Gentiles; and it arises from the adoration of the Wise Men, or *Magi*, commonly known as "the Three Kings," *Gaspar*, *Melchior*, and *Balthazar*, who were led by the miraculous star to Bethlehem, and there offered to the infant Christ gold, frankincense, and myrrh. The following carol is in the Harl. MSS. British Museum, and is of the time of Henry VII. :—

Now is Christmas i-come,
Father and Son together in One,
Holy Ghost as ye be One,
　　In fere-a;
God send us a good new year-a.

I would now sing, for and I might,
Of a Child is fair to sight;
His mother bare him this enders[2] night,
　　So still-a;
And as it was his will-a.

There came three kings from Galilee
To Bethlehem, that fair citie,
To see Him that should ever be
　　By right-a,
Lord, and King, and Knight-a.

As they came forth with their offering,
They met with Herod, that moody king,

He asked them of their coming
　　This tide-a;
And thus to them he said-a:

"Of whence be ye, you kings three?"
"Of the East, as you may see,
To seek Him that should ever be
　　By right-a,
Lord, and King, and Knight-a."

"When you to this Child have been,
Come you home this way again,
Tell me the sights that ye have seen,
　　I pray-a;"
Go not another way-a."

They took their leave, both old and young,
Of Herod, that moody king;
They went forth with their offering,
　　By light-a
Of the Star that shone so bright-a.
　　　　　　　　　Till

---

[1] Vallancey's *Collectanea de Rebus Hibernicis*, vol. i. No. 1. p. 124.　　[2] Last.

Till they came into the place
Where Jesus and his mother was,
There they offered with great solace,
  In fere-a,
Gold, incense, and myrrh-a.

When they had their offering made,
As the Holy Ghost them bade,
Then were they both merry and glad,
  And light-a;
It was a good fair sight-a.

Anon, as on their way they went,
The Father of Heaven an Angel sent,
To those three kings that made
  present,
  That day-a,
Who thus to them did say-a:

"My Lord hath warned you every
  one,
By Herod King ye go not home,

For, an' you do, he will you slone [1]
  And strye-a,[2]
And hurt you wonderly-a."

So forth they went another way,
Through the might of God, His lay,[3]
As the Angel to them did say,
  Full right-a,
It was a fair good sight-a.

When they were come to their
  countree,
Merry and glad they were all three,
Of the sight that they had see
  By night-a;
By the Star's shining light-a.

Kneel we now all here adown
To that Lord of great renown,
And pray we in good devotion
  For grace-a,
In Heaven to have a place-a.

This festival was held in high honour in England; and up to the reign of George III. our Kings and Queens, attended by the Knights of the three great Orders—the Garter, the Thistle, and the Bath—were wont to go in state to the Chapel Royal, St. James's, and there offer gold, frankincense, and myrrh, in commemoration of the *Magi;* but when George III. was incapacitated, mentally, from performing the functions of royalty, it was done by proxy, and successive sovereigns have found it convenient to perform this act of piety vicariously.

It must have been a magnificent function in the time of Henry VII., as we learn by Le Neve's *Royalle Book.* "As for Twelfth Day, the King must go crowned, in his royal robes, kirtle, surtout, his furred hood about his neck, his mantle with a long train, and his cutlas before him; his armills upon his arms, of gold set full of rich stones; and no temporal man to touch it but the King himself; and the squire for the body must bring it to the King in a fair kerchief, and the
             King

---

[1] Slay.   [2] Stay, hinder.   [3] Law.

King must put them on himself; and he must have his sceptre in his right hand, and the ball with the cross in his left hand, and the crown upon his head. And he must offer that day gold, myrrh, and sense; then must the Dean of the Chapel send unto the Archbishop of Canterbury, by clerk, or priest, the King's offering that day; and then must the Archbishop give the next benefice that falleth in his gift to the same messenger. And then the King must change his mantle when he goeth to meat, and take off his hood, and lay it about his neck; and clasp it before with a great rich ouche; and this must be of the same colour that he offered in. And the Queen in the same form as when she is crowned."

Now the ceremonial is as simple as it can be made. In the Chapel Royal, St. James's, after the reading of the sentence at the offertory, "Let your light so shine before men," etc., while the organ plays, two members of Her Majesty's household, wearing the royal livery, descend from the royal pew, and, preceded by the usher, advance to the altar rails, where they present to one of the two officiating clergymen a red bag, edged with gold lace or braid, which is received in an alms dish, and then reverently placed upon the altar. This bag, or purse, is understood to contain the Queen's offering of gold, frankincense, and myrrh.

CHAPTER XXXI

" The King of the Bean "—Customs on Twelfth Day—Twelfth Cakes—Twelfth
Night Characters—Modern Twelfth Night—The Pastry Cook's Shops—
Dethier's Lottery—The Song of the Wren—" Holly Night" at Brough—
" Cutting off the Fiddler's Head."

BUT another sovereign had a great deal to do with Twelfth
day, " The King of the Bean," who takes his title from a
bean, or a silver penny, baked in a cake, which is cut up
and distributed, and he is king in whose slice the bean is
found. Naogeorgus gives us the following account of
Twelfth day :—

The wise men's day here foloweth, who out from *Persia* farre,
Brought giftes and presents unto Christ, conducted by a starre.
The Papistes do beleeve that these were kings, and so them call,
And do affirme that of the same there were but three in all.
Here sundrie friendes togither come, and meete in companie,
And make a king amongst themselves by voyce, or destinie :
Who, after princely guise, appoyntes his officers alway.
Then, unto feasting doe they go, and long time after play :
Upon their bordes, in order thicke, the daintie dishes stande,
Till that their purses emptie be, and creditors at hande.
Their children herein follow them, and choosing princes here,
With pompe and great solemnitie, they meete and make good chere :
With money eyther got by stealth, or of their parents eft,
That so they may be traynde to knowe, both ryot here and theft.
Then also every housholder, to his abilitie,
Doth make a mightie Cake, that may suffice his companie :
Herein a pennie doth he put, before it comes to fire,
This he devides according as his housholde doth require.
And every peece distributeth, as round about they stand,
Which, in their names, unto the poore, is given out of hand :
But, who so chaunceth on the peece wherin the money lies,

Is

238

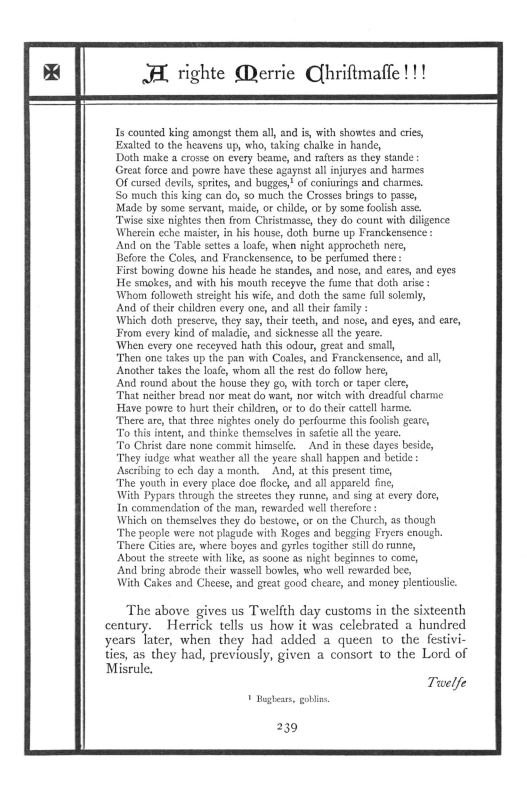

Is counted king amongst them all, and is, with showtes and cries,
Exalted to the heavens up, who, taking chalke in hande,
Doth make a crosse on every beame, and rafters as they stande :
Great force and powre have these agaynst all injuryes and harmes
Of cursed devils, sprites, and bugges,[1] of coniurings and charmes.
So much this king can do, so much the Crosses brings to passe,
Made by some servant, maide, or childe, or by some foolish asse.
Twise sixe nightes then from Christmasse, they do count with diligence
Wherein eche maister, in his house, doth burne up Franckensence :
And on the Table settes a loafe, when night approcheth nere,
Before the Coles, and Franckensence, to be perfumed there :
First bowing downe his heade he standes, and nose, and eares, and eyes
He smokes, and with his mouth receyve the fume that doth arise :
Whom followeth streight his wife, and doth the same full solemly,
And of their children every one, and all their family :
Which doth preserve, they say, their teeth, and nose, and eyes, and eare,
From every kind of maladie, and sicknesse all the yeare.
When every one receyved hath this odour, great and small,
Then one takes up the pan with Coales, and Franckensence, and all,
Another takes the loafe, whom all the rest do follow here,
And round about the house they go, with torch or taper clere,
That neither bread nor meat do want, nor witch with dreadful charme
Have powre to hurt their children, or to do their cattell harme.
There are, that three nightes onely do perfourme this foolish geare,
To this intent, and thinke themselves in safetie all the yeare.
To Christ dare none commit himselfe.   And in these dayes beside,
They iudge what weather all the yeare shall happen and betide :
Ascribing to ech day a month.   And, at this present time,
The youth in every place doe flocke, and all appareld fine,
With Pypars through the streetes they runne, and sing at every dore,
In commendation of the man, rewarded well therefore :
Which on themselves they do bestowe, or on the Church, as though
The people were not plagude with Roges and begging Fryers enough.
There Cities are, where boyes and gyrles togither still do runne,
About the streete with like, as soone as night beginnes to come,
And bring abrode their wassell bowles, who well rewarded bee,
With Cakes and Cheese, and great good cheare, and money plentiouslie.

The above gives us Twelfth day customs in the sixteenth
century.   Herrick tells us how it was celebrated a hundred
years later, when they had added a queen to the festivities, as they had, previously, given a consort to the Lord of
Misrule.

Twelfe

[1] Bugbears, goblins.

Twelfe night, or King *and* Queene.

Now, now the mirth comes
With the cake full of plums,
Where Beane's the *King* of the sport here ;
Besides, we must know
The Pea also
Must revell, as *Queene*, in the Court here.

Begin, then, to chuse
(This night, as ye use),
Who shall for the present delight here,
Be a *King* by the lot,
And who shall not
Be Twelfe-day *Queene* for the night here.

Which knowne, let us make
Joy-sops with the cake ;
And let not a man then be seen here
Who un-urg'd will not drinke
To the base, from the brink,
A health to the *King* and the *Queene* here.

Next, crowne the bowle full
With gentle lamb's-wooll ;
Adde sugar, nutmeg, and ginger,
With store of ale too ;
And thus ye must doe
To make the wassaile a swinger.

Give then to the *King*
And *Queene* wassailing ;
And though, with ale, ye be whet here,
Yet part ye from hence
As free from offence
As when ye innocent met here.

This custom of having a Twelfth cake and electing a king and queen has now died out, and is only known by tradition ; so utterly died out indeed, that in the British Museum Library there is not a single sheet of " Twelfth-night Characters " to show the younger race of students what they were like. The nearest approach to them preserved in that national collection of literature are some Lottery squibs, which imitated them ; and Hone, writing in 1838, says : " It must be admitted, however, that the characters sold
by

by the pastry cooks are either commonplace or gross; when genteel, they are inane; when humorous, they are vulgar."

A correspondent in the *Universal Magazine* for 1774 thus describes the drawing for King and Queen at that date. He says : " I went to a friend's house in the country to partake of some of those innocent pleasures that constitute a merry Christmas. I did not return till I had been present at drawing King and Queen, and eaten a slice of the Twelfth Cake, made by the fair hands of my good friend's consort. After tea, yesterday, a noble cake was produced, and two bowls, containing the fortunate chances for the different sexes. Our host filled up the tickets; the whole company, except the King and Queen, were to be ministers of state, maids of honour, or ladies of the bed-chamber. Our kind host and hostess, whether by design or accident, became king and queen. According to Twelfth-day law, each party is to support their character till midnight."

Here we see they had no sheets of " Twelfth-night Characters " (the loss of which I deplore), but they were of home manufacture. Hone, in his *Every-Day Book*, vol. i. p. 51, describes the drawing some fifty years later. "First, buy your cake. Then, before your visitors arrive, buy your characters, each of which should have a pleasant verse beneath. Next, look at your invitation list, and count the number of ladies you expect; and, afterwards, the number of gentlemen. Then take as many female characters as you have invited ladies; fold them up, exactly of the same size, and number each on the back, taking care to make the king No. 1 and the queen No. 2. Then prepare and number the gentlemen's characters. Cause tea and coffee to be handed to your visitors as they drop in. When all are assembled, and tea over, put as many ladies' characters in a reticule as there are ladies present; next, put the gentlemen's characters in a hat. Then call a gentleman to carry the reticule to the ladies, as they sit, from which each lady is to draw one ticket, and to preserve it unopened. Select a lady to bear the hat to the gentlemen for the same purpose. There will be one ticket left in the reticule, and another in the hat, which the lady and gentleman who carried each is to interchange, as having

fallen

241

fallen to each. Next, arrange your visitors according to their numbers; the king No. 1, the queen No. 2, and so on. The king is then to recite the verse on his ticket; then the queen the verse on hers, and so the characters are to proceed in numerical order. This done, let the cake and refreshments go round, and hey! for merriment!"

The Twelfth cakes themselves were, in the higher class, almost as beautiful as wedding cakes, but they might be had of all prices, from sixpence to anything one's purse might compass; and the confectioner's (they called them pastry cooks in those days) windows were well worth a visit, and crowds did visit them, sometimes a little practical joking taking place, such as pinning two persons together, etc. Quoting Hone again: "In London, with every pastry cook in the city, and at the west end of the town, it is 'high change' on Twelfth day. From the taking down the shutters in the morning, he and his men, with additional assistants, male and female, are fully occupied by attending to the dressing out of the window, executing orders of the day before, receiving fresh ones, or supplying the wants of chance customers. Before dusk the important arrangement of the window is completed. Then the gas is turned on, with supernumerary argand lamps and manifold waxlights, to illuminate countless cakes, of all prices and dimensions, that stand in rows and piles on the counters and sideboards, and in the windows. The richest in flavour and heaviest in weight and price are placed on large and massy salvers; one, enormously superior in size, is the chief object of curiosity; and all are decorated with all imaginable images of things animate and inanimate. Stars, castles, kings, cottages, dragons, trees, fish, palaces, cats, dogs, churches, lions, milkmaids, knights, serpents, and innumerable other forms in snow-white confectionery, painted with variegated colours, glitter by 'excess of light' from mirrors against the walls, festooned with artificial wonders of Flora."

As the fashion of Twelfth cakes declined, the pastry cooks had to push their sale in every way possible, not being very particular as to overstepping the law, by getting rid of them by means of drawings, raffles, and lotteries, which for a long time were winked at by the authorities, until they assumed dimensions

dimensions which could not be ignored, and M. Louis Dethier was summoned at Bow Street on 26th December 1860, under the Act 42 Geo. III. cap. 119, sec. 2, for keeping an office at the Hanover Square Rooms for the purpose of carrying on a lottery "under the name, device, and pretence of a distribution of Twelfth cakes." He had brought a similar distribution to a successful conclusion in 1851, but that was the exceptional year of the Great Exhibition, and he was not interfered with; but this was for £10,000 worth of cakes to be drawn for on ten successive days, beginning 26th December—tickets one shilling each. This was an undoubted lottery on a grand scale. The case was completely proved against Dethier, but he was not punished, as he abandoned his scheme, putting up with the loss.

There were some curious customs in different parts of the kingdom on Twelfth day, but I doubt whether many are in existence now. The following, taken from *Notes and Queries* (3 ser. v. 109), was in vogue in 1864. "It is still the custom in parts of Pembrokeshire on Twelfth night to carry about a wren.

"The wren is secured in a small house made of wood, with door and windows—the latter glazed. Pieces of ribbon of various colours are fixed to the ridge of the roof outside. Sometimes several wrens are brought in the same cage; and oftentimes a stable lantern, decorated as above mentioned, serves for the wren's house. The proprietors of this establishment go round to the principal houses in the neighbourhood, where, accompanying themselves with some musical instrument, they announce their arrival by singing the 'Song of the Wren.' The wren's visit is a source of much amusement to children and servants; and the wren's men, or lads, are usually invited to have a draught from the cellar, and receive a present in money. The 'Song of the Wren' is generally encored, and the proprietors very commonly commence high life below stairs, dancing with the maid-servants, and saluting them under the kissing bush, where there is one. I have lately procured a copy of the song sung on this occasion. I am told that there is a version of this song in the Welsh language, which is in substance very near to the following :—

"THE

"THE SONG OF THE WREN.

" Joy health, love, and peace
Be to you in this place,
By your leave we will sing
Concerning our King :
Our King is well drest,
In silks of the best ;
With his ribbons so rare,
No King can compare.
In his coach he does ride,
With a great deal of pride ;
And with four footmen
To wait upon him.

We four were at watch,
And all nigh of a match ;
With powder and ball,
We fired at his hall.
We have travelled many miles
Over hedges and stiles,
To find you this King,
Which we now to you bring.
Now Christmas is past,
Twelfth day is the last,
Th' Old Year bids adieu ;
Great joy to the New."

Hone, in his *Table Book*, p. 26, gives a description of "Holly Night" at Brough, Westmoreland, in 1838. "Formerly the 'Holly Tree' at Brough was really holly, but ash being abundant, the latter is now substituted. There are two head inns in the town, which provide for the ceremony alternately, although the good townspeople mostly lend their assistance in preparing the tree, to every branch of which they fasten a torch. About eight o'clock in the evening it is taken to a convenient part of the town, where the torches are lighted, the town band accompanying, and playing till all is completed, when it is removed to the lower end of the town ; and after divers salutes and huzzas from the spectators, is carried up and down the town in stately procession. The band march behind it, playing their instruments, and stopping every time they reach the town bridge and the cross, where the 'holly' is again greeted with shouts of applause. Many of the inhabitants carry lighted branches and flambeaus ; and rockets, squibs, etc., are discharged on the joyful occasion After the tree is thus carried, and the torches are sufficiently burnt, it is placed in the middle of the town, when it is again cheered by the surrounding populace, and is afterwards thrown among them. They eagerly watch for this opportunity ; and, clinging to each end of the tree, endeavour to carry it away to the inn they are contending for, where they are allowed their usual quantum of ale and spirits, and pass a merry night, which seldom breaks up before two in the morning."

According

244

According to Waldron, in his *Description of the Isle of Man*, 1859, p. 156, the following singular custom is in force on Twelfth day. In this island there is not a barn unoccupied on the whole twelve days after Christmas, every parish hiring fiddlers at the public charge. On Twelfth day the fiddler lays his head in the lap of some one of the wenches, and the *mainstyr fiddler* asks who such a maid, or such a maid, naming all the girls one after another, shall marry, to which he answers according to his own whim, or agreeable to the intimacies he has taken notice of during the time of merriment, and whatever he says is absolutely depended upon as an oracle ; and if he couple two people who have an aversion to each other, tears and vexation succeed the mirth ; this they call "cutting off the fiddler's head," for after this he is dead for a whole year.

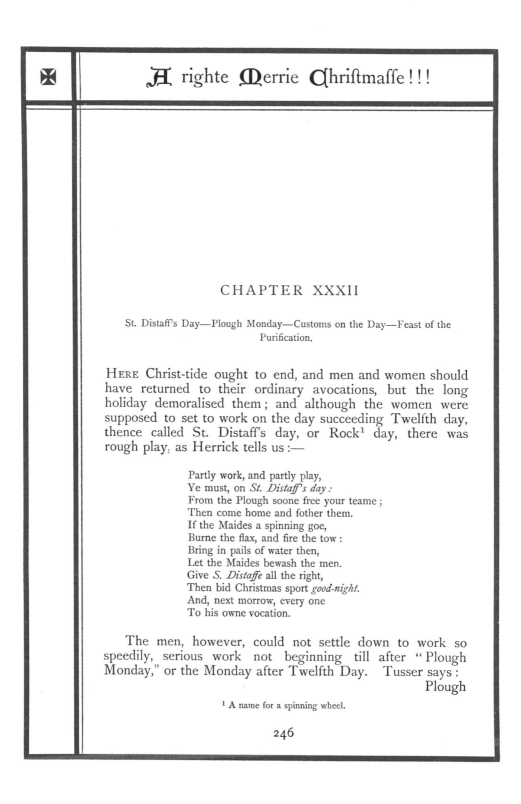
CHAPTER XXXII

St. Distaff's Day—Plough Monday—Customs on the Day—Feast of the
Purification.

HERE Christ-tide ought to end, and men and women should
have returned to their ordinary avocations, but the long
holiday demoralised them; and although the women were
supposed to set to work on the day succeeding Twelfth day,
thence called St. Distaff's day, or Rock[1] day, there was
rough play, as Herrick tells us :—

> Partly work, and partly play,
> Ye must, on *St. Distaff's day :*
> From the Plough soone free your teame ;
> Then come home and fother them.
> If the Maides a spinning goe,
> Burne the flax, and fire the tow :
> Bring in pails of water then,
> Let the Maides bewash the men.
> Give *S. Distaffe* all the right,
> Then bid Christmas sport *good-night.*
> And, next morrow, every one
> To his owne vocation.

The men, however, could not settle down to work so
speedily, serious work not beginning till after " Plough
Monday," or the Monday after Twelfth Day. Tusser says :

Plough

[1] A name for a spinning wheel.

246

Plough Munday, next after that twelf tide is past,
Bids out with the plough—the worst husband is last.
If plowman get hatchet, or whip to the skrene,
Maids loseth their cocke, if no water be seen.

This verse would be rather enigmatical were it not explained in *Tusser Redivivus* (1744, p. 79). "After Christmas (which, formerly, during the twelve days, was a time of very little work) every gentleman feasted the farmers, and every farmer their servants and task-men. *Plough Monday* puts them in mind of their business. In the morning, the men and the maid-servants strive who shall show their diligence in rising earliest. If the ploughman can get his whip, his ploughstaff, hatchet, or any thing that he wants in the field, by the fireside before the maid hath got her kettle on, then the maid loseth her Shrove-tide cock, and it belongs wholly to the men. Thus did our forefathers strive to allure youth to their duty, and provided them with innocent mirth as well as labour. On this Plough Monday they have a good supper and some strong drink."

In many parts of the country it was made a regular festival, but, like all these old customs, it has fallen into desuetude. However, Hone's *Every-Day Book* was not written so long ago, and he there says: "In some parts of the country, and especially in the North, they draw the plough in procession to the doors of the villagers and towns-people. Long ropes are attached to it, and thirty or forty men, stripped to their clean white shirts, but protected from the weather by waistcoats beneath, drag it along. Their arms and shoulders are decorated with gay coloured ribbons tied in large knots and bows, and their hats are smartened in the same way. They are usually accompanied by an old woman, or a boy dressed up to represent one; she is gaily bedizened, and called the *Bessy*. Sometimes the sport is assisted by a humourous countryman to represent a *fool*. He is covered with ribbons, and attired in skins, with a depending tail, and carries a box to collect money from the spectators. They are attended by music and Morris Dancers, when they can be got; but it is always a sportive dance with a few lasses in all their finery, and a super-abundance

abundance of ribbons. The money collected is spent at night in conviviality."

Chambers's *Book of Days* also gives an account of this frolic. "A correspondent, who has borne a part (cow-horn blowing) on many a Plough Monday in Lincolnshire, thus describes what happened on these occasions under his own observation:—Rude though it was, the Plough procession threw a life into the dreary scenery of winter as it came winding along the quiet rutted lanes on its way from one village to another; for the ploughmen from many a surrounding thorpe, hamlet, and lonely farm-house united in the celebration of Plough Monday. It was nothing unusual for at least a score of the 'sons of the soil' to yoke themselves with ropes to the plough, having put on clean smock-frocks in honour of the day. There was no limit to the number who joined in the morris dance, and were partners with 'Bessy,' who carried the money box; and all these had ribbons in their hats, and pinned about them, wherever there was room to display a bunch. Many a hard-working country Molly lent a helping hand in decorating her Johnny for Plough Monday, and finished him with an admiring exclamation of — 'Lawks, John! thou dost look smart, surely!' Some also wore small bunches of corn in their hats, from which the wheat was soon shaken out by the ungainly jumping which they called dancing. Occasionally, if the winter was severe, the procession was joined by threshers carrying their flails, reapers bearing their sickles, and carters with their long whips, which they were ever cracking to add to the noise, while even the smith and the miller were among the number, for the one sharpened the plough - shares, and the other ground the corn; and Bessy rattled his box, and danced so high that he showed his worsted stockings and corduroy breeches; and, very often, if there was a thaw, tucked up his gown-skirts under his waistcoat and shook the bonnet off his head, and disarranged the long ringlets that ought to have concealed his whiskers. For Bessy is to the procession of Plough Monday what the leading *figurante* is to the opera or ballet, and dances about as gracefully as the hippopotami described by Dr. Livingstone. But these rough antics

antics were the cause of much laughter, and rarely do we ever remember hearing any coarse jest that could call up an angry blush to a modest cheek.

"No doubt they were called 'plough bullocks' through drawing the plough, as bullocks were formerly used, and are still yoked to the plough in some parts of the country. The rubbishy verses they recited are not worth preserving, beyond the line which graces many a public-house sign, of 'God speed the Plough.' At the large farm-house, besides money, they obtained refreshment; and, through the quantity of ale they thus drank during the day, managed to get what they called 'their load' by night.

"But the great event of the day was when they came before some house which bore signs that the owner was well-to-do in the world, and nothing was given to them. Bessy rattled his box, and the ploughmen danced, while the country lads blew their bullock's horns, or shouted with all their might; but if there was still no sign, no forthcoming of either bread and cheese or ale, then the word was given, the ploughshare driven into the ground before the door or window, the whole twenty men yoked pulling like one, and, in a minute or two, the ground was as brown, barren, and ridgy as a newly ploughed field. But this was rarely done, for everybody gave something, and, were it but little, the men never murmured, though they might talk of the stinginess of the giver afterwards amongst themselves, more especially if the party was what they called 'well off in the world.' We are not aware that the ploughmen were ever summoned to answer for such a breach of the law, for they believe, to use their own expressive language, 'they can stand by it, and no law in the world can touch 'em, 'cause it's an old charter.'

"One of the mummers generally wears a fox's skin in the form of a hood; but, beyond the laughter the tail that hangs down his back awakens by its motion when he dances, we are at a loss to find a meaning. Bessy formerly wore a bullock's tail behind, under his gown, and which he held in his hand while dancing, but that appendage has not been worn of late."

On the 2nd of February—the Feast of the Purification of

of the Blessed Virgin Mary—all Christ-tide decorations are to be taken down, and with them ends all trace of that festive season.

Farwell, Crystmas fayer and fre ;
Farwell, Newers Day with the ;
Farwell, the Holy Epyphane ;
And to Mary now sing we.

" *Revertere, revertere*, the queen of blysse and of beaute."

THE END